T0154126

William Caxton

THE GAME AND PLAYE OF THE CHESSE

MIDDLE ENGLISH TEXTS SERIES

GENERAL EDITOR
Russell A. Peck, University of Rochester

ASSOCIATE EDITOR
Alan Lupack, University of Rochester

ASSISTANT EDITOR
John H. Chandler, University of Rochester

ADVISORY BOARD

Theresa Coletti
University of Maryland

Michael Livingston
The Citadel

Rita Copeland
University of Pennsylvania

R. A. Shoaf
University of Florida

Susanna Fein
Kent State University

Lynn Staley
Colgate University

Thomas G. Hahn
University of Rochester

Paul E. Szarmach
The Medieval Academy of America

David A. Lawton
Washington University in St. Louis

Bonnie Wheeler
Southern Methodist University

The Middle English Texts Series is designed for classroom use. Its goal is to make available to teachers and students texts that occupy an important place in the literary and cultural canon but have not been readily available in student editions. The series does not include those authors, such as Chaucer, Langland, or Malory, whose English works are normally in print in good student editions. The focus is, instead, upon Middle English literature adjacent to those authors that teachers need in compiling the syllabuses they wish to teach. The editions maintain the linguistic integrity of the original work but within the parameters of modern reading conventions. The texts are printed in the modern alphabet and follow the practices of modern capitalization, word formation, and punctuation. Manuscript abbreviations are silently expanded, and *u/v* and *j/i* spellings are regularized according to modern orthography. Yogh (ȝ) is transcribed as *g*, *gh*, *y*, or *s*, according to the sound in Modern English spelling to which it corresponds; thorn (þ) and eth (ð) are transcribed as *th*. Distinction between the second person pronoun and the definite article is made by spelling the one *thee* and the other *the*, and final *-e* that receives full syllabic value is accented (e.g., *charité*). Hard words, difficult phrases, and unusual idioms are glossed on the page, either in the right margin or at the foot of the page. Explanatory and textual notes appear at the end of the text, often along with a glossary. The editions include short introductions on the history of the work, its merits and points of topical interest, and brief working bibliographies.

This series is published in association with the University of Rochester.

Medieval Institute Publications is a program of
The Medieval Institute, College of Arts and Sciences

 WESTERN MICHIGAN UNIVERSITY

William Caxton

THE GAME AND PLAYE OF THE CHESSE

Edited by
Jenny Adams

TEAMS • Middle English Texts Series

MEDIEVAL INSTITUTE PUBLICATIONS
Western Michigan University
Kalamazoo

Library of Congress Cataloging-in-Publication Data

Jacobus, de Cessolis, fl. 1288-1322.
 [De ludo scachorum. English]
 The game and playe of the chesse / edited by Jenny Adams.
   p. cm. -- (Middle English texts series)
 Includes bibliographical references.
 ISBN 978-1-58044-130-8 (paperbound : alk. paper)
 1. Chess--Early works to 1800. I. Adams, Jenny, 1969- II. Title.
 GV1442.C415 2008
 794.1--dc22
                             2008015596

ISBN 978-1-58044-130-8

Copyright © 2009 by the Board of Trustees of Western Michigan University

Printed in the United States of America

P 5 4 3 2 1

❧ CONTENTS

ACKNOWLEDGMENTS

Various individuals and institutions contributed greatly to this edition. Foremost among the institutions is the Newberry Library, where I worked in the summer of 2006 as one of two Lester J. Cappon Fellows in Documentary Editing. Here I was helped by Mark Bland, the other Cappon Fellow for that year; Paul Gael, the custodian of the Newberry's John M. Wing Foundation on the History of Printing; and James Grossman, the Newberry's vice president for Research and Education. I am also grateful to the Newberry Library for allowing me to reproduce the woodcuts in Caxton's text. In Chicago I also had the privilege of working at the Regenstein Library at the University of Chicago and of attending a meeting of the Caxton Club, a lively group of bibliophiles who carry their love of print beyond the confines of academia. Their general good cheer and enthusiasm for early print culture were infectious, and I am grateful for their hospitality.

I also owe a huge debt of gratitude to Christina von Nolcken, who gave me support and shelter during my stay in Chicago. Among those at other universities who contributed their time and energy to this project are Lisa Cooper, Martha W. Driver, Suzanne Edwards, and Robert Upchurch.

Closer to home I would like to thank the University of Massachusetts and in particular the Department of English, which granted me time away from teaching for the final push. Within the department I am grateful to Joseph Black and Steven Harris, who gave me valuable feedback on the introduction to this volume. An even bigger thanks goes to Valerie Gramling, my tireless research assistant, who worked harder on this edition than I ever could have hoped. Her meticulous copyediting and indefatigable source tracking have saved me from many embarrassments, and any errors that remain can safely be attributed to me alone.

I am also indebted to the National Endowment for the Humanities and to Medieval Institute Publications for their sponsorship of this valuable series, and to Russell Peck, Alan Lupack, John H. Chandler, and Michael Livingston for their edits and emendations.

Finally, I would like to thank Jeff Sternal and Frankie Adams-Sternal, the latter of whom, by virtue of her arrival, gave me a firmer deadline than any editor could have set.

![decorative ornament] INTRODUCTION

Despite its title, Caxton's *The Game and Playe of the Chesse* does not, in fact, have much to say about a game or about playing it. First printed in 1474, then reprinted in 1483 with woodcuts added, it is instead a translation of Jacobus de Cessolis' thirteenth-century political treatise, the *Liber de moribus hominum et officiis nobilium ac popularium super ludo scachorum* (*The Book of the Morals of Men and the Duties of Nobles and Commoners, on the Game of Chess*).[1] Neither the *Liber* nor Caxton's translation contains any diagrams of boards set up for play, nor does the text itself suggest any advice for a player's improvement.[2] Instead, the work uses the chessboard and its pieces to allegorize a political community whose citizens contribute to the common good. Readers first meet the king, queen, bishops (imagined as judges), knights, and rooks, here depicted as the king's emissaries. They are then introduced in succession to the eight different pawns, who represent trades that range from farmers to messengers, and include innkeepers, moneychangers, doctors, notaries, blacksmiths, and several other professional artisans and tradesmen. Paired with each profession is a list of moral codes. The pawn who represents the moneychanger, for example, handles gold, silver, and valuable possessions, and thus "ought to flee avarice and covetyse, and eschewe brekyng of the dayes of payment" (3.600–601). The knights, entrusted with the safety of the realm, must be "wyse, lyberalle, trewe, strong, and ful of mercy and pyté" (2.448–49). The queen, charged with giving birth to the community's future ruler, should take care to be "chaste, wyse, of honest lyf, wel manerd" (2.136). And so on. These pairings reinforce the idea of a kingdom organized around professional ties and associations, ties that are in turn regulated by moral law, rather than around kinship.

Fleshing out what would otherwise be a dry list of moral qualities are *exempla*, short stories highlighting the advantages attendant on those professional workers who follow their moral law, and *sententiae*, maxims usually derived from classical sources. For instance, illustrating the importance of chastity among a community's doctors is the story of the ancient Greek physician Hippocrates, whose students pay a prostitute to seduce him. The prostitute uses all her wiles, even going so far as to lie next to him all night, but he remains immune to her charms and thus retains his good name. In the chapter on the queen we find the tale of Roman noblewoman Lucretia, whose suicide provides a model for women on the

---

[1] For an extended discussion of Caxton and his use of the *Liber*, see Adams, *Power Play*. Much of this introduction has been framed by my work in that volume.

[2] Such diagrams, more commonly known as chess problems, were popular in the Middle Ages, as they are today.

importance of their chastity.[3] And the rewards of integrity among moneychangers are made clear in the narrative of Albert, an honest Genoese merchant cheated out of a large sum of gold by a swindler, who invests the money, makes a fortune, and then bequeaths it to the ever-honest merchant. As the subsequent proverb states, "hit is fraude to take that thou wylt not ner mayst [not] rendre and paye agayn" (3.694–95). (Although one might question the moral clarity of a story that never overtly punishes the swindler, this tale does indeed support that notion that upstanding moneylenders will be rewarded.)

Stories like these comprise the bulk of the treatise, and only in the final chapter do readers learn the rules of the *playe*, rules that were and remain largely unchanged since chess entered Europe in the tenth century.[4] Yet even here the *Game and Playe* inscribes the board's structure and the moves of the pieces within its larger moral lessons. Thus the king has limited movement on the board because he "holdeth the dygnyté above alle other and the seignorye royall. . . . For whan he wyl meve hym, he ought not to passe at the first draught the nombre of three poyntes" (4.130–34). And the queen, who under medieval rules advanced diagonally like the bishop, does so because she should "have parfyt wysedom as the alphyns [bishops] have, whiche ben juges, as hit sayd above in the chappytre of the quene" (4.217–18). Even the layout of the pieces has social and moral significance: for "what may the knyght do yf he ne had tofore hym the smyth for to forge his armours, sadellys, axys, and speres, and suche thynges as aperteyneth to hym? And what is a knyght worth wythout hors and armes?" (4.46–49). Thus while many medieval readers might (and did!) find this text compelling, a serious chess player would have little use for Caxton's translation.

So what, then, was the value of the *Game and Playe*, or for that matter of the *Liber* itself to its non-chess-playing audience? Or, rephrasing this slightly, if the *Game and Playe* is not about playing a game, what exactly is it about?

Most scholars would describe the work as a *speculum regis*, or a mirror for a prince. A standard genre throughout Middle Ages, such *specula* reached an apex of popularity in the second half of the thirteenth century, a time when dozens of advice books appeared across Europe. Most were written under the pretext of offering counsel to the reigning ruler or to another well-placed member of the nobility. Yet in reality many *specula* also served as a forum for thinking about the nature and organization of government itself, and it is in this more philosophical mode that such works could become more daring. Giles of Rome's thirteenth-century *De regimine principum* [*On the Government of Princes*] is perhaps the best known (at least among medievalists) example of this genre, and it embodies this duality. On

---

[3] In this story, popular throughout the Middle Ages, Lucretia kills herself to preserve her honor after she is raped by Emperor Tarquin's son, also named Tarquin. Her act inspires a man named Brutus to kill the younger Tarquin and to chase the emperor from the throne. See, e.g., Gower, *Confessio Amantis* 7.4593–5123, and Chaucer, *Legend of Good Women* 1680–1885.

[4] Although most of the rules of chess have remained static since its entrance into Europe in the tenth century, there are several exceptions. Most notably, the medieval queen could move only along a diagonal line for a limited number of squares. This number differed throughout Europe. In some places she could move only one adjacent diagonal square. In other places her first move could be a three-square diagonal leap. Bishops, although moving diagonally like their modern counterparts, could in some places move only three squares at a time. The lack of universal rules was addressed in the Lombard universities, and lawyers there ultimately dictated that games should be played according to the customs of the country in which they took place (Murray, *History of Chess*, p. 456). For a complete explanation of the various medieval rules, see Murray, pp. 452–85.

the one hand, this work endorses the primacy of the royal body over all others in the realm, and the author, quite conservatively, addresses himself to this reader above all others. On the other hand, in the body of his treatise Giles encourages *all* citizens to read the text, a proposition that challenges the very nature of the *speculum* genre itself. Always his descriptions of moral self-governance emphasize royal restraint rather than royal prerogative.

Although writers varied in the powers they attributed to the king, almost all relied on the metaphor of the human body, a comparison that emphasized the naturalness of a community's hierarchical ordering and helped explain the elevation of some of its parts over others. Just as in a physical body, a foot could not wake up one day and be a stomach, so in a civic body an illiterate farmer was expected to spend his life working the land; he could not abruptly decide to become a tax collector. This image of the state as a naturally occurring and physiologically functioning unit owed much of its popularity to John of Salisbury, whose twelfth-century *Policraticus* describes the state as "a sort of body which is animated by the grant of divine reward and which is driven by the command of the highest equity and ruled by a sort of rational management."[5] The position of the head is occupied by the king; the ears, eyes, and mouth by the governors; the hands by the officials and soldiers; the flanks by the king's assistants; the stomach by the treasurers and record keepers; and the feet by the peasants, who are bound to the land.[6] These different versions of the allegory assigned different powers and virtues to the ideal monarch, yet all placed the monarch in the center as the heart or head of the kingdom.[7]

One of the few works to offer an alternative allegory of the political state was Jacobus' *Liber*, which appeared soon after Giles of Rome's *De regimine*.[8] Whereas a state-as-body model, such as that imagined by Giles and his contemporaries, saw its members bound by organic ties, Jacobus' chess allegory conceives of individuals as contractually connected. In the *Liber* each piece corresponds to a specific professional identity, with all pieces being interdependent; just as the knight needs the blacksmith, represented by the pawn before his square, so farmers depend for protection on the knights, who are found on an adjacent square.

In envisioning a social order as a game governed by rules rather than as a physical, organic body, the *Liber* did not offer the promise of complete independence for the various

---

[5] John of Salisbury, *Policraticus*, ed. and trans. Nederman, p. 66.

[6] John of Salisbury, *Policraticus*, ed. and trans. Nederman, pp. 66 and 67.

[7] Some writers positioned the monarch as the heart of the kingdom, although in these cases the heart, in keeping with medieval custom, contained the attributes we normally assign to the head or brain.

[8] Thanks to an allusion to a statue of Frederick II on a marble gate at Capua, we can be fairly sure that the *Liber* was not composed before 1240, the year that Frederick had the statue erected. Nor could it have been written much later than 1320. In a University of Chicago master's thesis, Judith Kolata notes that "Jean-Thiébaut Welter suggests that Cessolis must have written his sermons before 1325 because he speaks favorably of tournaments which were specifically prohibited that year by Pope John XXII's *Extravagantes*" (Welter, *L'Exemplum dans la littériuese et didactique du Moyen Age* [Paris: Occitania, 1927], p. 351, cited by Kolata, "*Livre des Echecs Moralisés*," p. 5). Burt notes that the earliest extant metrical translations of the text appeared in German in the 1320s and 1330s, which include the undated *Das Schachgedichte*, *Das Schachbuch des Pfarrers zu dem Hechte*, and Kunrats von Ammenhausen's *Schachzabelbuch* (Jacobus de Cessolis, *Libellus*, ed. Burt, pp. xxx–xxxi). These suggest that Latin versions of the treatise were in circulation well before this time.

members of a civic community. After all, everyone still had to follow the rules. But in breaking with the state-as-body model, the chess allegory imagined a more diverse social order organized primarily around associational and professional ties. Rather than having actions dictated by the "head" of the state, members of a civic community, including the king, would follow moral codes particularized to their own social stations. And while it is impossible to read this allegory as a reflection of a viable social order, it is notable that Genoa, the city in which Jacobus most likely lived while writing his treatise, was by the late thirteenth century governed by a much larger and diverse group of people than had been the case in the several centuries previous.[9] An illustration of this political shift can be seen in Genoa's reconfirmation, in 1257, of its trade pact with Sicily, a document signed by the *podestà*, or hired manager of the city, the *parlamento*, or parliament, the *anziani*, a council of elders, and the consuls of the craft guilds. As Steven A. Epstein notes, "no previous official act of the commune had included the guilds or their leaders as institutions or people having any say in the affairs of government."[10] Similarly, at the end of the Treaty of Nyphaeum, a trade agreement made with the Byzantines in 1261, a variety of Genoese representatives swore to uphold the accord, each signing his name and listing his trade. This diverse list included an innkeeper, a spicer, a draper, a dyer, a butcher, a barber, a cutler, and a smith, a list remarkably similar to the trades that Jacobus assigns to the *Liber*'s eight pawns.[11]

When, in the late fifteenth century, Caxton decided to translate and print the *Liber*, he capitalized on the text's broad scope and depiction of a diverse body politic. While his translation remains faithful to the original work, he uses his two prologues to frame *Game and Playe* as a text more concerned with the moral instruction of an entire community than with that of a single ruler. In the 1474 prologue, Caxton dedicates the work to his purported patron George, duke of Clarence, for whom he claims to have translated the book.[12] Clarence held the title of neither king nor prince, although he was one of the king's brothers. Several years later he would be executed for treason. Yet in this same prologue Caxton upends the text's *speculum regis* aspects by alluding to a readership far beyond that of a single ruler. He has, or so he claims, translated this book of "the auctorites, dictees, and stories of auncient doctours, philosophes, poetes," so that they may be "recounted and applied unto the moralité of the publique wele as well of the nobles as of the comyn peple."[13] Here, the *Game and Playe* becomes more of a mirror of a political body, a *speculum corpora politica*, than a *speculum regis*.[14]

---

[9] Kaeppeli, "Pour la biographie de Jacques de Cessole," pp. 149–50. As Kaeppeli observes, earlier scholars placed Cessolis in France, specifically at the convent of Rheims, an idea that he traces to a catalogue of Dominican writers composed in the mid-thirteenth century by a certain Laurent Pignon, who lists "Fr. Ioannes de Teryace, de conventu Remensi" as the author of "moralitates super ludum scacorum." For more on Jacobus see Murray, *History of Chess*, pp. 537–38.

[10] Epstein, *Genoa and the Genoese*, p. 149.

[11] Epstein, *Genoa and the Genoese*, p. 149.

[12] Most modern scholars believe that Caxton did not know the duke of Clarence and used his name only as a means to sell his book.

[13] Axon, *Caxton's Game and Playe of the Chesse, 1474*, p. 2.

[14] Medieval writers in general saw Jacobus' text as malleable. Two fourteenth-century French translators of the work, Jean de Ferron and Jean de Vignay, follow the text faithfully, retain most of its parts, and address their translations to noble patrons. Yet in the fifteenth century, Guillaume de

In the 1483 prologue Caxton draws even more attention to the text's potential for widespread application. "Wherfore bycause thys sayd book is ful of holsom wysedom and requysyte unto every astate and degree," he writes, "I have purposed to enprynte it, shewyng therin the figures of suche persons as longen to the playe, in whom al astates and degrees ben comprysed" (Pref.18–21). Presumably Caxton has little difficulty imagining a readership as diverse as the allegory itself. If this description of the text's scope is sweeping, so too is Caxton's entreaty to all those who read, or who hear the book read to them, to follow the precepts appropriate to their social role.

Caxton's own role as a fifteenth-century businessman, one with ties to the noble class, was a product of the same redistribution of political and social capital imagined in the *Game and Playe*. Before becoming a printer, Caxton had worked as a mercer, or merchant, with a trading circuit that kept him traveling between the Low Countries, the French seaport of Calais, and London.[15] By the mid-1450s, Caxton had become one of England's main importers of luxury goods, including cloth, silk, fur, and saffron, and his success as a merchant and financier provided entrée into powerful circles. Although no one has established the year Caxton began to serve as an envoy for the Crown, a 1458 charter referring to him as a person "of the Staple at Calais" provides the first record of this type of service, and other historical documents point to his ever-expanding role as a diplomat.[16] By 1462, Edward IV had appointed him governor of the English Nation at Bruges, and in this role he functioned on several occasions as the king's representative for trade negotiations with the dukes of Burgundy and the Hanseatic League, an alliance of German and Scandinavian trading groups that formed a monopoly in the Baltic region.

When Caxton, who was at this point most likely based in Bruges, turned to printing in the early 1470s, he was embedded in a matrix of commercial and political power, and his social position stood him in good stead. Although at least one scholar has recently downplayed his reliance on patronage and connections, there is no doubt that the young printer capitalized in the early stages of his business on regular trading allies and on royal

Saint André produced a 1,200-line French metrical version in which he omits most of the moral stories and moves the rules found in the *Liber*'s fourth book to the front. Such changes strip the work of any viable claim to the *speculum* tradition, turning it effectively into a book about chess. German poets had an even greater tendency than their French counterparts to redact Jacobus' text and transform it into verse. At least four different metrical versions appeared in Germany in the fourteenth century, and most of them considerably abbreviate the *Liber*'s scope. Nor was translation the only means used to reconfigure the original text. The anonymous author of the fourteenth-century *Les Echecs amoureux* frequently references the *Liber*'s symbolic system yet uses his poem to recast the chess pieces as the qualities and emotions of the two lovers who play the game. For more on the other translations of the *Liber*, see Murray, *History of Chess*, pp. 546–48. For a more complete discussion of *Les Echecs amoureux*, see Adams, *Power Play*, pp. 57–94.

[15] Details of Caxton's life before he began his career as a printer can be found in Blades, *Life and Typography of William Caxton*, 1:1–32; Blake, *Caxton and His World*, pp. 13–45; Painter, *William Caxton*, pp. 1–42; and Gill, "William Caxton and the Rebellion of 1483." The subsequent historical information has been taken primarily from Gill and Blake.

[16] A staple was a town or region in which a body of merchants had the exclusive right of purchase of certain goods for export. From 1390 to 1558, the Staple at Calais was the chief staple and was also known as The Staple.

support.[17] Caxton himself writes in his prologue to his first book, the *Recuyell of the Historyes of Troye*, that his translation was partially funded by the king's sister, Margaret of York, who gave Caxton a "yerly fee and other many goode and grete benefetes."[18] Caxton does not always provide accurate information about his channels of commercial and social support. As mentioned above, he dedicated the first edition of the *Game and Playe* to the king's brother, a man he had most likely never met, and this attribution suggests a tie between the two men that in reality probably never existed. Yet even if this particular attempt at forging a connection failed, it nonetheless bespeaks Caxton's attempts to promote himself as a printer who catered to royal tastes, who produced his texts for a courtly audience, and who endorsed the traditional authority of a patron over a producer, which in the case of Caxton functions as an extension of royal authority over lay power. Not just anyone bought Caxton's books; members of the king's household were his clients. Or at least this is the impression Caxton strives to create in his prologues and prefaces, which he uses to position his patrons as literary and political authorities.[19]

When Caxton returned to England, he continued to cultivate his connections to the royal household and the court, and continued to use their names in his prologues and epilogues, evidence that he needed or at least wanted such endorsements to publish his books. His most powerful patrons were members of the Woodville family, and foremost among them was Earl Rivers, for whom Caxton printed Rivers' own translations of Christine de Pizan's *Moral Proverbs* (1478) and *Cordial* (1479), the latter of which Caxton had printed earlier in French while still in Bruges.[20] For Elizabeth Woodville, wife of King Edward IV, Caxton translated and printed *Jason*, a continuation of the Troy story, which he presented to her son, the Prince of Wales, in 1477.[21]

In April of 1483, however, Edward IV died, thus initiating a shift in political power that would in turn have implications for Caxton's printing business and, by extension, for the ways he set about crafting his prologues. In June, after a struggle with the Woodvilles, Edward's brother Richard, duke of Gloucester, claimed the throne. Southern England never acknowledged King Richard III's legitimacy, and various dissidents planned a series of rebellions for October.[22] Rutter has surmised that Caxton's decrease of dedications around this time offers evidence of his increased independence from patrons.[23] Blake, observing the same phenomenon, has argued that the change was one of political necessity and sees *Caton*,

---

[17] Russell Rutter has argued that "the sustenance Caxton received from patrons was by comparison [to authors of manuscripts] thin and inconsequential" ("William Caxton and Literary Patronage," p. 444). Yet later in this same article Rutter argues that the printer did rely on patronage in the early parts of his career, and that it was only "once Caxton [had] begun to reach a larger public" that "patrons became less important to him" (p. 463).

[18] Caxton, *Recuyell of the Historyes of Troye*, 1:5.

[19] Describing Caxton's shop in Westminster, Blake refers to Caxton's patrons as "the nobility . . . litigants, professional men and merchants" (*Caxton and His World*, p. 80).

[20] Blake, *Caxton and His World*, pp. 86–87.

[21] Blake, *Caxton and His World*, pp. 86–87.

[22] While the principal figures included such high-placed people as Elizabeth Woodville and Henry Tudor, this rebellion was primarily a mutiny of Edward IV's household nobles, and it failed (Gill, "William Caxton and the Rebellion of 1483," p. 112).

[23] Rutter, "William Caxton and Literary Patronage," p. 463.

which was finished in December of 1483, as Caxton's attempt to change his approach to patronage.[24] "Up till now," Blake writes, "books had been produced without dedication or under the patronage of a nobleman. . . . *Caton* marks a break with the past for it is dedicated to the City of London. Not only did he dedicate it to London, but he stated his own allegiance to that city in no uncertain way; the prologue opens: 'I, William Caxton, cytezeyn & coniurye of the same [i.e., liveryman of London], & of the fraternyte & felauship of the Mercerye.'"[25] Rather than continue to foreground his affiliations with the nobility, as this argument goes, Caxton now addressed his fellow merchants and effectively severed his allegiance with the Woodville camp. While Caxton would continue to produce texts for the Woodvilles, and while the Woodvilles themselves would eventually return to power, the printer never again readopted the same glowing and florid style characteristic of his early prologues.

It is likely that Caxton's embracing of the merchant class represented a prudent business decision. But his writings also seem to be reacting to this changing landscape of royal power, which formed the backdrop for his mercantile activities. As noted above, his two editions of the *Game and Playe* ultimately reflect a continuation of the complex discourses that had surrounded fifteenth-century political organization. His dedication of the 1474 *Game and Playe* to Clarence and his prologue to this printing help him to present the text as a *speculum regis*, and this textual frame in turn gestures overtly to royal authority even as it simultaneously claims a larger audience.[26] His 1483 prologue, however, directs the work to all people, thus emphasizing the increasing importance of all classes and professions as arbiters of power at the expense of monarchial authority.

The changes Caxton made to his prologue might imply either a radical reformulation of political power or a sudden shift of sentiment on the part of Caxton or on the part of his readers, or even a more general change that affected both the printer and his audience. Such a reading, however, would be misleading at a time when there were many different models of royal authority available and in circulation, and when monarchial control was still strong.[27] While the death of his dedicatee furnished a reason to rewrite the volume's prefatory

---

[24] *Caton*, a translation of a French prose text of the writings of the classical author Cato, is not the same work as Benedict Burgh's *Cato*, a poem that Caxton printed three times.

[25] Blake, *Caxton and His World*, p. 92. Noting that "the book was designed to improve the morals of merchants rather than to amuse the nobility," Blake goes on to argue that Caxton "had previously printed books for the merchant market without stating his allegiance to the merchant community" and thus reads the change as an attempt by the printer to distance himself from the Woodvilles.

[26] Blake argues that Caxton's French manuscript copy most likely did not contain a prologue, thus forcing Caxton to return to the *Recuyell* for a model. As in the *Recuyell* he uses this space to launch into "a rather extravagant praise of [his patron] which is expressed in laudatory platitudes" ("Continuity and Change," pp. 75 and 76). In the introduction to his reprint, Axon posits that Caxton borrowed from Jean de Vignay's preface, in which the writer dedicates his French translation to Prince John of France. The parallels between Jean's preface and Caxton's prologue are striking. Yet it is not clear that Caxton had access to one of Jean de Vignay's manuscripts for his translation. It is also worthwhile to note that Jean de Ferron's translation of the *Liber* is prefaced by remarks that resemble Caxton's 1483 prologue.

[27] Gerald L. Harriss has shown that the emergence of a political society in which all ranks "came to be involved in the activity of governing" grew out of economic, social, and political changes that took place from the thirteenth to the fifteenth centuries, and that the changes in political order and descriptions thereof did not take place as a singular, rapid occurrence ("Political Society," p. 33).

matter, Caxton's decision to direct his 1483 prologue to all men rather than toward a specific person poses a challenge to received order by suggesting that a stable realm requires virtue on the part of all citizens, not simply on the part of a king. Or put another way, by emphasizing the need for all men to act virtuously, Caxton, like Jacobus, recognizes that a community consists of multiple nodes of power, and he foregrounds this fact in his prologue.

In the body of his translation Caxton makes even stronger suggestions about the importance of individual morality and of a shared responsibility for the common good. In a passage absent from Latin versions of the *Liber* and its French translations, and apparently original to Caxton himself, the printer includes a passage about communal property, which, as he sees it, is the form of life most acceptable to God:

> And also, it is to be supposid that suche as have theyr goodes comune and not propre is most acceptable to God. For ellis wold not thyse religyous men as monkes, freres, chanons, observauntes, and al other avowe hem and kepe the wylful poverté that they ben professyd to? For in trouth I have myself ben conversaunt in a religious hows of Whyt Freres at Gaunt, whiche have al thyng in comyn among them, and not one richer than another, insomoche that yf a man gaf to a frere three pence or four pence to praye for hym in his masse, as sone as the masse is don, he delyveryeth hit to his overest or procuratour, in whiche hows ben many vertuous and devout freris. And yf that lyf were not the best and the most holyest, Holy Chirche wold never suffre hit in religyon. (3.238–47)

Seeing this addition as an indication of Caxton's "communism" or as "an anti-clerical tirade of his own invention in which he praises egalitarianism as a better social arrangement than feudalism" is to push past reasonable interpretive limits, especially given the printer's own success as a businessman.[28] The White Friars that Caxton has met do not avoid profit; they sell their prayers and share the take. And it is not that they are not rich, but rather that there is "not one richer than another."[29] Nevertheless, Caxton's praise of common belongings gestures toward a fantasy of communal responsibility just as it acknowledges a more general dispersal of power already present. That private property forms a locus of concern means that property owners had some degree of economic and political power, and thus Caxton has good reason to address "the moralité of the publique wele as well of the nobles as of the comyn peple."[30]

In the second printing of the *Game and Playe*, a series of woodcuts, made especially for this text, further emphasizes the work's endorsement of associative political order, and they move the reader from the image of a literally fragmented king to a ruler who has mastered his role within the kingdom. In the first image, a decapitated body offers a striking commentary on royal authority. The king, reduced to a crowned head with closed eyes, lies on the ground in front of a chopping block as his executioner looks on. Four carrion birds

---

[28] For a reference to this moment as one of communism, see Wilson, "Caxton's Chess Book," p. 97. For the idea that Caxton promotes "egalitarianism," see Poole, "False Play," p. 53. Poole's idea that Caxton is responding to feudalism ignores the generally capitalist nature of late fifteenth-century London.

[29] Notably, this passage does not appear in the chapter about the judges but in the one dedicated to the blacksmiths.

[30] For a longer discussion of the historical incident that may have provoked Caxton's remarks, see the Explanatory Notes on this section of the *Game and Playe*, Book 3, chapter 2 (p. 132 n. 238–39).

swarm within the frame, each holding a body part it has seized from the corpse. In the text, this king is Nebuchadnezzar, a ruler in Babylon who, as the text explains, is killed by his despotic son, Evilmerodach.[31] One would be hard-pressed to make any claims about the identity of the king, nor does the picture match the narrative of Richard III's rise to power, which took place after his brother Edward IV had died of natural causes. Nevertheless, this representation of regicide would have had strong cultural reverberations in the context of Richard's assumption of the throne, an act that resulted in the execution of several people with royal connections, including Edward IV's two sons, who disappeared into the Tower never to be seen again. Even if the picture does not offer a specific reprimand of Richard's actions, it presents a graphic reminder of the destructibility of the royal body.[32]

At the same time, the subsequent woodcuts, like the chapters they introduce, do not wholly condemn such destruction. Although never sanctioning regicide, the image series positions this act as the fulcrum for the game's creation, which subsequently refashions the king's relationship both to his own body and to the body of the state. In the second woodcut we see Philometer, a philosopher who lives in Babylon, the kingdom depicted in the *Liber*.[33] Here the chaos and disorder of the swirling birds has given way to this single figure, who sits calmly in a room carefully studying the chessboard in front of him. The picture's symmetrical design and the frame around the image, which features thick pillars on both sides, highlight the logic and reason of his pastime and reinforce the idea of stability and permanence. By matching the checkered pattern of the floor with the checkered pattern of the board, the illustrator reminds us that the game should model real life.

In the third woodcut Philometer and Evilmerodach sit at a chessboard. Again, the board is located in a room and framed by pillars, although in this picture the differences between the two players disrupt the symmetry of the image. The king sits on a throne to the left, while the philosopher sits on the board's right, perched, it seems, on an invisible stool. The king's throne, crown, and fur-lined robe help us to identify him and also confer on him his political power. Yet the limits of his power are emphasized by Philometer, who holds a piece and shows the king the proper rules of play. Positioned to the right side of the board, the side that connotes his moral and intellectual authority, the philosopher prepares to explain to Evilmerodach the king's position on the board and the ways the game represents the

---

[31] A scriptural mention of Evilmerodach appears in 2 Kings 25:27 "And in the thirty-seventh year of the exile of Jehoiachin king of Judah, in the twelfth month, on the twenty-seventh day of the month, Evil-merodach king of Babylon, in the year that he began to reign graciously freed Jehoiachin king of Judah from prison." D. J. Wiseman describes Evilmerodach (Amēl-Marduk) as the son of Nebuchadnezzar, who took over his father's throne in 562 (*Nebuchadnezzar and Babylon*, p. 9). Wiseman adds that Amēl-Marduk's "reign was marred by intrigues, some possibly directed against his father." The historical Nebuchadnezzar was famous for his immense building in the city.

[32] In her study of early book illustration, Martha W. Driver remarks: "When we look at book illustration in particular, the movement from manuscript to print can be traced as a political act, with the print medium empowering newly literate readers, both women and men, to read and think for themselves" (*Image in Print*, p. 3).

[33] Jacobus initially refers to Philometer as "Xerxes" but then reverts to his "Greek" name for most of the rest of the *Liber*. This historical Xerxes was the king of Persia and the son of Darius of Persia. In Book 7 of his *Histories* Herodotus describes Xerxes' attacks on Egypt and Greece.

king's relationship to the other subjects in his realm.[34] The picture offers a blunt reminder that the king derives much of his power from his counselors, who represent him in his kingdom.

In the fourth woodcut we finally see the king alone. Once again, sturdy pillars frame the image, and an arch with two windows reinforces the scene's symmetry. The king sits on the throne facing the reader yet with his eyes closed, and he holds an apple of gold and a scepter. According to the text that follows, the apple indicates the king's ability to think about the administration of justice while the scepter represents the ruler's ability to punish any rebels.

In sum, these first four woodcuts thus move from an image of a king's fragmented body to a picture of a king intact. Between the two lies the process of reconstitution, namely, the creation of the chess game, which allows Philometer to reconceive of the king's body as one among many. "The kynge must be thus maad," explains the first sentence in the chapter, the verb "make" reminding the reader that the king's body as a manufactured entity over which the writer and illustrator have control. The piece itself is portrayed as a composite of the kings from the first two woodcuts; his robe, his smooth face, and his throne match those of Evilmerodach, while his closed eyes recall Nebuchadnezzar's corpse. The fifth woodcut, which shows the king seated next to the queen, pushes this point even further by adding a beard to the king's face while at the same time carrying over the scepter from the previous drawing. Although the beard can be taken as a sign of the king's maturity and readiness to marry, a contrast with his unshaved and youthful face in the previous woodcut, it also firmly links the picture back to the initial image of Nebuchadnezzar's decapitated head.

By showing the destruction and subsequent rebuilding of the king's body, Caxton offers a graphic reminder of the limits of monarchial authority. The royal body's transience, so graphically illustrated by the dismemberment depicted in the first image, enables the refashioning of the civic body in the form of a chess game. This new metaphor for social order reimagines the king as a member of the kingdom; the realm is no longer a reflection of royal will but rather a complicated matrix of different affiliations in which the king is one piece among many. The importance of all the pieces is made manifest by the woodcuts that follow, each of which illustrates a different piece/profession and emphasizes its contributions to the community as a whole. Just as the farmer's plow represents his identity as the provider of food for the kingdom, so too do the king's apple and scepter symbolize his job. As the manager of the realm, he has a responsibility to dispense justice. And if he fails to do his job correctly, he can be held accountable by the people he governs. The chess king, already a composite of both Evilmerodach and Nebuchadnezzar, is representative of all kings, including the one currently occupying the English throne.

The volume's appearance in 1483, the same year that Richard III seized the throne, thus reflects the complex state of royal authority and shifting political climate.[35] Again, this

---

[34] Although it is tempting to identify the piece in Philometer's hand as the chess king, it is most likely the rook. Not only does the board feature a rook identical to the piece he holds, but earlier diagrams such as Alfonso el Sabio's *Libros del axedrez, dados et tablas* depict the rook with a roughly similar shape.

[35] N. F. Blake claims that it is not possible to know "how many copies of any first edition were printed," yet also adds that "we must assume that he thought they would be sufficient to satisfy the expected demand" (*Caxton: England's First Publisher*, p. 184). It is thus significant that of the many translations Caxton printed, he reprinted only four: *Dictes or Sayengis of the Philosophres* (reprinted

is not to say that Caxton had a sudden change of heart about rule by monarch. But his two prologues to the *Game and Playe*, his story of London's White Friars, and his woodcuts all reflect an ambivalent attitude about governmental power, an ambivalence reflected in the instability of the politics and of the sociopolitical and literary discourse of the time. In a country torn apart by the Wars of the Roses and still recovering from the fiscal drain of the Hundred Years' War, the idea of a civic body with multiple and self-regulating nodes of power apparently held particular appeal.

THIS EDITION OF THE *GAME AND PLAYE*

In keeping with what would become his custom, Caxton used a French translation as the basis for the *Game and Playe*, although it is likely that he had access to an earlier Latin text as well. Robert H. Wilson has argued that the extant copy closest to Caxton's version is the "Cockerell" manuscript, now more commonly known as the Regenstein Library MS 392 at the University of Chicago. Judging from the illustrations, this manuscript was produced by Flemish scribes and illuminators working in the late fourteenth century. Although Wilson admits to numerous small differences between this manuscript and Caxton's translation, he also argues that "on the basis of the fundamental correspondence, one must believe that Caxton derived his combination of Faron and Vignay [the two main French translators of the *Liber*] from a MS related to the Cockerell."[36] Christine Knowles supports this claim: "a comparison of the English version with a microfilm of the Chicago manuscript shows an exact correspondence between the two, including the change-over to Jean de Vignay's translation towards the end of the chapter on the Rooks."[37] I tend to agree with Knowles and Wilson, with the caveat that it is impossible to know for sure if Caxton used this particular text as this manuscript is missing several lengthy sections.[38]

Roughly a dozen copies of each printing of Caxton's *Game and Playe* (eleven of the 1474 edition; thirteen of the 1483 edition) are currently extant.[39] There do not appear to be any textual variations or stop-press corrections within each edition. There are also only minimal customizations that various owners have made to their copies. For example, the Newberry Library version of the 1483 *Game and Playe* (fol. Inc. 9643) has large, lightly hand-painted initials opening each chapter, whereas the Yale Center for British Art's copy of the same (GV1442.C3 Oversize) has only lightly traced indications of where such initials should be. Excepting these differences, the copies of each text are identical.

By contrast, the 1474 and 1483 editions contain typographical differences, orthographic changes, subtractions (or occasionally additions) of individual words and phrases, and a

---

twice), the *Game and Playe of the Chesse*, *Mirrour of the World*, and the *Historye of Reynard the Foxe*.

[36] Wilson, "Caxton's Chess Book," p. 96.

[37] Knowles, "Caxton and His Two French Sources," p. 423. Knowles also observes that Caxton "seems to have made very careful and detailed use of the Latin [text]" (p. 420). N. F. Blake notes that the *Game and Playe* also resembles MSS fr. 2146 and 2471, both housed at the Bibliothèque nationale de France (*William Caxton: A Bibliographical Guide*, p. 31).

[38] The Regenstein manuscript is missing leaves between 7v and 8r (the end of Book 2, chapter 3, through the first part of Book 2, chapter 4), and between 28v and 29r (the end of Book 3, chapter 6, through the first part of Book 3, chapter 7).

[39] A list of extant copies follows this introduction.

recasting of the entire work from a 31-line to a 29-line layout. To give a sense of the ortho-graphic alterations, here is the opening to Book 2, chapter 5, the chapter on the rooks:

> 1474: "The rooks whiche ben vicaires and legats of the kynge ought to be made lyke a knyght upon an hors and a mantell on hood furryd with menevyer holdynge a staf in his hande."

> 1483: "The rookes whiche been vycayrs and legates of the kynge ought to be maad a knyght upon an hors and a mantel and hood furrid with menevier holdyng a staf in his hand."

Here the printer's changes consist of: *e*'s, some added (rooks/rookes), others dropped (hande/hand); *y*'s and *i*'s, some switched one way (vicaires/vycayrs) and some switched the other (menevyer/menevier); and the omission of the word "lyke." More substantial changes than these are rare. Nevertheless, more sizeable alterations occasionally do appear. In the third chapter of Book 3, for example, Caxton describes a sermon preached in the *Vitas Patrum* in which the priest notes that "deth spareth none. And as wel dyeth the yonge as the olde." This is a slight modification of the 1474 version, which reads "deth spareth none, ne riche ne poure. And as wel dyeth the yonge as the olde." While the deletion of "ne riche ne poure" might signal a larger shift of emphasis on class, economics, or monetary interest, such changes are not significant enough to note in this edition, and I leave it to others to examine more carefully these individual instances.[40]

Unlike Caxton's other publications — the *History of Troy*, the *Canterbury Tales*, and most notably the *Morte d'Arthur* — the *Game and Playe* has never been edited or published in a modern edition.[41] Currently, the only accessible copies are two facsimiles of Caxton's 1483 edition and one nineteenth-century transcription of the 1474 text.[42] I have chosen the 1483 edition as my base text for several reasons. First, it contains corrections to the 1474 text and

---

[40] Lisa Cooper has offered an enticing analysis of one particular change that Caxton made between the two editions. Of the 1483 version she notes that the artisans declare that "it is *not* [rather than *most*] necessary to studye for the comyn prouffit." As she points out, the artisans in this instance suddenly "serve as arrogant and ignorant foils, beside which the judges appear serenely wise and virtuous workers for the common good." She adds: "Although we find it in a passage about judges rather than kings, the irreconcilable difference here between Caxton's two editions of the *Game and Playe* neatly captures not only the paradoxical position artisans hold in this one text, but also the position they most often hold in every mirror for a prince in which they are found." I am extremely grateful to Cooper for sharing a draft of her forthcoming work on artisans, authors, and the literary artifact in late medieval England. My quotes are from that work. For a more complete analysis of orthographic changes that Caxton has made to his text, see Mizobata, "Caxton's Revisions."

[41] This lack of attention paid to editing the *Game and Playe* mirrors a more general scholarly disinterest in analyzing the text on its own merits or considering it in the context of Caxton's other publications. Indeed, only a handful of articles have addressed this work as a text in its own right. See the Bibliography.

[42] For facsimiles of the 1483 text, see N. F. Blake and Vincent Figgins. It should be noted that Figgins' "facsimile" does not reproduce the original text exactly but rather in a print type that imitates Caxton's own. For a transcription of the 1474 edition, see Axon's *Caxton's Game and Playe of the Chesse, 1474*. Axon's transcription is also accessible online through the Project Gutenberg at http://www.gutenberg.org/dirs/1/0/6/7/10672/10672-h/10672-h.htm (accessed on 11/2/06).

thus reflects Caxton's more finished copy.[43] But second, and more importantly, this edition was printed in England for an explicitly English audience. As noted above, Caxton's change in prologue, which is now freed from its ties to the nobility, and his addition of woodcuts reveal the printer's desire to reorient the text towards the body politic and to package it anew for a wider audience.

In keeping with standard editorial practices of the Middle English Texts Series, I have used modern punctuation and capitalization. I have also regularized *i/j*, *u/v*, and *f/s* spellings (thus *I* rather than *J*, *have* rather than *haue*, and *wysedom* rather than *wyfedom*) and have expanded any standard printer's abbreviations (thus *the admynystracion, founden, somme, commaundementis*, and *the ende* rather than *thadmynystracion, foûden, sôme, cômaûdementis*, and *thende*). I have differentiated between *the* and *thee* by silently expanding the latter, which appears almost uniformly as *the* in Caxton's text. In the very few instances where *ff* is used to designate a capital *F* I have used the latter. Finally, all Roman numerals in the body of the text have either been spelled out or replaced with Arabic numbers.

EARLY PRINTED EDITIONS

Caxton's *Game and Playe of the Chesse*, 1483 Edition (folio, 84 leaves, a–i[8] k–l[6]; type 2*)

Harry Ransom Center, University of Texas, Austin (missing thirty-eight leaves)
Huntington Library, San Marino, CA (complete)
Library of Congress, Washington, DC (one leaf in facsimile and one leaf blank)
Newberry Library, Chicago (complete) [copy text for this edition]
Pierpont Morgan Library, New York (complete)
Yale Center for British Art, New Haven (missing final folio)
British Library, London (missing six leaves, supplied in facsimile)
Bodleian Library, Oxford (two copies: one missing several leaves and one fragment)
St. John's College, Oxford (missing one leaf)
John Rylands Library, University of Manchester (complete)
Magdalene College Pepysian Library, Cambridge (incomplete)
Trinity College, Cambridge (complete)
Austrian National Library, Vienna (missing six leaves)

Caxton's *Game and Playe of the Chesse*, 1474 Edition (folio, 74 leaves, type 1)

Newberry Library, Chicago
Pierpont Morgan Library, New York
New York Public Library, New York
Huntington Library, San Marino, CA
Library of Congress, Washington, DC
Yale Center for British Art, New Haven

---

[43] Mizobata concludes that unlike the *Mirror of the World* and *Reynard*, texts whose second editions were inferior to the first, the 1483 edition of the *Game of Chess* represents a significant improvement in quality ("Caxton's Revisions," p. 262).

Bodleian Library, Oxford
British Library, London
British Library, London
John Rylands Library, University of Manchester
Austrian National Library, Vienna

References

Catalogue of Books Printed in the XVth Century Now in the British Museum. London: British Museum, 1908–. IX, p. 130.

Duff, E. Gordon. *Fifteenth Century English Books; a Bibliography of Books and Documents Printed in England and of Books for the English Market Printed Abroad.* London: Oxford University Press, 1917. Pp. 81–82.

Goff, Frederick R. *Incunabula in American Libraries; a Third Census of Fifteenth-century Books Recorded in North American Collections.* New York: Bibliographical Society of America, 1964. C 413 and C 414.

Pollard, A. W., and G. R. Redgrave. *A Short-title Catalogue of Books Printed in England, Scotland, & Ireland and of English Books Printed Abroad, 1475–1640.* 2nd edition. London: Bibliographical Society, 1976–1991. 4920 and 4921.

Proctor, Robert. *An Index to the Early Printed Books in the British Museum.* London: Holland Press, 1960. 9322 and 9323.

Facsimiles of *Game and Playe of the Chesse*

Caxton's Game and Playe of the Chesse, 1474. Ed. William E. A. Axon. London: Elliot Stock, 1883. (Available online at: http://www.gutenberg.org/dirs/1/0/6/7/10672/10672-h/10672-h.htm)

The Game of the Chesse by William Caxton. Ed. Vincent Figgins. London: John Russell Smith, 1860.

Jacobus de Cessolis, The Game of Chess: Translated and Printed by William Caxton, c. 1483. Ed. N. F. Blake. London: The Scholar Press, 1976.

The holy appostle and doctour of the peple, Saynt Poule, sayth in his Epystle:
"Alle that is wryten is wryten unto our doctryne and for our lernyng." Wherfore
many noble clerkes have endevoyred them to wryte and compyle many notable
werkes and historyes to the ende that it myght come to the knowlege and understondyng of suche as ben ygnoraunt, of which the nombre is infenyte. And accordyng
to the same saith Salamon, that the nombre of foles is infenyte. And emong alle
other good werkys, it is a werke of ryght special recomendacion to enforme and to
late understonde wysdom and vertue unto them that be not lerynd ne cannot
dyscerne wysdom fro folye. Thenne emonge whom there was an excellent doctour
of dyvynyté in the royame of Fraunce of the ordre of the Hospytal of Saynt John's
of Jherusalem whiche entende the same and hath made a book of the chesse
morlaysed, whiche as such tyme as I was resident in Brudgys in the counté of
Flaundres cam into my handes, which, whan I had redde and overseen, me semed
ful necessarye for to be had in Englisshe. And in eschewyng of ydlenes, and to the
ende that somme which have not seen it, ne understonde Frenssh ne Latyn, I
delybered in myself to translate it into our maternal tonge. And whan I so had
achyeved the sayd translacion, I dyde doo sette in enprynte a certeyn nombre of
theym, whiche anone were depesshed and solde. Wherfore bycause thys sayd book
is ful of holsom wysedom and requysyte unto every astate and degree, I have
purposed to enprynte it, shewyng therin the figures of suche persons as longen to
the playe, in whom al astates and degrees ben comprysed, besechyng al them that
this litel werke shal see, here, or rede to have me for excused for the rude and
symple makyng and reducyn into our Englisshe. And where as is defaute to
correcte and amende, and in so doyng they shal deserve meryte and thanke. And
I shal pray for them that God of His grete mercy shal rewarde them in His ever-
lastyng blisse in heven, to the whiche He brynge us, that wyth His precious blood
redemed us. Amen.

5

10

15

20

25

3 endevoyred them, put themselves to the task. **5 infenyte**, infinite. **6 foles**, fools; **emong**,
among. **9 dyscerne**, discern; **fro**, from. **11 entende the same**, (i.e., had the same desire
to educate people). **12 Brudgys**, Bruges. **13 Flaundres**, Flanders (now the Flemish region
of Belgium); **me semed**, it seemed to me. **18 depesshed**, distributed. **20 longen**, belong.
21 astates and degrees, estates and classes; **comprysed**, represented.

This book is devyded and departed into four traytyes and partyes.

---

28 traytyes, books.   **30 founden**, created.   **32 maad**, made.   **34 maners**, virtues or disposition.   **36 alphyns**, bishops.   **41 smyth**, blacksmith.   **42 notaries**, personal secretaries or clerks; **advocates**, those who plead cases in a court of justice; **scriveners**, professional scribes; **drapers**, makers of and/or dealers in cloth.   **44 chaungers**, money changers.   **45 leches**, doctors; **spycers**, spice dealers; **appotycaryes**, apothecaries.   **46 taverners**, tavern-keepers; **hostelers**, keepers of hostelries or inns; **vitaillers**, purveyors of victuals or provisions.   **47 kepars of townes, receyvers of custum, and tollenars**, officials who collect customs or tolls.   **48 currours**, couriers; **rybauldes**, ribald or dissolute characters.   **51 draught**, move; **eschequer**, chessboard.   **52 yssueth**, issues.   **55 her**, their.   **57 epilogacion**, conclusion.

This first chappitre of the first tractate sheweth under what kyng the playe of the chesse was founden and maad. **Capitulo primo.**

    Amonge alle the evyl condicions and signes that may be in a man, the first and the grettest is whan he fereth not ne dredeth to displese and make wroth God by synne and the peple by lyvyng disordonatly, whan he retcheth not nor taketh hede unto them that repreve hym and his vyces but sleeth them, in suche wyse as did the

5   emperour Nero, whiche did do slee his mayster, Seneque, for as moche as he myght not suffre to be reprevyd and taught of hym. In likewise was somtyme a kyng in Babilon that was named Evylmerodach, a jolye man without justyce and so cruel that he did do hewe his fader's body in thre hondred pieces and gaf hit to ete and devoure to thre hondred byrdes that men calle voultres. And [he] was of suche

10   condicion as was Nero, and right wel resemblid and was lyke unto his fader, Nabugodonosor, whiche on a tyme wold do slee all the sage and wise men of Babilone, for as moche as they coude not telle hym his dreme that he had dremyd

---

Title **maad** (made). **2 he fereth not ne dredeth**, does not fear or dread; **wroth**, angry. **3 disordonatly**, not according to order or moderation; **retcheth**, cares. **4 repreve**, reprove; **sleeth**, slays. **5 did do slee his mayster**, had his teacher slain. **6 somtyme**, once. **8 did do hewe his fader's body**, had his father's body cut up. **9 voultres**, vultures. **11 wold do slee**, would have slain.

17

on a nyght and had forgoten hit, like as hit is wreton in the Byble in the Book of
Danyel. Under this kyng, thenne, Evylmerodach, was this game and playe of the
15   chesse founden. Trewe it is that somme men wene that this play was founden in the
tyme of the bat; the tyme of the batailles and siege of Troye. But that is not so. For this playe cam to
the playes of the Caldees, as Diomedes the Greek saith and rehercech, that amonge
the philosophres was the most renomed playe amonge al other playes. And after
that cam this playe in the tyme of Alixander the Grete into Egypt, and so unto alle
20   the parties toward the south. And the cause wherfore this playe was so renomed
shal be sayd in the third chepitre.

This chappytre of the first tractate shewyth who fond first the playe of the chesse.

Capitulo two.

This playe fonde a phylosopher of the Oryent, whyche was named in Caldee
"Exerses," or in Greke "Philemetor," which is as moche to say in Englissh as "he
that lovyth justyce and mesure." And this philosopher was renomed gretly among
25   the Grekes and them of Athenes, whyche were good clerkys and phylosophers also
renomed of their connyng. This philosopher was so just and trewe that he had
lever dye than to lyve long and be a fals flaterer with the sayd kyng. For whan he
behelde the foul and synful lyf of the kyng, and that no man durst blame hym, for
by his grete cruelté he put them al to deth that displesid hym, he put hymself in
30   parel of deth, and lovyd and chees rather to dye than lenger to lyve. The evyl lyf,
and disfamed, of a kyng is the lyf of a cruel beste and ought not longe to be
susteyned. For he destroyeth hym that displesith hym.

15 **wene**, believe. **17 Caldees**, the Chaldeans (see Explanatory Notes); **saith and rehercech**,
says and recounts. **18 renomed**, renowned. **22 fonde**, invented; **Caldee**, the language
spoken by the Chaldeans. **26 connyng**, knowledge. **27 lever**, rather. **28 durst**, dared. **30
parel**, peril; **chees**, chose. **31 disfamed**, deprived of fame and honor; **beste**, beast.

And therfore reherceth Valerius that there was a wyse man named Theodore
Cerem whom his kyng dyd do hange on the crosse for as moche as he reprevyd
35 hym of hys evyl and foul lyf. And alwey, as he was in the torment, he sayd to the
kyng, "Upon thy counceyllours and theym that ben clad in thy clothyng and robys
were more reson that this torment shold come. For as moche as they dar not say
to thee the trouth for to do justyse rightwyslye. Of myself, I make no force whether
I dye on the lond or on the water or otherwyse," as who sayth he retched not to dye
40 for justyce.

In like wyse as Democreon the philosopher put out his owne eyen bycause he
wold not see that no good myght come to the evyl and vycious peple wythout right.

And also Desortes the philosophre, as he went toward his deth, his wyf that
folowed after hym sayd that he was dampned to deth wrongfully. Thenne he
45 answerd and sayd to her, "Holde thy pees and be stylle. Hit is better and more
meritorye to dye by a wrong and unrightful jugement than that I had deserved to
dye."

The thyrd chappitre of the first tractate treteth wherfore the playe was founden and maad.
Capitulo three.

The causes wherfore this playe was founden ben three. The first was for to
correcte and repreve the kyng. For whan this kyng Evylmerodach sawe this playe,
50 and the barons, knyghtes and gentilmen of his court playe wyth the phylosopher,
he merveylled gretly of the beaulté and noveltee of the playe and desired to playe
agaynst the philosopher. The philosopher answerd and sayd to hym that hit myght

---

34 **dyd do hange on the crosse**, had hung on a cross. **36 robys**, robes. **38 make no force**,
do not care. **39 as who sayth**, as much as who says. **41 eyen**, eyes; **bycause**, so that. **44
dampned**, condemned. **45 pees**, peace. **46 meritorye**, meritorious. **51 merveylled**,
marveled; **beaulté and noveltee**, beauty and novelty.

not be doon but yf he first lernyd the play. The kyng sayd hit was reson and that
he wold put hym to the payn to lerne hit. Than the phylosopher began to teche
55 hym and to shewe hym the maner of the table of the chesse borde and the chesse
meyne, and also the maners and the condycions of a kyng, of the nobles, and of the
comyn peple, and of theyr offyces, and how they shold be touchyd and drawen, and
how he shold amende hymself and become vertuous.

And when this kyng herde that, he reprevyd hym. He demaunded hym upon
60 payn of deth to telle hym wherefore he had founden and maad this playe. And he
answerd, "My right dere lord and kyng, the grettest and most thyng that I desire
is that thou have in thyself a glorious and vertuous lyf. And that may I not see, but
yf thou be endoctrined and wel manerd. And that had, so mayst thou be belovyd
of thy peple. Thus, than, I desire that thou have other governement thenne thou
65 hast had, and that thou have upon thyself first seignourie and maistrie suche as
thou hast upon other by force and not by right. Certeynly hit is not right that a
man be maister over other and comaundour when he cannot rewle nor may rewle
hymself, and that his vertues domyne above his vyces. For seignourie by force and
wylle may not longe endure. Thenne thus may thou see oon of the causes why and
70 wherfore I have founden and maad this playe, whiche is for to correcte and repreve
thee of thy tyrannye and vicious lyvyng. For all kynges ought specially to here her
corrigiours or correctours and her correccions to holde and kepe in mynde."

In like wyse, as Valerius reherceth, that the kyng Alixandre had a noble and
renomed knyght that sayd in reprevyng of Alixandre that he was to moche
75 covetous and in especial of the honours of the world. And sayd to hym, "Yf the
goddes had maade thy body as grete as is thy herte, alle the world coude not holde
thee. For thou holdest in thy right hond al the Oryent, and in thy lifte honde the
Occident. Sith than hit is so, or thou art a god, or a man, or nought. Yf thou be
God, doo than wel and good to the peple as God doth, and take not from them
80 that they ought to have and is theyres. Yf thou be a man, thynke that thou shalt
dye, and than thou shalt doo noon evyl. Yf thou be nought, forgete thyself." There
is no thyng so stronge and ferme but that sumtyme a feble thyng casteth doun and
overthrowe hit. How wel that the lyon be the strengest beest. Yet somtyme a lityl
byrde eteth hym.

85 The second cause wherfore this playe was founden and maad was for to kepe
hym from ydlenesse. Wherof Seneque sayth unto Lucylle "Ydlenes wythout ony
ocupacion is sepulture of a man lyvyng."

And Varro saith in his *Sentences* that in lyke wyse as men goo not for to goo, the
same wyse the lyf is not gyven for to lyve but for to doo wel and good.

---

53 **but yf**, unless; **hit was reson**, this was reasonable.   **55–56 chesse meyne**, chessmen.   **56 the maners and the condycions**, manners and moves.   **58 amende**, improve.   **63 endoctrined**, taught; **that had**, that achieved.   **64 than**, then; **thenne**, than.   **65 seignourie and maistrie**, governance and control.   **67 comaundour**, commander.   **68 domyne**, rule over.   **69 oon**, one. **71–72 here her corrigiours**, hear their correctors.   **73 reherceth**, recounts.   **74 renomed**, renowned.   **75 in especial**, in particular; **Yf**, If.   **77 lifte**, left.   **78 Sith than**, Because; **or . . . or . . . or**, either . . . or . . . or; **nought**, nothing.   **81 noon**, no.   **82 feble**, feeble; **casteth doun**, casts down.   **83 strengest**, strongest.   **86 ydlenesse**, idleness.   **87 sepulture**, sepulcher. **89 gyven**, given.

90   And therfore secondly the philosopher fond this playe for to kepe the peple
from ydlenes. For there is moche peple, whan so is that they be fortunat in worldly
goodes, that they drawe them to ease and ydlenes, wherof comyth ofte tymes many
evyllis and grete synnes. And by this ydlenes, the herte is quenchyd, wherof comyth
good desperacion.

95   The thyrd cause is that every man naturelly desireth to knowe and here noveltees
and tydynges. For this cause they of Athenes studyed, as we rede, and for as the
corporal or bodelye sight enpessheth and letteth otherwhyle the knowleche of
subtyl thynges.

          Therfore we rede that Democrite the philosopher put out his owen eyen, for
100   as moche as he myght have the better entendement and understondyng. Many
have ben made blynde that were grete clerkis, in like wyse as was Didimus, bysshop
of Alixandrie, that how wel that he sawe not, yet he was so grete a clerke that Gregore
Nazanz and Saynt Jerome, that were clerkes and maysters to other, cam for to be
his scolers and lernyd of hym. And Saynt Anthonye, the grete hermyte, cam for to
105   see hym on a tyme. And emonge alle other thynges, he demaunded hym yf he were
not gretly dysplesid that he was blynde and sawe not. And he answerd that he was
gretly abasshyd for that he supposid not that he was not displeasid in that he had
lost his sight. And Saynt Anthonye answerd to hym, "I mervaile moche that hit
displesith thee that thou hast lost that thyng whiche is comyn betwene thee and
110   bestes. And thou knowest wel that thou hast not lost that thyng that is comyn
betwene thee and the aungellis."

          And for thise causes forsayd, the phylosopher entended to put awey al
pensifnes and thoughtes, and to thynke onely on this playe, as shal be sayd and
appere in this book after.

---

92 drawe them, occupy themselves. **93 the herte is quenchyd**, the spirit is extinguished.
95 noveltees, new things. **97 enpessheth and letteth otherwhyle**, forbids and prevents
sometimes. **99–100 for as moche as**, so that. **100 entendement**, learning. **101 ben**, been.
105 emonge, among; **demaunded**, asked. **106 dysplesid**, displeased. **108 mervaile**,
marvel. **111 aungellis**, angels. **112 thise causes forsayd**, these forementioned causes. **113
pensifnes**, anxiety.

Book Two

The second tractate. The first chapiter treteth of the forme of a kyng, of his maners, and of his estate.   **Capitulo primo.**

The kynge must be thus maad. For he must sytte in a chayer clothyd in purpure, crowned on his heed, in his right hond a ceptre, and in the lift honde an apple of golde, for he is the most grettest and hyest in dygnyté above al other and most worthy. And that is signyfyed by the corone, for the glorie of the peple is the

5 dygnyté of the kyng. And above al other the kyng ought to be replenysshed with vertues and of grace. And this signyfieth the purpure, for in like wyse as the robes of purpure maketh fayr and enbelissheth the body, the same wyse vertues makyth the sowle. He ought alwey thynk on the governement of the royame and who hath the admynystracion of justyce, and this shold be by hymself pryncipally. This

10 signefyeth the appel of golde that he holdeth in his lift honde. And for as moche as it aperteyneth unto hym to punysshe the rebelles, hath he the septre in his right hond. And for as moche as mysericorde and trouth conserve and kepe the kyng in his trone, therfore ought a kyng to be merciful and debonayr. For when a kyng or prynce desireth or wyl be belovyd of his peple, lete hym be governed by debonayrté.

1 **purpure**, purple. 2 **ceptre**, scepter. 4 **corone**, crown. 5 **replenysshed**, filled. 8 **royame**, realm. 10 **appel**, apple. 11 **aperteyneth unto**, is the responsibility of. 13 **debonayr**, gracious or meek. 14 **debonayrté**, graciousness.

15   And Valerius saith that deboneyrté percyth the hertes of straungers, and
amolissheth and makyth softe the hertes of his enemyes. Wherof he rehercith that
Phylostratus, that was duc of Athenes, had a doughter whom a man lovyd so ardantly
that, on a tyme as he sawe her with her moder, sodaynly he cam and kyssed her.
Wherof the moder was so angry and sorouful that she went and requryed of her
20   lord, the duc, that his heed myght be smyten of. The prynce answerd to her and
sayd, "Yf we shold slee them that love us, what shal we do to our enemyes that hate
us?" Certeynly, this was the answer of a noble and debonayr prynce, that suffred
that vylonye doon to his doughter and to hymself yet more.
      This prynce had also a frende that was named Arispe that sayd on a tyme as
25   moche vylonye unto the prynce as ony man myght saye. And that myght not suffyse
hym, but he cratchid hym in the vysage. The prynce suffryd hym paciently in suche
wyse as though he had doon to hym no vylonye but curtesye. And whan his sones
wold have avengyd this vylonye, he comaunded them that they shold not be so
hardy so to doo. The next day folowyng, Arispe remembrid of the right grete
30   vylonye that he had doon to his frende and lord without cause. He fyl in dyspayr
and wold have slayn hymself. Whan the duc knewe and understood that, he cam
to hym and said, "Ne doubte thee no thyng," and swore to hym by hys faith that
also wel he was and shold be his frend fro than forthon as ever he had ben tofore,
yf he wold. And thus he respited hym of his deth by his debonayrté.
35   And in lyke wise rede we of the Kyng Pirre to whom was reported that they of
Tarente had sayd grete vilonye of hym, for which cause he maad al them to come
tofore hym and demaunded of them yf they had so said. Than one of them answerd
and said, "Yf the wyn and the candellis had not fayled, thys langage had ben but
a jape, in regarde of that we had thought to have doon." Than the kyng began to
40   lawhe, for they had confessyd that suche langage as was said and spoken was by
dronkenshyp. And for this cause of debonayrté, the peple of Tarante tooke for a
custome that the dronken men shold be punysshid, and the sobre men preysed.
      The kyng thenne thus ought to love humylité and hate falsyté after the Holy
Scripture, that speketh of every man generally. For the kyng in his royame
45   representeth God, and God is verité, and therfore hym ought to say no thyng but
yf hit were verrytable and stable.
      Valerius reherceth that Alyxandre, wyth alle his ooste, rood for to destroye a
cyté whiche was named Lapsare, whan than a phylosophre, whyche had to name
Anaxymenes, whych had ben tofore maistre and governour of Alixandre, herd and
50   understood of his comyng, cam agayn Alixandre to desire and requyre of hym.
And whan he sawe Alixandre, he supposid to have axyd his request. Alixandre

16 **amolissheth**, appeases. 19 **requryed of**, asked. 20 **smyten of**, cut off. 23 **vylonye**, shameful behavior or language. 25–26 **And that myght not suffyse hym**, And as if that were not enough. 26 **cratchid**, scratched; **vysage**, face; **suffryd**, endured. 27 **curtesye**, courtesy. 28 **avengyd**, avenged. 28–29 **so hardy so to doo**, so rashly bold to do such a thing. 30 **frende**, friend. 32 **"Ne doubte thee no thyng,"** Do not worry yourself. 33 **also wel he was**, he was not hurt; **fro than forthon**, from that time forth; **tofore**, before. 34 **respited hym**, granted respite to him. 38 **candellis**, candles. 39 **jape**, joke. 41 **dronkenshyp**, drunkenness. 42 **punysshid**, punished; **preysed**, praised. 45 **verité**, truth. 46 **verrytable and stable**, true and unchanging. 47 **ooste**, army. 50 **to desire and requyre of hym**, i.e., to plead for the city. 51 **supposid**, prepared; **axyd**, asked.

brake his demaunde tofore and swore to hym, tofore he axid ony thyng, by his goddes that suche thyng as he axyd or requyred of hym, he wold in no wyse doon. Thenne the phylosopher requyred hym to destroye the cyté. Whan Alixandre
55   understood his desyre and the oth that he had maad, he suffrid the cyté to stonde and not to be destroyed, for he had lever not to do his wyll than to be perjured and forsworn, and doo ageynst his oth.

Quyntilian sayth that no grete man ne lord shold not swere but where as is grete nede, and that the symple parole or worde of a prynce ought to be more
60   stable thenne the oth of a marchaunt. Alas, who kepe the prynces their promyses in thyse dayes! Not onely her promyses but their othes, her sealis and wrytynges, and signes of theyr propre handes alle faylleth, God amende hit.

A kyng also ought to hate all cruelté. For we rede that never dyed yet ony pietous persone of evyl deth ne cruel persone of good deth. Therfore recounteth
65   Valerius that there was a man named Therile, a werkman in metalle, that maad a boole of coppre and a lityl wyket on the syde wherby men myght put in them that shold be brent therin. And hit was maad in suche manere that they that shold be put and enclosyd therin shold crye no thynge lyke to the voys of a man but of an oxe. And thys maad he bycause men shold have the lasse pyté of them. Whan he
70   had maad thys boole of copper, he presentyd hit unto a kyng whiche was called Philarde, that was so cruel a tyraunt that he delited in no thynge but in cruelté, and he tolde hym the condicion of the bole. Whan Philerde herde and understood thys, he alowed and praisid moche the werke, and after sayd to hym, "Thou that art more cruel than I am shalt assay and prove first thy presente and gefte." And
75   so maad hym to go into the boole and dye an evyl deth.

Therfore, sayth Ovide, "there is no thyng more resonable thenne that a man dye of suche deth as he purchaseth unto other."

Also, the kyng ought soveraynly kepe justyce. Who maketh or kepeth a royame without justyce, of verry force there must be grete robberye and thefte. Therfore
80   reherceth Saynt Augustyn, in a book whyche is intituled *The Cyté of God*, that there was a theef of the see named Diomedes, that was a grete rovar and dyd so moche harme that the complayntes cam tofore Alixander, whiche dyd hym to be taken and brought afore hym. And he demaunded hym wherfore he was so noyous and cruel in the see. And he answerd to hym agayn, "For as moche as thou art oon a
85   londe in the worlde, so am I another in the see. But for as moche as the evyl that I doo is in oon galey or tweyn, therfore I am callyd a theef. But for as moche as thou doost in many shyppys and wyth grete puyssaunce and power, therfore arte thou callyd an emperour. But yf fortune were for me in suche wyse, I wold become a

52 **brake his demaunde**, interrupted his request. 53 **goddes**, gods. 55 **oth**, oath; **suffrid**, allowed. 56 **lever**, rather. 59 **parole**, oath. 60 **who**, how. 61 **her**, their; **sealis**, seals. 62 **faylleth**, fail. 64 **pietous**, merciful or good. 66 **boole of coppre**, a copper bull; **lityl wyket**, small door. 67 **brent**, burnt. 68 **voys**, voice. 69 **lasse pyté**, less mercy. 73 **alowed**, praised. 74 **assay**, try (test); **gefte**, gift. 77 **purchaseth unto other**, gives to another. 79 **of verry force**, necessarily. 80 **intituled**, entitled. 81 **theef of the see**, pirate; **rovar**, wanderer (pirate). 82 **dyd hym**, commanded him. 83 **afore**, before; **noyous**, annoying. 84 **agayn**, in reply. 86 **oon galey**, one galley or ship; **tweyn**, two. 88 **yf fortune were for me in suche wyse**, (i.e., if I were rich like you).

90   good man and better thenne I now am. But thou, the more rycher and fortunat that thou art, the more worse art thou."

    Alyxaunder said to hym, "I shal chaunge thy fortune in suche wise as thou ne say that thou shalt do it by poverté, but for evyl and mavaysté." And so he made hym ryche. And this was he that afterward was a good prynce and a good justicier.

95   The kyng ought to be soveraynly chaste. And this signefyeth a quene that is oonly on his right side. For it is to be belevyd and credyble that whan the kyng is a good man, juste, trewe, and of good maners and condicions, that his children shal folowe gladly the same, for a good sone and a trewe ought not to forsake and goo fro the good condicions of his fader. For certes it is agaynst God and nature in partye whan a man taketh other thenne his propre wyf. And that see we by byrdes,

100 of whom the male and female have togyder the charge in kepyng and norisshyng of their yonge fowles and byrdes. For somme maner of fowles kepen them to their females oonly, as hit appereth by storkes, dowves, and turtils. But the fowles that norisshith not their birdes have many wyves and femels, as the cok that nothyng norisshith his chekens. And therfore amonge al the bestes that been, man and

105 woman putteth most their entente, and have most cure and charge, in norisshyng of their chyldren. And therfore don they agaynst nature in partye whan they leve theyr wyves for other women.

    Of this chasteté reherceth Valerius an example, and saith that ther was a man of Rome whyche was named Scipio Affrican, for as moche as he had conquerd

110 Affrique, how wel that he was of Rome born. Whan he was of thirty-four yere of age, he conquerd Cartage and toke moche people in ostage, among whom he was presented with a right fayr mayde for his solas and plaisir, which was assured and handfast unto a noble yonge gentilman of Cartage, whiche was named Indivicible. And anon as this gentil Scipio knewe that, not withstondyng that he was a prynce

115 noble and lusty, dyd do calle anon the parents and kynnesmen of them, and delyverd to them their doughter without doyng of ony vylonye to her, and the raunson or gold that they had ordeyned for their doughter, gaf hit every deel in dowaire to her. And the yonge man that was her husbond sawe the fraunchise and gentilnes of hym torned hymself and the hertes of the noble peple unto the love

120 and alliaunce of the Romaynes.

    And this suffisith as touchyng the kyng.

91–92 as thou ne say that, so that you can no longer say that. **92 mavaysté,** badness. **93 justicier,** judge. **94 signefyeth,** is represented by. **95 oonly,** alone; **belevyd,** believed. **97 a trewe,** a true one. **98–99 in partye,** both. **100 togyder,** together. **101 kepen them to,** mate with. **102 dowves,** doves; **turtils,** turtledoves. **103–04 nothyng norisshith,** does not care for. **105 entente,** purpose. **106 don they agaynst,** they go against; **leve,** leave. **109 for as moche as,** because. **110 how wel that,** although. **111 ostage,** hostage. **112 solas,** comfort. **112–13 assured and handfast,** promised and engaged. **114 not withstondyng that,** although. **115 dyd do calle,** had summoned; **kynnesmen,** kinsmen. **117 ordeyned,** commanded; **deel,** part. **118 fraunchise,** generosity. **119 torned,** turned.

The second chapitre of the second book, and treteth of the forme and maners of the quene.
Capitulo secundo.

Thus ought the quene be maad. She ought to be a fayr lady sittyng in a chayer and crowned with a corone on her heed and cladde with a cloth of gold and a mantel above furrid wyth ermynes. And she shold sitte on the lift side of the kyng,

125   for the amplexions and enbrasynges of her husbond, like as it is sayd in Scripture in the Canticles: "Her lifte arme shal be under my heed, and her right arme shal beclyppe and enbrace me." In that she is sette on his lifte syde is by grace gevyn to the kynge by nature and of right. For better is to have a kyng by successyon thenne by eleccion. For often tymes the electours and chosers cannot ne wylle not accorde,

130   and so is the eleccion left. And otherwhyle they chese not the beste and most able and convenyent, but hym that they best love, or is for them most proffytable. But whan the kyng is by lignage and by trewe succession, he is taught, enseygned, and norisshyd in hys yougth all good and vertuous tatches and maners of his fader. And also, the prynces of the royame dar not so hardyly meve warre agaynst a kyng

135   havyng a sone for to reigne after hym.

And so a quene ought to be chaste, wyse, of honest lyf, wel manerd, and not curious in norysshyng of her chyldren. Her wysedom ought not onely to appere in fait and werkes, but also in spekyng, that is to wete that she be secrete and telle not suche thynges as ought to be holden secrete. Wherfore it is a comyn proverbe that

140   women can kepe no counceyl.

---

122 **chayer**, chair.   124 **mantel**, cloak; **furrid wyth ermynes**, lined with ermine.   125 **amplexions and enbrasynges**, embraces.   127 **beclyppe**, embrace.   129 **chosers**, choosers; **accorde**, be in accord.   131 **convenyent**, appropriate.   132 **lignage**, lineage; **enseygned**, taught.   133 **norisshyd**, nourished; **tatches**, gifts.   134 **meve**, make.   136–37 **not curious in norysshyng of her chyldren**, not fastidious in the rearing of her children.   138 **fait and werkes**, deed and works; **wete**, say.

And accordyng therto, Macrobe reherceth in the *Book of the Dremes of Scypyo*, that there was a chyld of Rome that was named Papirus that on a tyme went with his fader, whych was a senatour, into the chambre whereas they helde theyr counceyl. And that tyme they spake of suche maters as was comaunded and agreed
145   shold be kepte secret upon payn of theyr hedes, and so departed. And whan he was comen home from the Senatoyre and fro the counceyl wyth his fader, his moder demaunded of hym what was the counceyl and wherof they spake and had taryed so longe there. And the chylde answerd to her and sayd he durst not telle nor saye hit for so moche as hit was defended upon payn of deth. Thenne was the moder
150   more desirous to knowe than she was tofore, and began to flatere hym one tyme, and afterward to menace hym that he shold saye and telle to her what it was. And whan the chylde sawe that he myght have no reste of hys moder in no wyse, he made her first promyse that she shold kepe hit secrete and to telle hit to noon of the world. And that doon, he feyned a lesing, or a lye, and sayde to her that the
155   senatours had in counceyl a grete question and dyfference whiche was thys: whether hit were better and more for the comyn wele of Rome that a man shold have two wyves or a wyf to have two husbondys. And whan she had understonde thys, he defended hyr that she shold telle hit to none other body.

And after thys she went to her gossyb and tolde to her thys counceyll secretely,
160   and she tolde to another, and thus every wyf tolde hit to other in secrete. And thus hit happend anone after that alle the wyves of Rome cam to the Senatoyre where the senatours were assemblyd and cryed with an hygh voys that they had lever, and also hit were better for the comyn wele, that a wyf shold have two husbondys than a man two wyves. The senatours, heeryng this, were gretely abasshyd and wyst not
165   to say, ner what ner how to answere, tyl atte laste that the child, Papire, reherced to them all the caas and fayt how hit was happend. And whan the senatours herd and understood the mater, they were gretely abasshyd and commendyd gretly the ingenye and wytte of the chyld that so wysely contryved the lye rather than he wold discovere their counceyl, and forthwyth made hym a senatour, and establisshed and
170   ordeyned fro than forthon that no chyld in ony wise shold entre into the counceyl hows amonge them with their faders except Papirus, whome they wold that he shold alwey be amonge them.

Also a quene ought to be chaste. For as she is above al other in estate and reverence, so shold she be ensaumple unto al other in her lyvyng honestlye. Wherof
175   Jerome reherceth agaynst Jovynyan that there was a gentyl man of Rome named Duele, and this man was he that first fond the maner to fight on the water and had first the victorye. This Duele had to his wyf one of the best women, and so chaste that every woman myght take ensaumple of her. And at that tyme, the synne of the flesshe was the grettest synne that ony myght doo agaynst nature. And this sayd

---

145 payn, pain; **hedes**, heads. **146 Senatoyre**, Senate chamber. **149 defended**, prohibited. **150–51 one tyme, and afterward**, alternately or by turns. **152 in no wyse**, at all. **154 feyned a lesing**, told a lie. **156 comyn wele**, common good. **158 defended**, prohibited. **159 gossyb**, soulmate (gossip). **161 anone after**, soon after. **162 had lever**, would prefer. **164 abasshyd**, surprised. **164–65 wyst not to say**, did not know what to say. **165 tyl**, until. **166 caas and fayt**, reasons and circumstances. **168 ingenye**, ingenuity. **169 forthwyth**, immediately. **170 fro than forthon**, from that point on. **173 estate**, class.

180 good woman was named Ylie. And so hit happend that this Duele becam so olde
that he stowped and quaked for age. And on a tyme, one of his adversayres reprevyd
and reprochyd hym, sayeng that he had a stynkyng breeth. And forthwyth he went
home to his wyf al angry and abasshyd, and axed her why and wherfore she had
not tolde his defaute to hym that he myght have founden remedye to have ben
185 pourgyd therof. And she answerd that as for as moche as she supposyd that every
man had that same faute as wel as he, for she kyst never ony manne's mouth but
her husbonde's. O moche was this woman to be praysed and have a synguler lawde,
wenyng that this defaute had not ben onely in her husbond, wherfore she suffryd
hit paciently in suche wise that her husbond knewe his defaute sonner by other
190 thenne by her!

Also, we rede that there was a wedowe named Anna, whiche had a frende that
counceylled hyr to marye, for she was yonge, fayr, and ryche, to whom she answerd
that she wold not so doo in no wyse: "For yf I shold have an husbond as I have had,
and that he were as good as he was, I shold ever ben aferd to lose hym, lyke as I
195 lost that other, and thenne shold I lyve alwey in fere and drede, whiche I wyl not.
And yf hit happend me to have a worse, what shold hit proffyte me to have an evyl
husbond after a good?" And so she concluded that she wold kepe her chasteté.

Saynt Austyn reherceth in the book *De civitate dei* that in Rome was a noble lady,
gentyl of maners and of hygh kynrede, named Lucrecia. And [she] had an husbond
200 named Colatyne, whiche desired on a tyme the emperour's sone, named Torquyne
the Orguyllous, or the Proude, and he was calle Sixte, for to come dyne and sporte
hym in his castel or manoyr. And whan he was entred amonge many noble ladyes,
he sawe Lucrecia. And whan thys emperour's sone had seen and advertysed her
deportes, her countenaunce, her manere, and her beaulté, he was alle ravysshed and
205 esprysed wyth her love forthwyth, and espyed a tyme whan her husbond, Collatyn,
wente unto the oost of the emperour, and cam into the place where as Lucresse was
with her felawshyp, whom she receyved honourably. And whan tyme came to goo
to bedde and slepe, she maad redy a bedde rially for hym, as hit apperteyned to
the emperour's sone. And this Sixtus espyed where Lucrecia laye. And whan he
210 supposid and knewe that every body was in his first sleep, he cam unto the bedde
of Lucresse, and that one hand sette on her breste, and in that other honde a
nakyd swerd, and sayd to her, "Lucresse, holde thy pees and crye not. For I am
Sixte, Tarquynus' sone. For yf thou speke ony word, thou shalt be dede."

181 stowped, stooped; **on a tyme**, one time.   **182 stynkyng breeth**, bad breath; **184
defaute**, fault.   **185 pourgyd**, purged.   **186 kyst**, kissed.   **187 praysed**, praised; **synguler
lawde**, special praise.   **188 wenyng**, believing.   **189 sonner**, sooner.   **192 marye**, marry.
194 ever, always; **aferd**, afraid.   **195 alwey**, always; **fere and drede**, fear and dread; **wyl not**,
do not wish to.   **196 a worse**, (i.e., a worse husband).   **197 chasteté**, chastity.   **199 gentyl**,
noble; **hygh kynrede**, high birth.   **201 Orguyllous**, Proud; **calle Sixte**, called Sixtus.
201–02 dyne and sporte hym, dine and amuse himself.   **202 manoyr**, manor.   **203
advertysed**, taken note of.   **204 deportes**, deportment; **countenaunce**, bearing.   **204–05
ravysshed and esprysed wyth her love**, ravished and taken with love for her.   **205 espyed**,
spied.   **206 oost**, army.   **208 maad redy**, prepared; **rially**, royally; **apperteyned to**, befit.
210 first sleep, presumably the first period of deep sleep for the night.   **212 pees**, peace.

215 And for fere she helde her pees. Thenne he began to praye and promyse many thynges. And after, he menaced and thretened her that she shold enclyne to hym to doo his wylle. And whan he sawe he coude nor myght have his entente, he sayd to her, "Yf thou do not my wylle, I shal slee thee and one of thy servauntis and shal lay hym alle deed by thy syde. And thenne I shal say that I have slayn you for your rybaudrye."

220 And Lucresse, that than doubted more the shame of the world than the deth, consentyd to hym. And anone after, as the emperour's sone was departed, the lady sent lettres to her husbond, her fader, her brethern, and to her frendes, and to a man callyd Brute, counceyllour and nevewe to Tarquyn. And sayd to them that: "Yesterday, Syxte, the emperour's sone, cam into myn hows as an enemye in liknes

225 of a frende and hath oppressyd me. And knowe thou, Colatyn, that he hath dishonouryd thy bedde, and how wel that he hath fowled and dishonoured my body. Yet myn herte is not, wherfore I beseche thee of pardon, foryefnes, and absolucion of the trespas but not of the payne. And he that hath doon thys synne to me, hit shal ben to his myschaunce yf ye doo your devoyr. And bycause no woman

230 take ensaumple of Lucresse and lyve after the trespas, but that she in lyke wyse take ensaumple also of the payne."

And forthwyth with a swerde that she helde under her gowne or robe, she roof herself unto the herte and deyed forthwyth tofore them. And thenne Brute, the counceyller, and her husbond, Collatyn, and alle her other frendes swore by the

235 blood of Lucresse that they wold never reste unto the tyme that they had put out of Rome Tarquyn and al his lygne, and that never after none of them shold come to dygnyté. And al this was doon, for they bare the deed corps thrugh the cyté and mevyd the peple in suche wyse that Tarquyn was put in exyle and Syxte, his sone, was slayn.

240 A quene ought to be wel manerd, and amonge alle she ought to be tumerous and shamefast. For whan a woman hath lost shamefastnes, she may ner can not weel be chaste.

Wherfore sayth Symachus that they that ben not shamefast have no conscience of luxurye.

245 And Saynt Ambrose sayth that one of the best parementes and maketh a womman most fayr in her persone is to be shamefast.

Seneque reherceth that there was one named Archezylle, whiche was so shamefast that she put in a pelowe of fethers a certeyn somme of money and put hit under the heed of a poure frende of herys, whiche dissymyled his poverté and wolde not

250 nor durst not be a knowen of his poverté for shame. She durst not gyve it openly but had lever that he shold fynde hyt than that she had gyven hit hym. Wherfore otherwhile men shold gyve and helpe her frendes so secretly that they knowe not

---

215 enclyne, bow or bend. **220 that . . . doubted**, who . . . feared. **221 anone**, immediately. **225 oppressyd**, overcome. **227 foryefnes**, forgiveness. **229 myschaunce**, misfortune; **devoyr**, duty. **232–33 roof herself**, stabbed herself. **233 tofore**, before. **236–37 come to dygnyté**, assume the throne. **238 mevyd**, rallied. **240–41 tumerous and shamefast**, timorous and modest. **245 parementes**, accoutrements. **248 pelowe**, pillow. **249 dissymyled**, covered up. **250 a knowen of**, exposed for. **252 otherwhile**, sometimes; **her**, their.

whens it come, for whan we kepe it secret and make no boste therof, our dedes and werkes shal please God and them also.

255   A quene ought to be chosen whan she shal be weddyd of the moste honest kynrede and peple, for often tymes the doughters folowen the tatches and maners of theym that they ben dyscended from. Wherof Valeryus Maximus sayth that there was one that wold marye whiche cam to a philosopher and axyd counceyl what wyf he myght best take. He answerd that he shold "take her that thou knowest certeynly

260   that her moder and her grauntdame have ben chaste and wel condycioned. For suche moder, suche doughter, comunely."

Also, a quene ought to teche her chyldren to ben contynent and kepe chastité entierly, as hit is wryten in Ecclesiastes: "Yf thou have sones, enseigne and teche them. And yf thou have doughters, kepe wel them in chastyté."

265   For Helemonde reherceth that every kynge and prynce ought to be a clerke for to comaunde to other to studye and rede the lawe of our Lord God, and therfore wrote the emperour to the kyng of Fraunce that he shold do lerne his children sones the seven sciences liberal, and sayd amonge other thynges that a kyng not lettrid resembleth an asse coroned. The Emperour Octovyan maad his sones to be taught

270   and lerne to swymme, to sprynge and lepe, to juste, to playe wyth the axe and swerde, and al maner thyng that apperteyneth to a knyght. And his doughters he made hem to lerne to sewe, to spynne, to labour as wel in wolle as in lynen cloth, and al other werkis langyng to women. And whan his frendes demaunded wherfore he dyd so, he answerd how wel that he was lord and syre of alle the world, yet wyste

275   he not what shold befalle of his children and whether they shold falle or come to poverté or noo: "And therfore yf they conne a good crafte, they may alwey lyve honestly."

The quene ought to kepe her doughters in alle chastyté, for we rede of many maydens that for their virgynyté have ben maad quenes. For Poule the Historiagraph

280   of the Lombardes reherceth that ther was a duchesse named Remonde whiche had thre sones and [two] doughters. And hit happend that the kynge of Hongrye, Cantanus, assayled a castel where she and her chylddren were inne. And on a day, she behelde her enemyes, and amonge alle other, she sawe the kyng that he was a wel faryng and a goodly man. Anone she was esprysed and taken wyth his love, and

285   that so sore that forthwyth she sent to hym that she wold delyver over the castel to hym yf he wold take her to his wyf and wedde her. And he agreed therto and sware that he wold have her to his wyf on that condicion. Whan than the kyng was in the castel, his peple took men and women and alle that they fonde. Her soones fledde from her, of whome one was named Ermoaldus and was yongest, and after was duc

---

253 whens, whence; dedes, deeds. 254 them (i.e., the recipient of one's good deeds). 256 tatches, gifts. 260 grauntdame, grandmother. 261 comunely, usually. 263 enseigne, teach. 267 shold do lerne his children sones, should have his male children taught. 268 seven sciences liberal, seven liberal arts. 269 an asse coroned, a crowned donkey. 270 sprynge and lepe, jump and leap; juste, joust. 272 lynen, linen. 273 langyng to, appropriate for. 274 how wel that, although. 276 conne, know. 279 Historiagraph, Historian. 281 Hongrye, Hungary. 282 assayled, attacked. 284 wel faryng, handsome; esprysed, seized. 285 that so sore, it was so powerful; sent, sent word; delyver, deliver. 286 sware, swore. 288 soones, sons.

290   of Boneventan, and sithen kyng of the Lumbardis. And the two susters toke chykens and put hem under her armes next the flessh and bytwene her pappes, that of the hete and chauffyng, the flessh of the chikyns stanke. And whan so was that they of Hongrye wold have enforced and defowled, anone they felte the stenche and fledde awey and so lefte hem sayeng, "Fy! How these Lombardes stynke!" And so they

295   kepte theyr virgynyté. Wherfore that one of hem afterward was quene of Fraunce, and that other quene of Almayn.

       And hit happend thenne that the Kyng Catanus toke acordyng to his promyse the duchesse and lay wyth her one nyght for to save his ooth. And on the morne, he made her comune unto al the Hungres. And the thyrd day after, he dyd doo put

300   a staf of tree fro the nether parte of her thrugh her body unto her throte or mouthe. For by cause of the luste of her flessh, she betrayed her cyté. And sayd "suche husbond, suche wyf."

       And this suffyseth of the quene.

The thyrd chappytre of the second traytye treteth of the alphyns, her offyces and maners.

Capitulo tercio.

       The alphyns ought to be maad and formed in manere of juges sittyng in a

305   chayer wyth a book open tofore theyr eyen. And that is by cause that somme causes ben crymynel and somme ben cyvyle, as about possessions and other temporel thynges and trespaces. And therfore ought to be two juges in the royame, one in

---

290 Boneventan (see note); **sithen**, afterwards; **Lumbardis**, Lombards; **chykens**, chickens. **291 her armes**, their arms; **bytwene her pappes**, between their breasts. **292 chauffyng**, warming. **293 enforced and defowled**, violated and raped. **296 Almayn**, Germany. **298 morne**, morning. **299 made her comune** (i.e., shared her sexually with). **304 alphyns**, judges or chess bishops; **juges**, judges. **305 tofore**, in front of; **eyen**, eyes. **306 crymynel**, criminal; **cyvyle**, civil; **temporel**, worldly. **307 trespaces**, violations.

the black for the first cause and that other in whyt as for the second. Theyr offyce
is for to counceylle the kyng and to make by his commaundementis good lawes,
310   and to enforme alle the royame in good and vertuous maners, and to juge and gyve
sentence wel and trewly after the caas is had, and to counceyl wel and justely alle
them that axe counceyl of hem, wythout havyng of ony eye opene to ony persone,
and to estudye diligently in suche wyse, and to ordeigne alle that that ought to be
kept, be observyd, be faste and stable, so that they be not founde corupt for yefte,
315   for favour, ne for lignage, ne for envye varriable.

   And as touchyng the first poynt, Seneque saith in the *Book of Benefets* that the
pour Diogenes was more strong than Alixandre, for Alixandre coude not gyve so
moche as Diogenes wold refuse.

   Marcus Cursus, a Romayn of grete renomee, saith thus: that whan he had
320   besieged and assayled them of Samente and Beneventans, which herde that he was
poure, they took a grete masse and wedge of gold and sendyd hit to hym, prayeng
hym that he wold reseyve hit and leve his assault and siege. And whan they came
with the present to hym, they fond hym sittyng on the erthe and ete his mete out
of platers and dysshes of tree and of wode, and did than her message. To whom he
325   answerd and said that they shold goo home and saye to them that sente them that
"Marcus Cursus loveth better to be lord and wynne richesses than richesse shold
wynne hym. For by batayle he shal not be overcome and vaynquysshed, nor by
gold, ne silver he shal not be corrupt ne corompid." Oftentymes that thyng taketh
an evyll ende that is untrewe for gold and silver, and that a man is subget unto
330   money may not be lord therof.

   Helymond rehercheth that Demostene demaunded of Aristodone how moche he
had wonne for pletyng of a cause for hys client. And he answerd, "A mark of golde."
Demostenes answerd to hym agayn that he had wonne as moche for to holde hys
pees and speke not. Thus the tunges of advocates and men of lawe ben perilous and
335   dommegeable, yet they must be had yf thou wolt wynne thy cause, for with money
and yefte thou shall wynne. And oftentymes they selle as wel theyr scilence as their
utteraunce.

   Valerius rehercith that the senatours of Rome took counceil togeder of two
persones, that one was poure and that other riche and covetous, whiche of hem
340   bothe were most apte for to sende to governe and juge the contré of Spayne. And
Scipyon of Affrique said that none of hem bothe were good ne proffytable to be
sent theder. For that one hath no thyng, and to that other may no thyng suffyse,
and despysed in hys sayeng alle poverté and avarice in a juge. For a covetous man

---

310 enforme, educate.   **312 axe**, ask; **ony eye opene to ony persone** (i.e., showing
favoritism).   **313 ordeigne**, ordain or confirm.   **314 faste**, fixed; **yefte**, gift.   **315 lignage**,
lineage.   **319 Romayn**, Roman; **renomee**, renown.   **321 prayeng**, praying to.   **322 reseyve**,
receive.   **323 fond**, found; **ete**, eating; **mete**, food.   **324 dysshes**, dishes; **wode**, wood; **her**,
their.   **327 vaynquysshed**, vanquished.   **328 corompid**, spoiled.   **329 subget**, subject.   **332
pletyng**, pleading; **mark**, a monetary unit used for silver and gold.   **335 dommegeable**,
corruptible; **wynne**, win.   **336 yefte**, gift.   **338 togeder**, together.   **341 none of hem bothe**,
neither one.   **342 theder**, thither; **may no thyng suffyse**, nothing is sufficient.

hath nede of an halpeny, for he is servaunt and bonde unto money, and not lorde
345   therof. But poverté of herte and of wylle ought to be gretely alowed in a juge.

Therfore we rede that as longe as the Romayns lovyd poverté, they were lordys
of alle the world. For many there were that exposed al theyr goodes for the comyn
wele, and for that was most proffitable for the comynalté, that they were so poure
that whan they were dede they were buryed and brought to erthe wyth the comyn
350   good. And theyr doughters were maryed by the commaundement of the senatours.
But sithen that they despised poverté and begonne to gadre richesses and have
made grete bataylles, they have used many synnes. And so the comyn wele perisshed.
For ther is no synne but that it reigneth there, where is none that is so blisful as he
that hath al the world in despite. For he is in pees that dredith no man, and he is
355   riche that coveiteth no thyng.

Valere reherceth that he is not riche that moche hath, but he is riche that hath
lityl and coveyteth no thyng.

Than thus late the juges take hede that they enclyne not for love or for hate in
ony jugement. For Theofrast saith that all love is blynde. Where love is, there can
360   not right jugement by gyven, for all love is blynde. And therfore love is none evyn
juge. For ofte tymes love jugeth a fowle and lothly woman to be fayr.

And so reherceth Quinte Curse in his first book that the grete Godaches sayth
the same to Alyxandre. Men may saye in this caas that nature is evyl, for every man
is lasse advysed and worse in his owne feet and cause than in another mannys. And
365   therfore the juges ought to kepe hem wel from ire in jugement.

Tullyus sayth that an angry and yrous persone weneth that for to doo evyl is
good counceyl.

And Socrates saith that two thynges ben contrarious to counceyl, and they ben
hastynes and wrath.
370   And Galeren sayth in *Alexandrye*: "Yf yre or wrath overcome thee whan thou
sholdest geve jugement, weye all thyng in the balaunce so that thy jugement be not
enclyned by love, ne by yeft ne favor of persone torne not thy corage."

Helemond reherceth that Cambyses, kyng of Perce, whiche was a right wis
kyng, had an unrightwis juge, whiche for envye and evyl wyll had dampned a man
375   wrongfully and agaynst right. Wherfore he dyd hym to be flayn al quyk and made
the chayer or siege of jugement to be coverid with his skyn, and made his sone juge
and to sitte in the chayer on the skyn of his fader, to the ende that the sone shold
juge rightwisly and abhorre the jugement and payne of his fader.

---

344 **halpeny**, halfpenny or coin worth one-half of a penny.   347 **exposed**, rendered.
347–48 **comyn wele**, common good.   351 **sithen that**, since the time that.   352 **used**,
engaged in.   354 **in despite**, in contempt; **dredith**, fears.   355 **coveiteth**, covets.   358 **late**,
let.   360 **evyn**, even or just.   361 **fowle and lothly**, foul and ugly.   364 **worse in his owne
feet and cause**, i.e., has less of an ability to present his own case dispassionately; **mannys**,
man's.   365 **hem**, themselves.   366 **yrous**, ireful; **weneth**, believes.   368 **contrarious**,
opposed.   369 **hastynes**, hastiness.   371 **geve**, give.   372 **yeft**, gift.   373 **Perce**, Persia; **right
wis**, upstanding or honest.   374 **unrightwis**, dishonest.   375 **he dyd hym** (i.e., Cambyses
ordered the false judge); **flayn al quyk**, flayed alive.   376 **chayer or siege**, chair or seat.

380 Juges ought to punysshe the defaultes egally and fulfille the lawe that they ordeyne. Caton saith: "Accomplisshe and do the lawe in suche wyse as thou hast ordeigned and geven."

Valerius rercheth that Calengius, a consul, had a sone whiche was taken in advoultrye, and therfore, after the lawe at that tyme, he was dampned to lose bothe his eyen. The fader wold that the lawe shold be accomplisshed in his sone wythout
385 favour. But al the cité was mevyd herewyth and wold not suffre hit. But in the ende his fader was vaynquysshed by theyr prayers and ordeyned that his sone shold lese one eye, whyche was put out, and he hymself lost an other eye. And thus was the lawe observyd and kept, and the prayer of the people was accomplisshed.

We rede that there was a counceyllour of Rome that had gyven counceylle to
390 make a statute that whosommeever that entryd into the Senatoyr and a swerde gyrt aboute hym shold be deed. Than hit happend on a tyme that he came from without and entrid into the Senatoir and his swerd gyrt about hym, wherof he toke none hede. And one of the senatours told hym of hit. And whan he knewe hit and remembrid the statute, he drewe out his swerde and slewe hymself tofore them,
395 rather to dye than to breke the lawe, for whos dethe alle the senatours maad grete sorowe.

But alas we fynde not many in thyse dayes that so do. But they do lyke as Anastasyus saith, that the lawes of somme ben like unto the nettis of spyncoppis, that take no grete bestes and fowles but let goo and flee thrugh. But they take flyes
400 and gnattes and suche smale thynges. In like wise, the lawes nowadayes ben not executed but upon the poure peple. The grete and riche breke hit and goo thrugh with al, and for this cause sourden batailles and discordes, and make the grete and riche men to take by force and strengthe lordshippis and seignories upon the smale and poure peple. And this don they specially that ben gentil of lignage and poure
405 of goodes, and causeth them to robbe and reve, and yet constreyne them by force to serve them. And thys is no mervayle, for they that drede not to angre God, ner to breke the lawe and to false hit, falle often tymes by force in moche cursidnes and wickednes. But whan the grete peple do accordyng to the lawe and punysshe the transgressours sharply, the comyn peple absteyne and withdrawe hem fro doyng
410 of evyl and chastiseth hemself by theyr example.

And the juges ought to entende for to studye. For yf the smythes, the carpentiers, the vignours, and other craftymen say that it is not necessarye to studye for the comyn proffit, and glorefye them in their connyng and say that they ben proffitable, than shold the juges studye and contemplaire moche more than they in that that
415 shold be for the comyn wele.

---

379 **egally**, equally. 382 **consul**, a member of the ancient Roman Senate. 383 **advoultrye**, adultery. 384 **accomplisshed**, enacted. 385 **mevyd**, moved; **suffre**, allow. 386 **vaynquysshed**, overcome. 390 **whosommeever**, whosoever; **entryd**, entered; **Senatoyr**, Senate chamber; **gyrt**, girded. 391 **from without** (i.e., from outside the Senate building). 395 **rather to**, preferring to. 398 **spyncoppis**, spiders. 399 **flee**, fly. 402 **sourden**, spring up. 403 **seignories**, feudal domains. 404 **lignage**, lineage. 405 **robbe and reve**, rob and plunder. 407 **false**, cheat. 410 **hemself**, themselves. 411 **entende for** (i.e., direct themselves); **smythes**, blacksmiths. 412 **vignours**, vine tenders. 413 **connyng**, knowing. 414 **contemplaire**, reflect.

Wherfore saith Seneke: "Beleve me that they seme that they do no thyng, they do more than they that laboure, for they do spirituel and also corporal werkis." And therfore, amonge artificers ther is no plesaunt rest but that reson of the juges hath maad and ordeyned hit.

420 And therfore Angelius saith in *Libro Atticors de Socrate* that Socrates was on a tyme so pensif that in an hole naturel day, he helde one estate, that he ne meved mouth, ne eye, ne foot, ne hand, but was as he had ben deed or ravysshed. And whan one demaunded hym wherfore he was so pensif, he answerd, "In al worldly thynges and labours of the same," and helde hym bourgeys and cytézeyn of the world.

425 And Valerius rehercith that Carnardes, a knyght, was so sage, wyse, and laborous in pensifnes of the comyn wele, that whan he was sette atte table for to ete, he forgate to put his hond unto the mete to fede hymself. And therfore his wyf, that was named Mellyse, whom he had taken more to have her companye and felawshyp than for ony other thynge, fedde hym to the ende that he shold not dye for hongre 430 in his pensifnes.

Didimus sayd to Alixandre: "We be not deynseyns in the world but straungers, nor we ben not born in the world for to dwelle and abyde alwey therein, but for to goo and passe thrugh hit. We have doon noon evyl dede but that it is worthy to be punysshed, and we to suffre payne therfore, and thenne we may goon with open 435 face and good conscience. And so may we goo lightly and apertly the way that we hope and purpose to goo."

Thys suffyseth as for the alphyns.

416 that they seme, that they who seem. **421 pensif**, pensive; **estate**, position; **meved**, moved. **422 ravysshed**, ravished or taken off. **423–24 "In al worldly thynges and labours of the same"** (i.e., Socrates explains that he is thinking about all worldly things and labors, which is bound to make anyone pensive). **424 bourgeys**, a burgess or an inhabitant of a borough who possesses full municipal rights. **429 hongre**, hunger. **431 deynseyns**, denizens. **432 abyde**, abide or stay. **435 apertly**, publicly.

The fourth chappitre of the second book treteth of the ordre of chevalrye and knyghthoode, and of her offyces and maners.   **Capitulo   quarto.**

The knyght ought to be maad al armed upon an hors in suche wise that he have an helme on his heed and a spere in his right hond, and coverid with his shelde, a
440   swerd and a mace on his lyft syde, clad with an hawberk and plates tofore his breste, legge harnoys on his legges, spores on his heelis, on hys handes hys gauntelettes, hys hors wel broken and taught, and apte to bataylle, and coveryd with his armes. Whan the knyghtes ben maad, they ben bayned or bathed. That is the signe that they shold lede a newe lyf and newe maners. Also, they wake alle the nyght in prayers
445   and orisons unto God that He wil geve hem grace that they may gete that thyng that they may not gete by nature. The kyng or prynce gyrdeth aboute them a swerde in signe that they shold abyde and kepen hym of whom they taken their dispences and dignyté. Also, a knyght ought to be wyse, lyberalle, trewe, strong, and ful of mercy and pyté, and kepar of the peple and of the lawe.
450   And right as chevalrye passeth other in vertue, in dignyté, in honour, and in reverence, right so ought he to surmounte alle other in vertue. For honour is nothyng ellys but to do reverence to another persone for the good and vertuous disposicion that is in hym. A noble knyghte ought to be wyse and provyd tofore he be maad knyght. Hit behoved hym that he had long tyme usid the warre and
455   armes, that he may be expert and wyse for to governe the other. For sithen that a knyght is capitayn of a batayle, the lyf of them that shal be under hym lyeth in his

Title **chevalrye**, knights;   **439 helme**, helmet; **shelde**, shield.   **440 hawberk and plates**, hauberk (a short protective shirt of mail) and metal armor.   **441 harnoys**, armor.   **445 orisons**, prayers; **geve hem**, give them.   **446 gyrdeth aboute**, belts around.   **447 abyde**, wait on; **dispences**, upkeep.   **448 lyberalle**, generous; **trewe**, honest.   **449 pyté**, mercy; **kepar**, keeper.   **450 right as chevalrye**, just as knightly prowess.   **451 surmounte**, surpass.   **452 ellys**, else; **for**, on account of.   **453 provyd**, tested.   **454 Hit behoved**, It behooved; **usid**, been used to.   **455 the other** (i.e., other people); **sithen**, since.   **456 batayle**, battalion.

honde. And therfore behoveth hym to be wyse and wel advysed, for somtyme art, craft, and engyne is more worthe than strengthe or hardynes of a man that is not proved in armes. For otherwhile it happeth that whan the prynce of the batayl affyeth and trusteth in his hardynes and strengthe, and wol not use wisedom and engyne for to renne upon his enemyes, he is vaynquysshed and his people slayn.

460

Therfore saith the philosopher that no man shold chese yong peple to be captayns and governours, for as moche as ther is no certeynté in her wisdom. Alixandre of Macedone vaynquysshed and conquerd Egipte, Judé, Caldee, Affrique, and Assyrie, unto the Marches of Bragmans, more by the counceyl of olde men than by the strengthe of the yong men.

465

We rede in the *Historye of Rome* that there was a knyght whiche had to name Malechete, that was so wyse and trewe that whan the Emperour Theodosius was dede, he made mortal warre agenst his broder germayn, which was named Gyldo or Guye, for as moche as this sayd Guye wold be lord of Affrique without leve and wylle of the senatours. And thys sayd Guy had slayn the two sones of his broder Malechete, and dyd moche torment unto the Crysten peple. And afore that he shold come into the felde ayenst his broder Guyon, he went into an Yle of Capayre, and ladde with hym al the Cristen men that had ben sent theder in exyle, and maad hem alle to praye with hym by the space of thre dayes and thre nyghtes, for he had grete affyaunce and truste in the prayers and orisons of good folk, and specially that no man myght counceyl ne helpe but God. And thre dayes tofore he shold fight, Saynt Ambrose, whiche was deed a litil tofore, apperyd to hym and shewed hym by revelaconn the tyme and howre that he shold have victorye. And for so moche as he had ben [three] dayes and thre nyghtes in orysons and prayers, and that he was assuryd for to have victorye, he faught wyth fyve thousand men ayenst his broder that had in his companye four score thousand men. And by Godde's helpe, he had victorye. And whan the barbaryans that were comen to helpe Guyon sawe the discomfiture, they fledde awey, and Guyon fledde also into Affryque by shyppe. And whan he was there aryved, he was sone after stranglid. These two knyghtes of whom I speke were two brethern germayns, whyche were sent into Affrique for to deffende the comyn wele.

470

475

480

485

In lyke wyse, Judas Machabeus, Jonathas, and Symon, his brethern, put them self in the mercy and garde of our Lord God and ageyn the enemyes of the lawe of God, with litil people in regarde of the multitude that were agayn them, and had also victorye.

490

The knyghtes ought to ben trewe to theyr prynces, for he that is not trewe leseth the name of a knyght. Unto a prynce, trouth is the grettest precious stone whan hit is medlid wyth justice.

457–58 art, **craft**, **and engyne**, artfulness, craftiness, and ingenuity.   **459 otherwhile**, otherwise.   **460 affyeth and trusteth**, places faith in and trusts.   **461 engyne**, skill.   **462 chese**, choose.   **464 Judé**, Judea; **Caldee**, Chaldea.   **465 Assyrie**, Assyria; **Bragmans**, The Isle of the Bragmans (see Explanatory Notes).   **469 agenst**, against; **broder germayn**, full brother.   **470–71 leve and wylle**, permission and consent.   **472 Crysten**, Christian.   **473 Yle of Capayre**, Island of Caprara off the eastern coast of Italy.   **474 ladde**, led; **theder**, thither.   **476 affyaunce**, faith.   **479 revelaconn**, revelation; **howre**, hour.   **484 discomfiture**, complete defeat or rout.   **489 ageyn**, against.   **490 litil**, few; **in regarde of**, with respect to.   **492 leseth**, loses.   **494 medlid**, melded.

495   Paule the Historiagraph of the Lombardes reherceth that there was a knyght
          named Enulphus, and was of the cyté of Papye, that was so trewe and faythful to his
          lord and kyng named Pathariche that he put hym in parylle of deth for hym. For hit
          happend that Grymald, duc of Buneventayns, of whom we have touched tofore in
          the chapytre of the quene, dyd do slee Godebert, whyche was kyng of the Lombardes
500   by the hande of Goribert, duc of Tarente, whiche was descended of the crowne of
          Lombardes. And this Grymalde was maad kyng of Lombardye in his place, and
          after this put and banysshed out of the contraye this Patharich, whiche was broder
          unto the Kyng Godebert, that for fere and drede fledde into Hongrye. And thenne
          this knyght Enulphus dyd so moche that he gate the pees agayn of his lord Patharich
505   agaynst the Kyng Grymalde, and that he had licence to come out of Hongrye,
          where he was alwey in parell. And so he came and cryed hym mercy. And the Kyng
          Grymalde gaf hym leve to dwelle and to lyve honestly in his contré, alwey forseen
          that he took not upon hym and named hymself kyng, how wel he was kyng by right.
               This doon, a lityl whyle after the kyng, that belevyd evyl tonges, thought in
510   hymself how he myght brynge this Pathariche unto the deth. And al thys knewe wel
          the knyght Enulphus, whiche came the same nyght wyth his squyer for to vysite his
          lord, and maad hys squyer to unclothe hym and to lye in the bedde of his lord, and
          maad his lorde to rise and clothe hym wyth the clothes of his squyer. And in this
          wyse brought hym out, brawlyng and betyng hym as his servaunt by them that were
515   asigned to kepe the hows of Patharich that he shold not escape, which supposid
          that hit had been his squyer that he entreted so outragyously, and so he brought
          hym unto his hows which joyned wyth the walles of the toun. And at mydnyght,
          when al men were aslepe, he lete adoun his maistre by a corde, whiche took an
          hors out of the pasture and fledde unto the cyté of Aast, and there cam to the kyng
520   of Fraunce. And whan it cam unto the morne, hit was founden that Enulphus and his
          squyer had deceyved the kyng and the watchemen, whom the kyng commaunded
          shold be brought tofore hym and demaunded of them the maner how he was
          escapyd. And they tolde hym the trouthe.
               Thenne the kyng demaunded his counceyl of what deth they had deservyd to dye
525   that had so doon and wrought agayn the wylle of hym. Somme said that they shold
          ben honged. And somme said they shold be flayn. And other said that they shold
          be beheded. Than said the kyng, "By that Lord that maad me, they ben not worthy
          to dye but for to have moche worshyp and honour. For they have ben trewe to theyr
          lord." Wherfore the kyng gaf hem a grete lawde and honour for theyr feet. And after,
530   it happend that the propre squyer and servaunt of Godeberd slewe the traytre
          Gorybalde, that by treson had slayn his lorde at a feste of Saynt John in his cyté of
          Tarente, wherof he was lord and duc.

495 **Lombardes**, people from the Lombard region in northern Italy. 496 **Papye**, Pavia.
497 **parylle**, peril. 498 **Buneventayns**, citizens of Benevento, a town and *comune* northeast
of Naples. 500 **Tarente**, Tarento. 503 **fere**, fear; **Hongrye**, Hungary. 504 **gate**, obtained.
507 **forseen**, making sure. 509 **doon**, done. 514 **wyse**, fashion; **betyng**, beating; **by**, passed
by. 516 **entreted**, treated. 519 **Aast**, Asti. 520 **morne**, morning. 525 **doon and wrought
agayn**, done and acted against. 526 **flayn**, flayed. 529 **feet**, deed; **after**, afterwards. 531
feste of Saynt John, the Feast of Saint John (usually held in midsummer on June 24).

Thus ought the knyghtes to love togyder, and eche to put his lyf in aventure for other, for so been they the strenger and the more doubted, lyke as were the noble
535 knyghtes Joab and Abysay, that fought ageynst the Syryens and Amonytes, and were so trewe, that one to that other, that they vaynquysshed theyr enemyes, and were so joyned togyder that yf the Siriens were strenger thenne that one of them, that other helpe hym.

We rede that Damon and Phisias were so right parfight frendes togyder that
540 whan Dionysius, whiche was kyng of Zecille, had jugged one to deth for his trespaas in the cyté of Siracusane, whom he wold have executed, he desired grace and leve to goo into his contré for to dispose and ordeyne his testament. And his felawe pledgyd hym and was sewrté for hym upon his heed that he shold come agayn. Wherof they that herde and sawe this helde hym for a fool and blamed hym. And
545 he sayd alwey that he repentyd hym no thyng at all, for he knewe wel the trouth of his felawe. And whan the day cam and the howre that execucion shold be doon, his felowe cam and presented hymself tofore the juge and dischargid his felowe that was pledge for hym, wherof the kyng was gretely abasshyd. And for the grete trouthe that was founden in hym, he pardonyd hym and prayed hem bothe that they wold
550 receyve hym as theyr grete frende and felowe. Lo, here the vertues of love, that a man ought not to doubte the deth for his frende! Lo, what it is to doo for a frende and to lede a lyf debonayr, and to be wythout cruelté, to love and not to hate, whyche causeth to doo good ayenst evyl, and to torne payne into benefete, and to quenche cruelté!

555 Anthonyus sayth that Julius Cesar lefte not lightly frendshyp and amytye, but whan he had hit, he reteyned hit faste and mayntened hit alwey.

Scipion of Affrique saith that there is no thyng so stronge as for to maynteyne love unto the deth. The love of concupissence and of lecherye is sone dissolvyd and broken. But the verray trewe love of the comyn wele and proffyt nowadayes is selde
560 founden. Where shal thou fynde a man in thyse dayes that wyl expose hymself for the worshyp and honour of his frende or for the comyn wele? Selde or never shal he be founden.

Also, the knyghtes shold be large and liberal. For whan a knyght hath regarde unto his synguler prouffyt by his covetyse, he dyspoyleth his peple. For whan the
565 souldyours se that they put hem in parel, and their mayster wyl not paye hem theyr wages lyberally, but entendeth to his owne propre gayn and proffyt, than whan the enemyes come, they torne sone her backes and flee often tymes. And thus hit happeth by hym that entendeth more to gete money than vyctorye that his avaryce is ofte tymes cause of his confusion. Thenne lete every knyght take hede to be
570 lyberalle in suche wyse that he wene not ne suppose that his scarceté be to hym a

---

533 in aventure, at risk. **534 doubted**, feared. **535 Syryens and Amonytes**, Syrians and Ammonites. **539 parfight**, perfect. **540 Zecille**, Sicily. **541 Siracusane**, Syracuse. **542 ordeyne**, ordain or put in order. **543 sewrté**, sworn or given as a surety. **545 trouth**, honesty. **551 doubte**, fear. **552 debonayr**, debonair (in the archaic sense of gracious). **553 torne**, turn; **benefete**, benefit (in the archaic sense of a kind deed). **558 concupissence**, concupiscence. **559 selde**, seldom. **564 covetyse**, covetousness; **dyspoyleth**, dispoils. **565 souldyours**, soldiers; **put hem in parel**, put themselves in peril. **567 sone**, soon. **570 wene not**, does not think or believe; **scarceté**, frugalness.

grete wynnyng or gayn. And for thys cause, he be the lasse lovyd of his peple, and that his adversarye wythdrawe to hym them by large gevyng. For ofte tyme batayle is avaunced more for getyng of silver than by the force and strengthe of men. For men see alle day that suche thynges as may not be achyevyd by force of nature ben
575 goten and achyevyd by force of money. And for so moche it behoveth to see wel to that whan the tyme of bataille cometh, that he borowe not ne make no tayllage, for no man may be riche that levyth his owne, hopyng to gete and take of other. Than alwey al her gayn and wynnyng ought to be comyn emong [them], exept theyr armes. For in like wyse, as the vyctorye is comune, so shold the dispoyle and botye
580 be comune unto them.

        And therfore Davyd, that gentyl knyght in the first Book of Kynges, in the last chappytre made a lawe that he that abode behynde by maladye or sekenes in the tentes shold have as moche parte of the butyn as he that had ben in the batayle. And for the love of this lawe, he was maad afterward kyng of Israel.
585   Alixandre of Macedone cam on a tyme lyke a symple knyght unto the court of Porus, kyng of Ynde, for to espye the astate of the kyng and of the knyghtes of the court. And the kyng receyvyd hym right worshypfully and demaunded of hym many thynges of Alixander, and of his constance and strengthe, nothyng wenyng that he had ben Alixander but Antygone, one of his knyghtes. And after he had
590 hym to dyner. And whan they had servyd Alixander in vessayl of gold and sylver with dyverse metes, after that he had eten suche as plesid hym, he voyded the mete and toke the vessayl, and helde hit to hymself and put hit in his bosom or slevys, wherof he was accusid unto the kyng. After dyner, thenne, the kyng callyd hym and demaunded hym wherfore he had taken hys vayssayl. And he answerd: "Sir kyng,
595 my lord, I pray thee to understonde and take heed thyself, and also thy knyghtes. I have herd moche of thy grete hyghnes, and that thou art more myghty and puyssaunt in chevalrye and in dispencis than is Alixaunder. And therfore I am come to thee, a poure knyght whiche am named Antygone, for to serve thee. Than hit is the custome in the courte of Alixander that what thyng a knyght is servyd
600 wyth, alle is hys, mete and vaissel and cuppe. And therfore I had supposid that this custome had ben kept in thy court, for thou art richer than he."

        Whan the knyghtes herde this, anone they lefte Porus and went to serve Alixaunder. And thus he drewe to hym the hertes of hem by yeftes, whiche afterward slewe Porus that was kyng of Ynde, and they maad Alixandre kyng
605 therof. Therfore, remembre knyght alwey that wyth a closid and shette purse shalt thou never have victorye.

        Ovyde saith that he that taketh yeftes, he is glad therwyth, for they wynne wyth yeftes the hertes of the goddes and of men. For yf Jupyter were angrid, with yeftes he wold be plesid.

---

572 wythdrawe to hym them, withdraw them to him; **large gevyng,** generous giving. **575 achyevyd,** gained. **576 tayllage,** a tallage or tax. **577 levyth,** leaves. **578 her,** their. **579 armes,** armor; **dispoyle and botye,** dispoil and booty. **582 abode,** stayed. **583 butyn,** spoils. **586 Ynde,** India. **590 vessayl,** vessels. **591 voyded,** cleared. **592 slevys,** sleeves. **593 accusid,** betrayed or disclosed. **597 puyssaunt,** powerful; **dispencis,** dispensing. **598 poure,** poor. **603 yeftes,** gifts. **605 shette,** shut.

610   The knyghtes ought to be stronge not onely of body but also in corage. There ben many stronge and grete of body that ben faynt and feble in the herte. He is stronge that may not be vaynquysshed and overcome, how wel that he suffrith moche otherwhyle. And so we beleve that they that be not overgrete ne over litel ben most corageous and beste in bataylle.

615   We rede that Cadrus, duc of Athenes, shold have a bataylle agayn them of Polipe. And he was warned and had a revelacion of the goddes that they shold have the vyctorye of whom the prynce shold be slayn in the bataile. And the prynce, whiche was of a grete corage and trewe herte, took other armes of a poure man and put hymself in the fronte of the bataylle to the ende that he myght be slayn, and so he
620   was. For the right trewe prynce had lever dye than his peple shold be overcomen. And so they had the victorye. Certes hit was a noble and fayr thynge to expose hymself to the deth for to deffende his contraye. But no man wold do so but yf he hopyd to have a better thyng therfore. Therfore the lawe sayth that they lyve in her sowles gloriously that ben slayn in the warre for the comyn wele.

625   A knyght ought also to be merciful and pietous, for there is no thyng that maketh a knyght so renomed as is whan he savyth the lyf of them that he may slee. For to shede and spylle blood is the condicyon of a wylde beste and not the condycion of a good knyght. Therfore we rede that Scilla, that was duc of the Romayns without, had many fair victories agaynst the Romayns. And within, that were contrayre to
630   hym, in so moche that in the Bataylle of Puylle he slewe eighteen thousand men, and in champayne seventy thousand, and after in the cyté he slewe thre thousand men unarmed. And whan one of his knyghtes that was named Quyntus Catulus sawe this cruelté, sayd to hym: "Sesse now and suffre them to lyve and be merciful to them wyth whome we have ben vyctorious and wyth whom we ought to lyve. For
635   it is the most hyest and fair vengeaunce that a man may do as to spare them and gyve hem her lyf whom he may slé."

Therfore Joab ordeyned, whan Absalon was slayn, he sowned a trompette that his peple shold nomore renne and slee theyr adversaries. For there were slayn about twenty thousand of them. And in like wyse dyd he whan he faught ayenst Abner,
640   and Abner was vaynquysshed and fledde. For where that he went in the chaas, he commaunded to spare the people.

The knyghtes ought to kepe the peple. For whan the peple ben in their tentis or castellis, the knyghtes ought to kepe the watche. For this cause, the Romayns callyd them "legyons," and they were made of dyverse provynces and of dyverse
645   nacions to the entente to kepe the peple. And the peple shold entende to theyr werke, for no crafty man may bothe entende to his crafte and to fight. How may a crafty man entende to his werke sewrely in tyme of warre but yf he be kept? And

---

612 **how wel that**, even if. 615 **Polipe**, the Peloponnese. 620 **lever**, rather. 622 **but yf**, unless. 625 **pietous**, full of pity. 628 **without**, this seems to be a translation from the Latin version of the *Liber*, which states that Sulla governed "*exterae partis*," or in the outer regions. 630 **Bataylle of Puylle**, Battle of Apulia, a region in southeast Italy. 631 **champayne**, the countryside or the field. 633 **Sesse**, Cease. 637 **sowned**, sounded. 640 **where that**, wherever; **chaas**, pursuit. 644 **"legyons,"** a body of an infantry ranging from three to six thousand soldiers. 645 **entente**, goal or end; **entende to**, attend to. 647 **sewrely**, surely.

right in suche wyse as the knyghtes shold kepe the peple in tyme of pees, in like
wyse the peple ought to purveye for theyr dispencis. How shold a plowman be
650 sewre in the felde but yf the knyghtes made dayly watche to kepe hem. For like as
the glorye of a kyng is upon his knyghtes, so it is necessarye to the knyghtes that
the marchauntes, crafty men, and comyn peple be defended and kepte. Therfore
late the knyghtes kepe the peple in suche wyse that they may enjoye pees, and gete
and gadre the costis and expencis of them bothe.

655 We rede that Athis sayd to Davyd, whiche was a knyght: "I make thee my kepar
and defendar alwey." Thus shold the knyghtes have grete zele that the lawe be
kept. For the magesté ryal ought not onely to be garnysshed wyth armes but also
wyth good lawes. And therfore shold they laboure that they shold be wel kepte.

Turgeus Pompeus rehercith of a noble knyght named Ligurgyus that had made
660 auncient lawes, the whiche the peple wold not kepe ne observe, for they semed
hard for them to kepe, and wold constreyne hym to rapelle and sette hem aparte.
Whan the noble knyght sawe that, he dyd the peple to understonde that he had not
made them, but a god that was named Apollo Delphynus had made them and had
commaunded hym that he shold do the peple kepe them. Thyse wordes avayled
665 not. They wold in no wyse kepe them. And than he sayd to them that it were good
that or the sayd lawes shold be broken that he had gyven to them, that he shold goo
and speke wyth the god Appollo, for to gete of hym a dispensacion to breke hem,
and that the peple shold kepe and observe them tyl that he retorned agayn. The
peple accorded therto and swore that they shold kepe them unto the tyme he
670 retorned. Than the knyght went into Grece in exyle and dwellyd there alle his lyf.
And whan he shold dye, he commaunded that hys body shold be cast in the see.
For as moche as yf his body shold be borne theder, the peple shold wene to be quyt
of theyr othe and shold kepe no lenger his lawes that were so good and resonable
that the knyght had lever to forsake his owne contré and to dye so than to repele
675 his lawes.

And his lawes were suche:

The first lawe was that the people shold obeye and serve the prynces, and the
prynces shold kepe the peple and doo justyce on the malefactours.

The second lawe that they shold be al sobre, for he wyst wel that the labour of
680 chevalrye is most stronge whan they lyve sobrely.

The thyrd was that no man shold bye ony thyng for money, but they shold
chaunge ware for ware, and one marchaundyse for another.

The fourth was that men shold sette nomore by money ner kepe hit more than
they wold dunge or filthe.

649 **purveye**, provide; **dispencis**, upkeep. 650 **sewre**, secure (or possibly "sower," although there is no instance of this spelling in other texts). 652 **crafty men**, tradesmen. 653–54 **gete and gadre**, obtain and gather. 655 **kepar**, keeper. 656 **alwey**, perpetually. 657 **magesté ryal**, royal greatness; **garnysshed**, decorated. 660 **auncient**, ancient. 661 **rapelle**, repeal; **sette hem aparte**, set them aside. 662 **dyd**, caused. 664–65 **avayled not**, did not succeed. 666 **or**, before. 668 **tyl**, until. 669 **accorded therto**, agreed to this. 672 **For as moche as yf**, For if; **theder**, thither. 674 **lever**, rather. 678 **malefactours**, transgressors. 679 **sobre**, temperate; **wyst**, knew. 682 **chaunge ware for ware**, exchange goods. 684 **dunge**, dung.

685   The fifthe he ordeyned for the comyn wele alle thynge by ordre, that the prynces myght meve and make bataylle by her power. To the maisters' counceyllours he commysed the jugementis and the annuel rentes. To the senatours, the kepyng of the lawe. And to the comyn peple he gaf power to chese suche juges as they wold have.

690   The sixte he ordeyned that alle thynge shold be departed egally and al thyng shold be comyn, and none richer than other in patrimony.

   The seventh that every man shold eete lyke wel in comyn opynly, that richesse shold not be cause of luxurye whan they ete secretly.

   The eighth that the yonge peple shold not have but one gowne or garment in
695 the yere.

   The ninth that men shold sette poure children to laboure in the felde to the ende that they shold not enploye theyr yongthe in playes and folye but in laboure.

   The tenthe that the maydens shold be maried wythout dowaire, in suche wyse that no man shold take a wyf for money.

700   The eleventh that men shold rather take a wyf for her good maners and vertues than for her richesses.

   The twelfth that men shold worshyp the olde and auncient men for theyr age and more for theyr wysedom than for her riches.

   This knyght made none of thyse lawes but he first kepte hem.

The fyfthe chappytre of the second book, of the forme and maners of the rookes.
Capitulo quinto.

---

  686 meve, initiate; **maisters' counceyllours**, royal council. **687 commysed**, commissioned or entrusted. **690 departed**, divided. **691 patrimony**, inheritance. **692 eete**, eat. **697 enploye**, employ or direct. **698 dowaire**, dowry.

705   The rookes, whiche been vycayrs and legates of the kynge, ought to be maad a knyght upon an hors and a mantel and hood furrid with menevier, holdyng a staf in his hand. And for as moche as a kyng may not be in al places of his royame, therfore the auctorité of hym is gyven to the rookes, whiche represente the kyng. And for as moche as a royame is grete and large, and that rebellyon or noveltees

710   myght sourde and aryse in one partye or other, therfore ther ben two rookes, one on the right syde and that other on the lift syde. They ought to have in hem pyté, justice, humylité, wylful poverté, and lyberalyté.

First justyce, for it is most fayr of the vertues. For hit happeth ofte tyme that the mynystres, by theyr pryde and orgueyl, subverte justyce and doo no right, wherfore

715   the kynges otherwhyle lose theyr royames wythout theyr culpe or gylte. For an untrewe juge or offycer maketh his lord to be named unjuste and evyl. And contrarye wyse, a trewe mynystre of the lawe and rightwys causeth the kyng to be reputed just and trewe. The Romayns therfore maad good lawes and wold that they shold be juste and trewe. And they that establisshid them for to governe the peple wold in no wyse

720   breke them but kepe them for to dye for them. For the auncient and wyse men said comynly that it was not good to make and ordeygne that lawe that is not just.

Wherof Valeryus reherceth that there was a man that was named Themystydes, whiche came to the counceyllours of Athenes and sayd that he knewe a counceyl whiche was right proffytable for them, but he wold telle hit but to one of them whom

725   that they wold. And they assygned to hym a wyse man named Aristydes. And whan he had understonde hym, he cam agayn to the other of the counceyl, and sayd that the counceyl of Themystides was wel proffytable, but "hit was not just, how be hit ye may revolve hit in your mynde." And the counceyl that he sayd was thys: that there were comen two grete shippes fro Lacedome and were arryved in theyr

730   londe, and that hit were good to take them. And whan the counceyl herde hym that sayd that hit was not juste ner right, they left hem al in pees, and wold not have a doo with al.

The vicair or juge of the kyng ought to be so just that he shold enploye al his entente to save the comyn wele, and yf hit were nede to put his lyf and lose hit

735   therfore. We have an ensaumple of Marcus Regulus, wherof Tullyus reherceth in the *Book of Offyces*, and Saynt Augustyn also [in] *De Civitate dei*, how he faught agayn them of Cartage by see in shyppes and was vaynquysshed and taken. Than hit happend that they of Cartage sent him in her message to Rome for to have theyr prysoners there for them that were taken, and so to chaunge one for another, and

740   made hym swere and promyse to come ageyn. And so he came to Rome and made proposicion tofore the Senate and demaunded them of Cartage of the senatours to be chaunged as afore is sayd. And than the Senatours demaunded hym what

---

705 vycayrs and legates, representatives and delegates.   **706 furrid with menevier**, lined with fur.   **707 royame**, kingdom.   **709 noveltees**, news.   **710 sourde**, spring up.   **712 wylful**, voluntary; **lyberalyté**, generosity.   **714 orgueyl**, pride.   **715 otherwhyle**, in these cases; **culpe**, culpability.   **717 rightwys**, upstanding.   **723 counceyl**, used in this section to refer both to advice and to the Senate as a whole.   **724 but to one**, only to one.   **727–28 how be hit ye may revolve hit** (i.e., however you may consider it).   **729 Lacedome**, Lacedaemon (Sparta).   **733–34 enploye al his entente**, direct all his energy.   **734 save**, preserve; **nede**, necessary.   **738 in her message**, as their messenger.   **742 demaunded**, requested.

counceyl he gaf. "Certeyn," sayd he, "I counuceyll yow that ye doo hyt not in no wyse, for as moche as the peple of Rome that they of Cartage holde in pryson of youris byn olde men and brusid in the warre as I am myself. But they that ye holde in pryson of theyr peple is alle the floure of alle theyr folke." Whyche couunceyl they took. And than his frendes wold have holden hym and counceilled them to abyde there and not retorne agayn prisoner into Cartage. But he wold never do so, ner abyde, but wold goo agayn and kepe his oth, how wel that he knewe that he went toward his deth, for he had lever dye than to breke his oth.

Valerius rehercith in the sixth book of one Emelie, duc of the Romayns, that in the tyme whan he had assiegid the Phalistes, the scole maistre of the children deceyvyd the children of the gentilmen that he drewe hym a litil and a litil unto the tentis of the Romayns by fayr speche. And sayd to the Duc Emelye that by the moyan of the chyldren that he had brought to hym, he shold have the cyté, for theyr faders were lordes and governours. Whan Emelye had herde hym, he said thus to hym: "Thou that art evyl and cruel, and thou that woldest gyve a gyfte of grete felonye and of mavastye, thou shalt ner hast not founden here duc ne peple that resembleth thee. We have also wel lawes to kepe in batayle and warre, as in our contrees and other places. And we wol observe and kepe them unto every man as they ought to be kept. And we ben armed ayenst our enemyes that wol defende them, and not ayenst them that can not save their lyf whan their contré is taken, as thise litil children. Thou hast vaynquysshed them as moche as is in thee by thy newe deceyvable falsnes and by subtilnes and not by armes. But I that am a Romayn shal vaynquysshe them by craft and strength of armes."

And anone he commaunded to take the sayd scole maister and to bynde his handes behynde hym as a traytour, and lede hym unto the parentis of the chyldren. And whan the faders and parentes sawe the grete curtoysye that he had doon to them, they opened the gates and yelded them unto hym.

We rede that Hanybal had taken a prynce of Rome whyche upon his othe and promyse suffred hym to goo home and to sende hym hys raunson or he shold come agayn within a certeyn tyme. And whan he was at home in his place, he said that he had deceyved hym by a false oth. And whan the Senatours knewe therof, they constrayned hym to retorne agayn unto Hanybal.

Amos Florus tellith that the phisicien of Kyng Pirrus cam on a nyght to Fabrice, his adversarye, and promysed hym yf he wold geve hym for his labour that he wold enpoysone Pirrus, his mayster. Whan Fabricius understood this, he dyd to take hym and bynde hym hand and foot, and sent hym to his maistre, and dyd do say to hym word for word like as the phisicien had said and promysed hym to do. And whan Pirrus understood this, he was gretly admervaylid of the loyalté and trouth of Fabrice, his enemye, and said "certeynly that the sonne myght lightlyer and sonner

745

750

755

760

765

770

775

780

---

743 Certeyn, Certainly. **744 for as moche as,** because. **745 brusid,** wounded. **747 holden hym,** kept him; **them** (presumably Marcus travels with other prisoners). **748 abyde,** stay. **749 how wel that,** although. **750 lever,** rather. **752 assiegid,** attacked; **Phalistes,** citizens of Falerii, an ancient city in central Italy; **scole maistre,** schoolmaster. **754 moyan,** means. **758 mavastye,** evil; **shalt ner hast not,** shall not nor have not. **769 them,** themselves. **773 hym,** them. **774 constrayned,** made. **777 enpoysone,** poison. **780 admervaylid of,** astounded by. **781 lightlyer and sonner,** more easily and more quickly.

be enpesshid of his cours thenne Fabrice shold be letted to holde loyalté and
trouthe." Yf they than that were not Crysten were so juste and trewe, and lovyd
theyr contréy and theyr good renomee, what shold we now doon, than, that been
785   Cristen, and that our lawe is sette al upon love and charité? But now a dayes there
is nothynge ellis in the world but barate, treson, deceit, falsenes, and trecherye. Men
kepe not their covenauntes, promyses, othes, writynges, ne trouth. The subgettis
rebelle agayn their lord. Ther is now no lawe kepte, nor fydelyté, ne othe holden.
The people murmure and ryse agayn theyr lord and wol not be subget.

790   They [the vicars] ought to be pietous in herte, whiche is avaylable to alle thyng.
There is pyté in effect by compassyon and in worde by remyssyon, and pardon by
almesse for to enclyne hymself unto the poure. For pyté is no thyng ellis but a right
grete wylle of a debonayr herte for to helpe alle men.

Valerius rehercith that there was a juge named Sangis whiche dampned a
795   woman that had deservyd the deth for to have her heed smyten of or ellys that she
shold dye in pryson. The jayler that had pyté on the woman put not her anon to deth
but put her in the pryson. And this woman had a doughter whiche came for to see
and comforte her moder. But alwey or she entrid into the prison, the jayler serchyd
hyr that she shold bere no mete ne drynke to her moder, but that she shold dye for
800   honger. Than hit happend after thys that he mervayled moche why this woman
dyed not, and began to espye the cause why she lyvyd so long and fonde atte laste
how her doughter gaf sowke to her moder and fedde her with her mylke. Whan the
jayler sawe thys merveyle, he went and tolde the juge. And whan the juge sawe this
grete pyté of the doughter to the moder, he pardoned her and made her to be
805   delyverd out of her pryson. What is that that pité ne amolissheth? Moche peple
wene that it is agaynst nature and wondre that the doughtre shold gyve the moder
to souke. Hit were agaynst nature but the children shold be kynde to fader and
moder.

Seneka sayth that the kyng of bees hath no prykke to stynge wyth as other bees
810   have, and that nature hath take hit away from hym by cause he shold have none
armes to assayle them. And this is an example unto prynces that they shold be of
the same condycion.

Valerius rehercith in his fifthe book of Marchus Martellus that whan he had
taken the cyté of Syracusane and was sette in the hyest place of the cyté, he behelde
815   the grete destruccyon of the peple and of the cyté. He wepte and said: "Thou
oughtest to be sorowful, for so moche as thou woldest have no pyté of thy self. But
enjoye thee, for thou art fallen in the hande of a right debonair prynce."

782 enpesshid of his cours, thrown off his course; **letted to holde**, prevented from
keeping.   **783 than**, then; **Crysten**, Christian.   **784 renomee**, reputation.   **786 barate**,
trouble or suffering.   **788 fydelyté**, fidelity.   **790 avaylable to**, beneficial to.   **791 in effect**,
in deed.   **792 almesse**, alms; **enclyne**, turn.   **793 debonayr**, gracious.   **795 smyten of**, cut
off.   **798 or she entrid**, before she entered.   **800 mervayled**, marveled.   **802 gaf sowke to**,
nursed (with her breast).   **805 that that**, that which; **amolissheth**, soften.   **806 wene**, know.
807 Hit were agaynst nature but, But it would really be against nature unless.   **814
Syracusane**, Syracuse.   **815 destruccyon**, destruction.   **817 enjoye thee**, comfort yourselves;
debonair, gracious.

Also, he recounteth when Pompeeé had conquerd the kyng of Germanye, that
often tymes had foughten ayenst the Romayns, and that he was brought tofore hym
820   bounden. He was so pyetous that he wold not suffre hym to be longe on his knees
tofore hym, but he receyved hym curtoysly and sette the crowne agayn on his heed,
and put hym in the estate that he was tofore. For he had oppynyon that it was as
worshypful and fittyng to a kyng to pardone as to punysshe.

Also, he reherceth of a counceyllour that was named Poule, that dyd do brynge
825   tofore hym a man that was prysoner. And or he knelid tofore hym, he toke hym up
fro the grounde and made hym to sitte besyde hym for to geve hym good esperaunce
and hope, and sayd to the other stondyng by in thys wyse: "Yf hit be grete noblesse
that we shewe ourself contrarye to our enemyes, than this fete ought to be alowed,
that we shewe ourself debonayr to our caytyfs and prisoners."

830   Cesar, whan he hard the deth of Cathon, whiche was his adversarye, sayd that
he had grete envye of hys glorye and nothyng of his patrymonye. And therfore, he
lefte to his chyldren frely al hys patrymonye.

Thus taught Virgyle and enseygneth the glorious prynces to rewle and governe
the peple of Rome.

835   And Saynt Austyn [in] *De Civitate dei* sayth thus: "Thou emperour, governe the
peple pyetously and make pees overall, deporte and forbere thy subgettis, repreve
and correcte the prowde, for so enseyne and teche thee the lawes."

And hyt was wryten unto Alixaunder that every prynce ought to be pyetous in
punysshyng and redy for to rewarde. Ther is nothyng that causeth a prynce to be
840   so belovyd of his peple as whan he spekyth to hem swetely and concervyth wyth
hem symply. And al this cometh of the rote of pyté.

We rede of the Emperour Trajan that his frendes reprevyd hym of that he was
to moche pryvé and famulier wyth the comyn peple more than an emperour ought
to be. And he answerd that he wold be suche an emperour as every man desyred
845   to have hym.

Also, we rede of Alisaunder that on a tyme he ladde his hoost forth hastely. And
in that haste he beheld where satte an olde knyght that was sore acolde, whom he
dyd do aryse and sette hym in his owne sete or siege. What wondre was hit though
the knyghtes desyred to serve suche a lorde that lovyd better theyr helthe than his
850   dignyté?

The rookes ought also to be humble and meke after the Holy Scripture, whiche
sayth: "The gretter or in the hyer astate that thou art, so moche more oughtest thou
be meker and more humble."

Valerius rehercheth in his seventh book that ther was an emperour named
855   Publius Cesar, that dyd doo bete doun his hows, whyche was in the myddes of the

---

820 pyetous, merciful. **822 estate**, condition. **826 esperaunce**, expectation or hope. **828
fete**, deed. **829 caytyfs**, prisoners. **830 hard**, heard of. **831 patrymonye**, patrimony or
estate. **831–32 he lefte to his chyldren** (i.e., Caesar leaves Cato's inheritance to Cato's
children). **833 enseygneth**, instructs. **836 deporte and forbere**, spare and be forbearing
towards. **837 for so enseyne**, and in this way instruct. **840 concervyth**, should probably
be "convercyth," or converses. **843 pryvé**, private. **847 acolde**, chilled. **848 sete or siege**,
seat; **though** (best taken as "that"). **855 dyd doo bete doun his hows**, who caused his house
to burn down; **myddes**, middle.

marketplace, for as moche as hit was hyer than other howses. For as moche as he was more gloryous in estate than other, therfore wold he have a lasse hows than other.

And Scipion of Affrique, that was so poure of valuntarye poverté, that whan he was dede, he was buryed at the dyspencis and in costes of the comyn good. They should be so humble that they shold leve theyr offyces and suffre other to take hem whan her tyme cometh, and doo honour to other. For he governeth wel the royame that may governe hit when he wyl.

Valerius rehercith in his third book that Fabyan the Grete had ben maystre counceyllour of his fader, his grauntsire, and of his grauntsir's fader, and of alle his antecessours. And yet dyd he al his payn and labour that his sone shold never have that offyce after hym. But for no thynge that he mystrusted his sone, for he was noble and wyse and more attempered than other. But he wold that the offyce shold not alwey reste in the famylye and hows of the Fabyans.

Also, he rehercith in his seventh book that they wold make the sayd Fabyan emperour, but he excusyd hym, and sayde that he was blynde and myght not see for age. But that excusacion myght not helpe hym. Than sayd he to hem: "Seke ye and gete you another! For yf ye make me your emperour, I may not suffre your maners, nor ye may not suffre myn."

There was a kyng of so subtyl engyne that whan men brought hym the crowne, tofore that he toke hit, he remembrid hym a litil, and sayd, "O thou crowne that art more noble thenne happy! For yf a kyng knewe wel and parfaytly how that thou art ful of parylles of thoughte and of charge, yf thou were on the grounde, he wold never lyfte nor take thee up. Remembre thee that whan thou art most glorious, thenne have somme men moste envye on thee. And whan thou hast most seignorye and lordshyps, than shalt thou have most care, thought, and anguysshes."

Vaspasian was so humble that whan Nero was slayn, alle the peple cryed for to have hym emperour. And many of his frendes came and prayed hym that he wold take hit upon hym. So at the last he was constreyned to take hit upon hym, and sayd to hys frendys, "Hit is better and more to prayse and alowe for a man to take the empyre agaynst his wylle than for to laboure to have hit and to put hymself therin."

Thus ought they to be humble and meke for to receyve worshyp. Therfore saith the Byble that Joab, the sone of Saryne, that was captayne of the warre of the Kyng Davyd, whan he cam to take and wynne a cyté, he sente to Davyd and desyred hym to come to the warre, that the victorye shold be geven to Davyd and not to hymself.

Also, they ought to be ware that they chaunge not ofte tymes her offycers. Josephus rehercith that the frendes of Tyberius mervaylled moche why he helde his officers so longe in theyr offyces wythout chaunchyng. And they demaunded

---

856 hyer, higher. **857 lasse**, more modest. **859 at the dyspencis**, at the expense. **861 royame**, kingdom. **864 grauntsire**, grandfather. **865 antecessours**, ancestors; **dyd he al his payn and labour**, did he work to the end that. **866 offyce**, responsibility; **But for no thynge**, But not for the reason. **867 attempered**, well-balanced. **870 excusyd hym**, exempted himself. **871 for age**, on account of his age. **872–73 suffre your maners**, endure your customs. **874 engyne**, genius. **875 remembrid hym**, reminded himself. **877 parylles**, perils. **879 seignorye**, power. **884 alowe for**, sanction. **892 chaunchyng**, changing.

of hym the cause, to whom he answerd, "I wolde chaunge them gladly yf I wyst that hit shold be good for the peple. But I sawe on a tyme a man that was royneous and

895 ful of sores, and many flyes satte upon the sores and souked hys blood, that hit was mervayle to see. Wherfore I smote and chaced them away. And he than sayd to me 'Why chasest and smytest thou away thyse flyes that been ful of my blood? And now shalt thou lete come other that be hongrye, which shal doon to me double payne more than the other dyd. For the prick of the hongry is more poygnaunt the half

900 thenne of the fulle.'"

"And therfore," sayde he, "I leve the offycers in theyr offyces, for they ben al riche and do not so moche evyll and harme as the newe shold do and were poure yf I shold sette hem in her places."

They ought also to be pacient in heryng of wordes and in suffryng payne on her

905 bodyes. As to the first, one sayd to Alisaunder that he was not worthy to reigne, specially whan he suffred that lecherye and delyte to have seignorye in hym. He suffrid hit paciently and answerd none otherwyse but that he wold correcte hymself, and take better maners and more honeste.

Also, hit is rehercid that Julyus Cesar was ballyd, wherof he had displasir so

910 grete that he kempt hys heeris that laye on the after parte of his heed forward for to hyde the bare tofore. Than sayd a knyght to hym, "Cezar, hit is lightlier and soner to be maad that thou be not ballyd than that I have usid ony cowardyse in the warre of Rome, or here after shal doo ony cowardyse." He suffryd hyt paciently and sayd not one word. Another reprochyd hym by his lignage and called hym "baker."

915 He answerd that "Hit is better that noblesse begynne in me than hit shold faylle in me." Another callyd hym tyraunt. He answerd, "Yf I were one, thou woldest not say so."

A knyght callyd on a tyme Scipyon of Affrique "fowle and olde knyght in armes," and that he knewe lytyl good. And he answerd, "I was borne of my moder a lytyl

920 chylde and feble, and not a man of armes." And yet he was at alle tymes one of the best and most worthyest in armes that lyvyd.

Another sayd to Vaspasion: "And a wolf shold sonner chaunge his skyn and heer than thou sholdest chaunge thy lyf. For the lenger thou lyvest, the more thou coveytest." And he answerd of thyse wordes: "We ought to laughe. But we ought to

925 amende ourself and punysshe the trespaces."

Seneke rehercith that the Kyng Antygonus herde certeyn peple speke and say evyl of hym, and there was betwene hem nomore but a courtyne. And than he sayd, "Make an ende of your evyl langage lest the kyng here you, for the courtyne heeryth yow wel ynough."

930 Than, as touchyng to the paynes that they ought to suffre paciently, Valerius reherceth that a tyraunt dyd do torment Anamaxymenes and thretenyd hym for to cutte of his tunge, to whom he sayd, "Hit is not in thy power to do so." And forthwith

---

894 royneous, ruinous/broken down. **895 souked**, sucked. **897 smytest**, smite. **898 lete come**, cause to come. **899 poygnaunt**, powerful. **904 heryng**, hearing. **909 ballyd**, bald; **displasir**, displeasure. **910 kempt**, combed. **911–12 lightlier and soner**, more easily and sooner. **922 sonner**, sooner. **928 courtyne**, curtain. **932 cutte of**, cut off.

he bote of his owne tongue and chewid hit wyth his tethe, and caste hit in the
vysage of the tyraunt.

935   Hit is a grete vertu in a man that he forgete not to be pacient in correccions of
wronges. Hit is better to leve a gylty man unpunysshed than to punysshe hym in
a wrath or yre.

Valerius rehercith that Archyta of Tarente, that was mayster to Plato, sawe that
his feldes and landes were destroyed and lost by the necligence of his servaunt, to
940   whom he sayd: "Yf I were not angry with thee, I wolde take vengeaunce and
turmente thee." Lo, there ye may see that he had lever to leve to punysshe than to
punysshe more by yre and wrath than by right.

And therfore sayth Seneque: "Do not thyng that thou oughtest to doo whan
thou arte angrye. For whan thou art angry, thou woldest do alle thynges after thy
945   playsir. And yf thou canst not vaynquysshe thyn yre, than must thyn yre overcome
thee."

After thys ought they to have wylful poverté, lyke as hit was in the auncient
prynces. For they coveyted more to be riche in wytte and good maners thenne in
money. And that rehercith Valerius in his eighth book that Scypyon of Affryque
950   was accused unto the Senate that he shold have grete tresour. And he answerd,
"Certes, whan I submysed Affrique into your poesté, I helde no thyng to myself that
I myght say 'This is myn' save onely the surname of Affrique. Ner the Affriquans
have not founden in me, ner in my broder, ony avaryce, ner that we were so
covetouse that we had, ne had gretter envye to be riche of name than of richesses."

955   And therfore sayth Seneque that the Kyng Altagone usyd gladly in his hows
vessels of erthe. And somme sayd he dyd hit for covetyse. But he sayd that hit was
better and more noble thynge to shyne in good maners than in vasseyll. And whan
somme men demaunded hym why and for what cause he dyd so, he answerd, "I am
now Kyng of Secylle and was sone of a potter. And for as moche as, I doubte fortune.
960   For whan I yssued out of the hows of my fader and moder, I was sodaynly maad
riche, wherfore I beholde the natyvyté of me and of my lignage, whyche is humble
and meke." And al these thynges cometh of wylful poverté, for he entended more
to the comyn proffyt than to his owen.

And of this poverté speketh Saynt Augustyn in the *Book of the Cyté of God*, that
965   they that entende to the comyn proffyt sorowe more that wylful poverté is lost in
Rome than the richesses of Rome, for by the wylful poverté was the renomee of
good maners kepte entierly. Thus by this richesse, poverté is not onely corrupt in
thyse dayes, ner the cyté, ner the maners, but also the thoughtes of the men ben
corrupt by this covetise and by felonye that is worse than ony other enemye.

970   And of the cruelté of the peple of Rome speketh the good man of noble
memorye, John the Monke, late cardynal of Rome, in the *Decretal the Sixte*, in the

---

933 bote of, bit off; **tethe**, teeth.   **934 vysage**, face.   **941 turmente**, torment; **to leve to
punysshe**, not to punish.   **948 wytte**, wit or intellect.   **950 accused unto**, accused before.
951 submysed Affrique, made Africa submit; **poesté**, poustie or pousté, an archaic word
that means power.   **955 hows**, house.   **956 erthe**, clay.   **957 vasseyll**, vessels.   **959 Secylle**,
Sicily; **for as moche as**, because of this.   **960 yssued**, issued.   **961 natyvyté**, nativity (in the
sense of family origins).   **962 entended**, inclined himself.   **965 sorowe**, regret.   **966
renomee**, renown.   **968 ner the . . . ner the**, both in . . . and in.

chappytre *Gens sancta*, where he sayth that they ben felons ayenst God, contrarye
to holy thynges, trayters one to that other, envyous to her neyghbours, proud unto
straungers, rebell and untrewe unto their soverayns, not suffryng to them that been
975   of lower degree than they, and no thyng shamefast to demaunde thynges
discovenable, and not to leve tyl they have that they demaunde, and not plesyd but
disagreable whan they have receyved the gefte. They have theyr tongues redy for
to make grete boost and do lityl. They ben large in promysyng and smale gyvers.
Thyy ben right fals deceyvours, and right mordent and bytyng detractours, for
980   whiche thyng hit is a grete sorowe to see the humylité, the pacyence, and the good
wysdom that was wonte to be in this cyté of Rome, whiche is chyef of al the world,
and is perverted and torned into maleheurte and thyse evylles. And me thynketh
that in other parties of Cristenté, they have taken ensaumple of them to do evyl.
They may say that this is after the *Decretale of Seygnorye and Dysobeysaunce*, that sayth
985   that suche thynges that the soverayns do is lightly and sone taken in ensaumple of
theyr subgettis.

And also, thyse vycayres shold be large and liberall, in so moche that suche peple
as serve them ben duly payd and guerdoned of her labour. For every man doth his
labour the better and lightlyer whan he seeth that he shal be wel payed and
990   rewarded. And we rede that Titus, the sone of Vaspasian, was so large and so
lyberal that he gaf and promysed sumwhat to every man. And whan his most prevy
frendes demaunded of hym why he promysed more thenne he myght gyve, he
answerd, "For as moche as it aperteyneth not to a prynce that ony man shold departe
sorowful or tryste fro hym." Than hit happend on a day that he gaf ner promysed
995   no thyng to ony man. And whan hit was even and advysed hymself, he sayd to his
frendes: "O ye my frendes, thys day have I lost. For this day have I don no good."

And also, we rede of Julius Cesar that he never sayd in alle his lyf to his knyghtes
"Goo on," but alwey he sayd "Come, come! For I love alwey to be in your companye."
And he knewe wel that hit was lasse payne and travaylle to the knyghtes whan the
1000   prynce is in her companye that loveth hem and comforteth hem.

And also, we rede of the same Julyus Cesar in the *Book of Truphes of Philosophers*
that there was an auncient knyght of his that was in parelle of a caas hangyng
tofore the juges of Rome. So he callyd Cesar on a tyme and sayd to hym tofore al
men that he shold be his advocate. And Cesar delyveryd and assygned to hym a
1005   right good advocate. And the knyght sayd to hym, "O Cesar, I put no vycayr in my
place when thou were in paryl in the Batayl of Assise, but I faught for thee."

And than he shewyd to hym the places of his woundes that he had receyved in
the bataylle. And than cam Cesar in his propre persone for to be his advocate and

---

975 no thyng shamefast, and in no way ashamed.   **976 discovenable**, unsuitable; **leve**,
leave; **plesyd**, pleased.   **977 gefte**, gift.   **979 mordent and bytyng**, mordant and biting.   **981
wonte**, wont; **chyef**, chief.   **982 maleheurte**, misfortune.   **983 Cristenté**, the Christian
world.   **984 *Seygnorye and Dysobeysaunce***, *Rule and Disobedience*.   **985 lightly and sone**,
quickly and soon.   **987 large and liberall**, generous and openhearted.   **988 guerdoned**,
rewarded.   **991 most prevy**, closest.   **994 tryste**, sad.   **995 whan hit was even and advysed
hymself**, when it was evening and he considered to himself.   **999 travaylle**, distress.   **1002
parelle**, peril; **hangyng**, pending.   **1006 Batayl of Assise**, Battle of Assisi.   **1008 in his
propre persone**, himself.

to plete his cause for hym. He wold not have the name of unkyndenes, but doubted
1010   that men shold say that he were proude and that he wold not doo for them that
had servyd hym. They that can not do so moche as for to be belovyd of her knyghtes
can not love the knyghtes.

     And this suffiseth of the rookes.

1009 plete, plead; **doubted**, feared.

BOOK THREE

The third tractate of the offices of the comyn peple. The first chappitre is of the offyce of the labourers and werkmen. **Capitulo primo.**

For so moche as noble persones cannot rewle ne governe without the servyse and werke of the people, than hit behoveth to devyse the oultrages and the offyces of the werkmen. Than I shal begynne first at the first pawn that is in the play of the chesse and signefieth a man of the comyn peple on fote. For they be al named "pietons," that is as moche to say as footmen. And thenne we wyl begynne at the pawn whyche standeth tofore the rooke on the right syde of the kyng, for as moche as thys pawne apperteyneth to serve the vycayre or lyeuetenaunt of the kyng and other officers under hym of necessaries of vytaylle.

And this maner of peple is figured and ought be maad in the forme and shappe of a man holdyng in his right honde a spade or shovel, and a rodde in the lyft hand. The spade or shovel is for to delve and labour therwyth the erthe, and the rodde is for to dryve and conduyte wyth al the bestys unto her pasture. Also, he ought to have on hys gyrdel a sarpe or crokyd hachet for to cutte of the superfluytees of the vignes and trees.

5

10

2 **devyse**, consider; **oultrages**, exertions. 4 **fote**, foot; **"pietons,"** foot soldiers. 7 **vycayre**, representative. 8 **vytaylle**, food. 11 **delve**, dig. 12 **conduyte**, steer through. 13 **gyrdel**, girdle or belt; **sarpe or crokyd hachet**, a pruning hook or crooked hatchet; **cutte of**, cut off; **superfluytees**, overgrowth; **vignes**, vines.

15   And we rede in the Bible that the first labourer that ever was was Caym, the first
sone of Adam, that was so evyl that he slewe his broder Abel, for as moche as the
smoke of his tithes went strayt unto heven, and the smoke and fume of the tythes
of Caym went dounward upon the erthe. And how wel that thys cause was trewe.
Yet was there another cause of envye that he had unto his broder. For when Adam,
20   theyr fader, maryed them for to multeplye the erthe of his ligne, he wold not marye
ner joyne togyder the two that were borne attones, but gaf unto Caym her that was
born with Abel, and to Abel her that was borne wyth Caym. And thus began the
envye that Caym had ayenst Abel, for hys wyf was fayrer than Caym's wyf. And for
this cause he sle[we] Abel wyth the chekebone of a beste. And at that tyme was never
25   no maner of yron blody of manne's blood. And Abel was the fyrst martir in the
Olde Testament. And thys sayd Caym dyd many other evyl thynges whiche I leve,
for it apperteyneth not to my mater.
        But it behoveth for necessyté that somme shold laboure the erthe after the
synne of Adam. For tofore or Adam synned, the erthe brought forth fruyt without
30   labour of handes. But sithe he synned, hit must nedes be laboured with the handes
of men. And for as moche as the erthe is moder of al thynges, and that we were first
formed and took our begynnyng of the erthe, the same wyse at the last, she shal be
the ende unto al us and to al thynges. And God that formed us of the erthe hath
ordeyned that by the labour of men she shold gyve nourysshyng unto al that lyveth.
35   And first the labourer of the erthe ought to knowe his God that formed and
made heven and erthe of nought, and ought to have loyalté and trouth in hymself,
and despise deth for to entende to his labour. And he ought to geve thankynges
to hym that made hym and of whom he receyveth al his goodes temporal, wherof
his lyf is susteyned. And also, he is bounden to paye the dismes and tythes of al his
40   thynges, and not as Caym dyd but as Abel dyd of the beste that he chese out alwey
for to gyve to God and to plese Hym. For they that grutche and be greved in that
they rendre and geve to God the tienthes of her goodes, they ought to be aferd and
have drede that they shal falle in necessyté, and that they myght be despoylyd or
robbyd by warre or by tempest that myght falle or happen in the contray. And hit
45   is no merveylle, though hyt so happen for that man that is disagreable unto God
and weneth that the multeplyeng of his goodes temporel cometh by the vertu of
his owne counceyl and his witte, the whiche is made by the only ordenaunce of
Hym that made al, and by the same ordenaunce is sone taken awey fro hym that
is disagreable. And hit is reson that whan a man haboundeth by fortune in goodes
50   and knowith not God by whom it cometh, that to hym come somme other fortune
by the whiche he may requyre grace and pardon, and to knowe his God.

16 for as moche as, because. **20 maryed**, married. **21 attones**, at once. **23 fayrer**, fairer.
24 chekebone, cheekbone. **28 behoveth**, is requisite. **32 at the last**, in the end. **37
entende**, direct himself towards; **geve thankynges**, give thanks. **38 goodes temporal**,
worldly goods. **39 dismes**, obsolete meaning for *dime* or a tenth part, a tithe paid to the
church or to a temporal ruler. **40 beste**, beast; **chese out**, selected. **41 grutche and be
greved**, complain and are vexed. **42 rendre**, offer up; **tienthes**, tenth; **her**, their. **43 falle
in necessyté**, fall into want; **despoylyd**, despoiled. **44 contray**, country. **45 merveylle**,
marvel. **46 weneth**, believes; **multeplyeng**, multiplying. **47 counceyl**, deliberation; **witte**,
intellect; **ordenaunce**, decree. **48 sone**, soon. **49 haboundeth**, abounds. **51 requyre**, ask.

And we rede of the Kyng Davyd, that was first symple and one of the comyn peple, that whan fortune had enhauncid and sette him in grete estate, he left and forgate his God, and fyl to advoultrie and homycide and other synnes. Than anone his owne sone, Absalon, assaillid and began to persecute hym. And than whan he sawe that fortune was contrarye to hym, he began to take ageyn his vertuous werkis and requyred pardon and so retorned to God agayn.

We rede also of the children of Ysrael, that were nygh enfamyned in desert, and sore hungry and thrusty, that they prayed and requyred of God for remedye. Anone He chaunged His wille and sent to hem manna and flessh. And whan they were replenysshed and fatte of the flessh of bestes and of the manna, they made a calf of gold and worshipped hit, whiche was a grete synne and inyquyté. For whan they were hongry, they knewe God. And whan theyr belies were filled and fatted, they forgid ydolles and were ydolatreres.

After this every labourer ought to be faithful and trewe, that whan his maister delyvereth to hym his lande to be laboured, that he take nothyng to hymself but that he ought to have and is his, but laboure truly and take cure and charge in the name of hys maystre, and do more diligently hys mayster's labours than his owen, for the lyf of the most grete and noble men next God lieth in the handes of the labourers. And thus al craftes and occupacions ben ordeyned not only to suffise to them only but to [the] comyn. And so it happeth oft tyme that the labourer of the erth useth grete and boistous metis, and bryngeth to his maister more subtile and more deynteous metes.

And Valerius rehercith in his sixt book that there was a wyse and noble maistre that was named Anthonius, that was accusid of a caas of avoultry. And as the cause henge tofore the juges, his accusers or denonciatours brought a labourer that closed his lande, for so moche as they sayd whan his mayster went to do the advoultrye, this same servaunt bare the lanterne, wherof Anthonius was sore abasshid and douted that he shold depose agaynst hym. But the labourer, that was named Papirion, said to his maister that he shold denye his cause hardily unto the juges, for to be tormentid, his cause shold never be enpeyred by hym, ner nothyng shold yssue out of his mouth wherof he shold be noyed or grevyd. And than was the labourer beten and tormentid, and brent in many places of his body. But he sayd never thyng wherof his maister was hurt or noyed. But the other that accused his maister were punysshed, and Papirion was delyverd of his paynes.

And also tellith Valerius that there was another labourer that was named Penapion, that servyd a maister whos name was Themes, which was of mervaillous

52 symple, humble. 53 enhauncid, elevated or lifted up. 54 advoultrie, adultery. 56 to take ageyn, to resume. 58 nygh enfamyned, nearly starved. 59 Anone, Immediately. 60 hem, them; manna and flessh, heavenly drink and food. 63 belies, bellies. 64 forgid ydolles, built idols. 65 that whan, so that when. 67 cure, care. 70–71 to suffise to them only, to be sufficient to them alone. 72 boistous metis, coarse food. 73 deynteous metes, delicate morsels. 75–76 cause henge, case was pending. 76 closed, guarded. 78 bare the lanterne (i.e., the servant guides Antonius to his secret rendezvous); abasshid, ashamed. 79 douted, feared; depose, testify. 81 for to be tormentid, for even if he were tortured; enpeyred, impaired or made worse. 82 noyed or grevyd, harmed or vexed. 83 brent, burned.

faith to his maister. For hit befel that certeyn knyghtes cam to his maister's hows for
to slé hym. And anone as Penapion knewe hit, he went into his maister's chambre
90   and wold not be knowen, for he did on his mayster's gowne and his rynge on his
fyngre, and lay in his bedde, and thus put hymself in parelle of deth for to respyte
hys mayster's lyf. But we see nowadayes many fooks that daigne not to use grose
metis of labourers and flee the cours clothyng and maners of a servaunt. Every
wyse man [who is] a servaunt that trewly servyth his maister is free and not bonde.
95   But a fool that is over proud is bonde. For the debylité and feblenes of corage that
is broken in conscience by pryde, envye, or by covetyse is right servytude. Yet they
ought not to doubte to laboure. For fere and drede of deth, no man ought to love
to moche his lyf, for hit is a foul thyng for a man to renne to the deth for the envye
of his lyf. And a wyse man and a stronge man ought not to fle for his lyf, but to
100   yssue. For there is no man that lyveth but he must nedes dye.
         And of this speketh Claudyan, and saith that al tho thynges that the ayer goth
about and envyronneth, and alle thyng that the erthe laboureth, al thynges that
ben conteyned within the see, al thynges that the flodes brynge forth, alle thynges
that ben norisshed, and al the bestes that ben under the heven shal deporte alle
105   from the world. And al shal goo at His commaundement, as wel kynges, prynces,
and al that the world envyronneth and goeth about. Alle shal goo this way. Than
he ought not to doubte for fere of deth. For as wel shal dye the ryche as the poure.
Deth maketh alle thynge lyke and putteth al to an ende.
         And therof made a noble versefyer two versis whiche folowe: "*Forma, genus,*
110   *mores, sapiencia, res, et honores / Morte ruant subita sola manent merita.*" Wherof the
Englissh is: "Beauté, lignage, maners, wysedom, thynges and honoures / Shal ben
deffetid by sodeyn deth; nothyng shal abyde but the meritis."
         And herof fynde we in *Vitas patrum* that ther was an erle, a riche and noble man,
that had a sone onely. And whan thys sone was of age to have knowleche of the
115   lawe, he herde in a sermone that deth spareth none. And as wel dyeth the yonge
as the olde. And that the deth ought specially to be doubted for thre causes. One
was that no man knoweth whan he comyth. And the second, ner in what state he
taketh a man. And the thyrd, he wote never whether he shal goo. Therfore eche
man shold dispyse and flee the world, and lyve wel, and holde hym toward God.
120   And whan this yonge man herde this thyng, he wente out of his contray and
fledde unto a wyldernesse unto an hermytage. And whan his fader had loste hym,
he made grete sorowe and dyd do enquere and seke hym so moche that atte last
he was founden in the hermytage. And thenne his fader cam theder to hym and

---

87–88 mervaillous faith, great loyalty. **90 knowen**, recognized; **did on**, put on. **91 parelle**,
peril; **respyte**, save (obsolete use of "respite"). **92 fooks**, folks (Caxton's spelling is
questionable here); **daigne**, deign. **92–93 grose metis**, coarse foods. **93 cours**, coarse. **94
bonde**, bound. **95 debylité and feblenes**, debility and feebleness. **96 covetyse**,
covetousness; **right**, truly. **97 doubte**, fear. **99 fle**, flee. **100 yssue**, issue (in the sense of
sallying forth). **101 ayer**, air. **102 envyronneth**, encompasses; **laboureth**, produces. **103
conteyned**, contained; **flodes**, floods. **104 deporte alle**, depart entirely. **105 as wel**, even.
109 versefyer, poet; **versis**, verses. **112 deffetid**, destroyed; **meritis**, good works. **118
whether**, where (whither). **119 holde hym**, incline himself. **120 contray**, country. **121
hermytage**, hermitage. **122 enquere and seke**, inquire and seek. **123 theder**, thither.

125 sayd, "Dere sone, come from thens! Thou shalt be after my dethe erle and chyef of my lignage. I shal be lost yf thou come not out from thens."

And he than, that wyst none otherwyse to eschewe the yre of his fader, bethought hym and sayd, "Dere fader, there is in your contré and lande a right evyll custume. Yf hit plese you to put that awey, I shal gladly come out of this place and goo with you."

130 The fader was glad and had grete joye, and demaunded of hym what hit was. And yf he wolde telle hym, he promysed hym to take hit awey, and hit shold be lefte and sette aparte. Than he sayd, "Dere fader, there dyen as wel the yonge folke as the olde in your contray. Do that awey, I praye you."

Whan his fader herde that, he sayd, "Dere sone, that may not be, ner no man 135 may put that awey but God onely."

Than answerd the sone to the fader, "Than wyl I serve Hym and dwelle here wyth Hym that may do that." And so abode the childe in the hermytage and lyved there in good werkis.

After this, hit apperteyneth to a labourer to entende to his labour and flee 140 ydelnes. And thou oughtest to knowe that Davyd preyseth moche in the Sawlter the trewe labourers and sayth, "Thou shalt ete the labour of thyn handes and thou art blessyd, and He shal doo to thee good."

And hit behoveth that the labourer endende to his labour on the werkedayes for to recuyel and gadre togydre the fruyt of hys laboure. And also, he ought to reste 145 on the holy day, bothe he and hys bestys. And a good labourer ought to norisshe and kepe his bestys. And this is signyfyed by the rodde that he hath, whiche is for to lede and dryve them to the pasture.

The first pastour that ever was was Abel, whyche was juste and trewe, and offrid to God the bestis unto hys sacrefise. And hym ought he to folowe in craft and 150 maners. But no man that useth the malyce of Caym maye ensue and folowe Abel.

And thus hit apperteyneth to the labourer to sette and graffe trees and vygnes, and also to plante and cutte them. And so dyd Noe, whyche was the first that planted the vygne after the deluge and flood. For as Josephus reherceth in the *Book of Naturel Thynges*, Noe was he that fonde first the vigne, and he fonde hym bytter 155 and wylde. And therfore he took four maners of blood, that is to wete the blood of a lyon, the blood of a lamb, the blood of a swyne, and the blood of an ape, and medlid them al togeder wyth the erthe. And than he cutte the vigne and put thys about the rotes therof, to the ende that the byttirnes shold be put awey, and that hit shold be swete. And whan he had dronken of the fruyt of thys vygne, hit was so 160 good and myghty that he becam so dronke that he despoyled hym in suche wyse that his pryvy membres myght be seen. And his yongest sone, Cham, mocqued

---

124 thens, thence. **125 lignage**, descendants. **126 wyst**, knew; **eschewe**, avoid. **126–27 bethought hym**, collected his thoughts. **137 abode**, stayed. **140 preyseth**, praises; **Sawlter**, Psalter. **143 behoveth**, is fitting; **endende**, attend (the text should probably read *entende* here). **144 recuyel**, collect (recueil); **gadre togydre**, gather together. **145 bestys**, animals or livestock. **146 kepe**, protect. **148 offrid**, offered. **151 graffe**, graft; **vygnes**, vines. **154 hym bytter**, it bitter. **155 to wete**, to wit. **157 medlid**, mixed. **158 about the rotes**, around the roots; **byttirnes**, bitterness. **160 despoyled hym**, stripped himself of clothes. **161 pryvy membres**, sex organs.

and skorned hym. And whan Noe was awaked and was sobre and fastyng, he assemblid his sones and shewed to them the nature of the vygne and of the wyn, and tolde to them the cause why that he had put the blood of the bestes about the rote of the vigne, and that they shold knowe wel that otherwhile, by the strengthe of the wyn, men be maad as hardy as the lyon and yrous. And otherwhile, they be made symple and shamefast as a lambe, and lecherous as a swyne, and curious and ful of play as an ape. For the ape is of suche nature that whan he seeth one doo a thyng, he enforceth hym to do the same, and so don many whan they ben dronke. They wyl meddle them with al offycers and maters that apperteyne nothyng to them. And whan they ben fastyng and sobre, they can scarcely accomplisshe theyr owne thynges.

And therfore, Valerian reherceth that of auncient and in olde tyme women dranke no wyn, for as moche as by dronkenshyp, they myght falle in ony filthe or vylony.

And as Ovyde saith, that the wynes otherwhyle apparaylle the corages in suche manere that they ben covenable to al synnes, whiche take awey the hertes to do wel. They make the poure, riche, as longe as the wyn is in his heed. And shortly, dronkenshyp is the begynnyng of alle evylles, and corrupteth the body, and destroyeth the sowle, and mynyssheth the goodes temporels.

And this suffiseth for the labourers.

The second chappytre of the thyrd tractate treteth of the forme and maner of the second pawne and of the maner of a smyth.   **Capitulo secundo.**

161–62 **mocqued and skorned**, mocked and scorned.   166 **yrous**, fierce; **otherwhile**, sometimes.   167 **symple and shamefast**, timid.   169 **enforceth**, strives.   170 **apperteyne**, pertain.   174 **dronkenshyp**, drunkenness.   175 **apparaylle the corages**, enhance the boldness.   177 **covenable**, open to; **hertes**, desire.   178 **shortly**, briefly.   180 **sowle**, soul; **mynyssheth**, diminishes; **goodes temporels**, worldly goods.

The second pawn that stondeth tofore the knyght on the right syde of the kyng hath the forme and fygure of a man as a smyth and that is reson. For hit apperteyneth to the knyghtes to have bridellys, sadellis, spores, and many other

185 thynges maad by the handes of smythes, and ought to holde an hamer in his right hond, and in his lift hande a squyer. And he ought to have on his gyrdel a trowel, for by this is signefyed alle maner of werkmen as goldsmythes, marchallis, smythes of alle forges, forgers and makers of money. And al maner of smythes ben signefyed by the martel or hamer. The carpenters ben signefyed by the dolabre or squyer.

190 And by the trowel we understonde al masons and kervers of stones, tylers, and al those that make howses, castels, and towres.

And unto al thyse crafty men hit aperteyneth that they be trewe, wyse, and stronge. And hit is nede that they have in hemself fayth and loyaulté. For unto the goldsmythes behoveth golde and sylver, and alle other metallys, yren and steel, to

195 other. And unto the carpentiers and masons ben put to theyr edefyces the bodyes and goodes of the peple. And also men put in the handes of the maroners body and goodes of the peple. And in the garde and sewerté of them, men put body and sowle in the parilles of the see. And therfore ought they to be trewe unto whom men commytte suche grete charge and so grete thynges upon her fayth and truste.

200 And therfore sayth the phylosopher: "He that leseth his fayth and beleve may lose no gretter ne more thynge." And fayth is a soverayn good and cometh of the good wylle of the herte and of his mynde, and for no necessyté wyl deceyve no man, and is not corrupt for no mede.

Valerius rehercith that Fabius had receyved of Hanybal certeyn prysoners that he

205 helde of the Romayns for a certeyn somme of money, whiche he promysed to paye to the sayd Hanybal. And whan he cam unto the senatours of Rome and desyred to have the money lente for hem, they answerd that they wold not paye nor lene. And than Fabius sent his sone to Rome and made hym to selle hys heritage and patrymonye, and sent the money that he receyvyd therof unto Hanybal, and had

210 lever and lovyd better to be poure in his contréy of heritage than of beleve and fayth. But in thyse dayes it were grete folye to have suche affyaunce in moche peple but yf they had ben prevyd afore. For oftentymes men truste in them by whom they ben deceyvyd at theyr nede.

And it is to wete that these crafty men and werkmen ben soveraynly proffytable

215 unto the world. And wythout artificers and werkmen, the world myght not be governed. And knowe thou verily that alle tho thynges that ben engendrid on the erthe and on the see ben maad and formed for to do proffyt unto the lignage of

---

183 **reson**, logical.   184 **bridellys**, bridles; **sadellis**, saddles; **spores**, spurs.   186 **squyer**, a carpenter's square, an implement for determining, measuring, or setting out right angles; **gyrdel**, belt.   187 **marchallis**, a person who tends horses.   188 **of alle forges**, of all types of manufacturing.   189 **martel**, hammer; **dolabre**, an adz or axe-like tool; **squyre**, square.   190 **kervers**, carvers; **tylers**, those who lay tiles.   193 **hit is nede**, it is necessary.   194 **behoveth**, belongs.   195 **edefyces**, buildings.   196 **maroners**, mariners.   197 **sewerté**, surety.   200 **leseth**, loses; **beleve**, belief.   202 **deceyve**, deceive.   203 **mede**, reward or recompense.   207 **lene**, loan.   208–09 **heritage and patrymonye**, inheritance and estate.   211 **affyaunce**, affiance or confidence.   212 **prevyd**, tested.   214 **soveraynly proffytable**, supremely profitable.   216 **verily**, truly.

man, for man was formed for to have generacion that the men myght helpe and
proffyt eche other. And here in ought we to folowe nature, for she sheweth to us that
220 we shold do comyn proffyt, one to another. And the first fondement of justyce is
that no man shold noye ne greve other, but that they ought do the comen proffyt.
For men say in reproche, "That I see of thyn, I hope hit shal be myn." But who is
he in thyse dayes that entendeth more to the comyn proffyt than to his owne?
Certeynly none. But alwey a man ought to have drede and fere of his owne hows
225 whan he seeth his neyghbour's hows afyre. And therfore ought men gladly helpe
the comyn prouffyt, for men otherwhyle sette not by a lytyl fyre and myght quenche
hit in the begynnyng that afterward maketh a grete blasygng fire.

And fortune hath of nothyng so grete plesure as for to torne and werke alwey.
And nature is so noble a thyng that whereas she is, she wyl susteyne and kepe. But
230 thys rewle of nature hath faylled longe tyme.

How wel that the decree saith that alle the thynges that been ayenst the lawe of
nature ought to be taken awey and put aparte. And he sayth tofore in the eighth
distinccion that the ryght lawe of nature defferenceth ofte tymes fro custom and
statutes establisshyd. For by lawe of nature al thyng ought to be comyn to every man.
235 And thys lawe was of olde tyme. And men wene yet specially that the Trojans kept
this lawe, and we rede that the multitude of the Trojans was one herte and one sowle.
And verayly we fynde that in tyme passid the philosophres dide the same.

And also, it is to be supposid that suche as have theyr goodes comune and not
propre is most acceptable to God. For ellis wold not thyse religyous men as monkes,
240 freres, chanons, observauntes, and al other avowe hem and kepe the wylful poverté
that they ben professyd to? For in trouth I have myself ben conversaunt in a
religious hows of Whyt Freres at Gaunt, whiche have al thyng in comyn among
them, and not one richer than another, insomoche that yf a man gaf to a frere
three pence or four pence to praye for hym in his masse, as sone as the masse is
245 don, he delyveryeth hit to his overest or procuratour, in whiche hows ben many
vertuous and devout freris. And yf that lyf were not the best and the most holyest,
Holy Chirche wold never suffre hit in religyon.

And accordyng therto, we rede in Plato, whiche sayth that the cyté is wel and
justly governed and ordeyned in the which no man may say by right, by custome, ne
250 by ordenaunce, "Thys is myn." But I say to thee certeynly that sythen this custome
came forth to say "This is myn, and this is thyn," no man thought to preferre the
comyn prouffyt so moche as his owne.

---

220 **fondement**, fundament or foundation. **221 noye ne greve**, annoy or aggravate. **223
entendeth**, inclines. **224 hows**, house. **225 afyre**, on fire. **226 sette not by**, do not heed.
227 blasygng, blazing. **229 whereas**, wherever. **233 distinccion**, class or category;
defferenceth, differs. **235 wene**, believe. **237 verayly**, truly; **tyme passid**, past times. **238
supposid**, known. **239 For ellis wold not**, Otherwise, why would. **240 freres**, friars;
chanons, canons; **observauntes**, Franciscans. **241 professyd**, promised or bound; **ben
conversaunt in**, had social dealings with. **242 Whyt Freres**, White Friars or Carmelites;
Gaunt, possibly Gaunt Street, a central street in Southwark by the river. **245 overest or
procuratour**, superior or steward. **248 accordyng therto**, on this topic. **249 ordeyned**,
ruled.

And al werkmen ought to be wyse and wel advysed so that they have none envye
ne none evyll suspecion one to another. For God wyl that our humayn nature be
255   covetous of two thynges, that is of religyon and of wysedom. But in this caas ben
somme often tymes deceyved. For they take often tymes religyon and leve wysedom,
and they take wysedom and refuse religion. And none may be veray and trewe
wythout other. For it apperteyneth not to a wyse man to do onythyng that he may
repente hym of hit, and he ought to do nothyng ayenst his wylle but to do al thyng
260   nobly, meurely, fermely, and honestly. And yf he have envye upon ony, hit is folye,
for he on whom he hath envye is more honest and of more havoyr than he whiche
is so envyous. For a man may have none envye on another, but bycause he is more
fortunat and hath more grace than hymself. For envye is a sorowe of corage that
cometh of this ordenaunce of the prouffyt of another man.
265   And knowe thou verily that he that is ful of bounté shal never have envye of
another. But the envyous man seeth and thynketh alwey that every man is more
noble and more fortunat that hymself, and saith alwey to hymself, "That man
wynneth more than I!" and "Myn neyghbours have more plenté of bestes!" and "Her
thynges multeplye more than myn!" And therfore thou oughtest knowe that envye
270   is the most grettest dedely synne that is, for she tormenteth hym that hath her within
hym wythout tormentyng or doyng ony harme to hym on whom he hath envye.
And an envyous man hath no vertu in hymself, for he corrumpeth hymself, for
as moche as he hateth alwey the welthe and vertues of other. And thus ought they
to kepe them that they take none evyl suspecion. For a man naturelly, whan his
275   affeccion hath suspecion in ony man that he weneth that he doth, hit semeth to
hym veryly that it is don.
And it is an evyl thyng for a man to have suspecion on hymself. For we rede
that Dyonyse of Zecyle, a tyraunt, was so suspecious that he had so grete fere and
drede. For as moche as he was hated of alle men, that he put his frendes out of
280   theyr offyces that they had and put other straungers in their places for to kepe his
body, and chese suche as were right cruel and felons. And for fere and doubte of the
barbours, he made his doughters to lerne shave and kembe. And whan they were
grete, he wold not they shold use ony yron to be occupyed by them but to brenne and
senge his heeris, and menaced them and durst not truste in them. And in like wyse
285   they had none affyaunce in hym. And also, he did do envyronne the place where
he lay wyth grete dyches and brode lyke a castel. And he entrid by a drawe bridge,
whiche closid after hym. And his knyghtes laye wythout wyth his gardes, whiche
watched and kept straytly thys forteresse. And whan Plato sawe thys said Dionyse,
Kyng of Zecille, thus envyroned and sette about wyth gardes and watchemen for
290   the cause of his suspecion, sayd to hym openly tofore alle men, "Kynge, why has

253 **advysed**, provided for. 254 **God wyl**, God ordains. 257 **veray**, true. 260 **meurely**, with consideration; **fermely**, steadfastly. 261 **more havoyr**, better deportment. 262 **but bycause**, unless. 263 **sorowe**, affliction. 264 **ordenaunce**, decree. 265 **bounté**, goodness. 268–69 **Her thynges**, Their things. 272 **corrumpeth**, corrupts. 275 **weneth**, supposes. 278 **Zecyle**, Sicily. 279 **For as moche as**, For it was because. 282 **kembe**, comb. 283 **grete**, grown or adult; **yron**, iron; **occupyed**, used. 283–84 **brenne and senge his heeris**, burn and singe his hair. 285 **affyaunce**, affiance or confidence; **envyronne**, surround. 286 **brode**, broad. 287 **laye wythout**, lay outside.

thou don so moche evyl and harme that thee behoveth to be kept wyth so moche peple? And therfore I say that it apperteyneth not to ony man that wylle truly behave hymself in his werkes to be suspecious."

295   And also, they ought to be stronge and seure in theyr werkys. And specially they that ben maysters and maronners on the see. For yf they be tumerous and ferdful, they shold make aferde them that ben in theyr shippis that knowe not the parilles. And so hit myght happen that by that drede and fere, al men shold leve theyr labour, and so they myght be perisshed and dispeyrid in theyr corages. For a shyppe is soon perisshed and lost by a litil tempest whan the governour faylleth to

300   governe his shyppe for drede and can geve no counceyl to other. Thenne it is no mervaylle though they be aferde that ben in his governaunce. And therfore ought to be in them strengthe, force, and corage, and [they] ought to considere the paryls that myght falle. And the governour specially ought not to doubte. And yf hyt happyn that ony parril falle, he ought to promyse to the other good hoop. And hit

305   aperteyneth wel that a man of good and hardy corage be sette in that office, in suche wyse that he have ferme and seure mynde ayenst the parylles that oft tymes happen in the see. And wyth this ought the maronners have good and ferme creaunce and beleve in God, and to be of good recomforte and of fayr langage unto them that he governeth in suche parellys.

310   And thys suffyseth to you as touchyng the labourers.

The thyrd chappytre of the thyrd book treteth of the office of notaries, advocates, skryvenars, and drapers or clothmakers.   **Capitulo tercio.**

291 **thee behoveth**, it is necessary for you. **294 seure**, sure. **295 maronners**, mariners; **tumerous**, timorous; **ferdful**, fearful. **296 parilles**, perils. **298 perisshed and dispeyrid**, damaged and deprived of. **301 mervaylle**, wonder. **304 hoop**, hope. **307 creaunce**, faith. *Title* **notaries**, personal secretaries or clerks; **advocates**, those who plead cases in a court of justice; **skryvenars**, professional scribes; **drapers**, makers of and/or dealers in cloth.

The third pawn, whiche is sette tofore the alphyn on the right syde, ought to be fygured as a clerke. And hit is reson that he shold so be. For as moche as emonge the comune peple of whom we speke in this boke they plete the differences, contencions, and causes, otherwhyle the whiche behoveth the alphyns to geve

315 sentence and juge as juges. And hit is reson that the alphyn or juge have his notarye, by whom the processe may be wreton.

And this pawn ought to be maad and figured in this manere. He must be made like a man that holdeth in his right hand a payr of sheris or forcettis, and in the lyfte hand a grete knyf, and on his gurdel a penner and an ynkhorn, and on his eere

320 a penne to wryte with. And that been the instrumentis and the offyces that been maad and putte in wrytyng autentique, and ought to have passyd tofore the juges as libelles, writes, condempnacions, and sentences. And that is signefied by the scripture and the penne. And on that other parte, hit aperteyneth to them to cutte clothe, shere, dyght, and dye. And that is signefyed by the forcettis or sheris. And

325 the other ought to shave berdis and kembe the heeris. And the other ben coupers, coryers, tawyers, skynners, bouchers, and kordwanners. And these ben signefyed by the knyf that he holdeth in hys hand. And somme of thyse forsayd crafty men been named drapers or clothmakers, for so moche as they werke with wolle. And the notaries, skynnars, coryours, and cordwaners werke by skynnes and hydes as

330 perchymyn, velume, peltrie, and cordewan. And the tayllours, cutters of cloth, wevars, fullars, dyers, and many other craftes ocupye and use wulle.

And al thyse crafty men, and many other that I have not named, ought to do theyr craft and mestier, where as they ben duly ordeyned curiously and trewly. Also, there ought to be amonge thyse crafty men amyable companye and trewe, honest

335 contenaunce, and trouthe in theyr wordes. And hit is to wete that the notaryes ben ryght prouffytable and ought to be good and trewe for the comyn. And they ought to kepe them from appropryyng to them self that thyng that aperteyneth to the comyn. And yf they be good to themself, they ben good to other. And yf they be evyl for themself, they ben evyl for other. And the processes that ben maad tofore the

311 alphyn, chess bishop or judge. **312 reson**, logical; **emonge**, among. **313 plete**, debate or plead in a legal sense. **314 otherwhyle**, sometimes. **316 processe**, proceedings. **317 figured**, depicted. **318 sheris or forcettis**, shears or scissors. **319 gurdel**, belt; **penner**, pen case; **ynkhorn**, an ink horn, a small vessel for holding ink; **eere**, ear. **321 autentique**, authoritative. **322 libelles**, formal pleas; **writes**, writs or written orders; **condempnacions**, judicial decisions; **sentences**, judgments. **323 scripture**, writings; **aperteyneth to**, is fitting to. **324 dyght**, clean or prepare. **325 coupers**, barrel makers. **326 coryers**, craftsmen who prepare leather; **tawyers**, those who "taw" or prepare white leather; **skynners**, skinners; **bouchers**, butchers; **kordwanners**, cordwainers or those who work in cordovan leather; also shoemakers. **329 skynnes and hydes**, skins and hides. **330 perchymyn**, parchment; **velume**, vellum, a finer type of parchment made from lambs or calves; **peltrie**, peltry or undressed skins; **cordewan**, leather. **331 fullars**, those who "full" or beat cloth in order to thicken it. **332 crafty men**, craftsmen. **333 mestier**, profession; **duly ordayned**, appointed or arranged; **curiously**, skillfully. **334 amyable companye**, friendly camaraderie. **336 prouffytable**, beneficial. **337 appropryyng**, appropriating; **aperteyneth**, belongs. **339 processes**, proceedings.

340 juges ought to ben wreton and passyd by them. And it is to wete that by their writyng
in the processis may come moche prouffit. And also, yf they wryte otherwyse than
they ought to doo, may ensewe moche harme and domage to the comyn. Therfore
ought they to take good hede that they chaunge not, ne corumpe in no wise, the
content of the sentence. For than ben they first forsworne and ben bounden to
345 make amendis to them that by their trecherye they have endomaged.
        And also ought they to rede, visite, and to knowe the statutes, ordenaunces, and
the lawes of the citees of the contré where they dwelle and enhabite. And they
ought to considere yf there be onythyng therin conteyned ayenst right and reson.
And yf they fynde onythynge contraire, they ought to admoneste and warne them
350 that governe that suche thynges may be chaunged in to better estate. For custume
establisshed ayenst good maners and ageynst the fayth ought not to be holden by
ryght.
        For as hit is sayd in the decree in the chappytre tofore all ordenaunce maad
ayenst right ought to be holden for nought. Alas, who is now that advocate or notarye
355 that hath charge to wryte and kepe sentence that putteth his entente to kepe more
the comyn prouffyt or as moche as his owen! But alle drede of God is put aback, and
they deceyve the symple men and drawen them to the courtes disordenatly, and
constrayne them to swere and make othes not covenable. And in assemblyng the
peple thus togyder, they make mo traysons in the cytees thenne they make good
360 alyaunces. And otherwhile they deceyve theyr soverayns, whan they may do hit
covertly. For there is nothyng at this day that so moche greveth Rome and Italie
as doth the College of Notaryes and Advocates Publique, for they ben not of one
accorde.
        Alas! And in Engelond, what hurte doon the advocates, men of lawe, and
365 attorneyes of court to the comyn peple of the royame, as wel in the spirituel lawe
as in the temporalle! How torne they the lawe and statutes at their plesure! How ete
they the peple! How enpovere they the comynté! I suppose that in alle Cristendom
are not so many pletars, attorneys, and men of the lawe as been in England onely.
For yf they were nombrid, alle that longe to the courtes of the chaunserye, kynge's
370 benche, comyn place, cheker, ressayt, and helle, and the bagge berars of the same,
hit shold amounte to a grete multitude. And how al thyse lyve and of whom, yf hit
shold be uttrid and tolde, hit shold not be belevyd, for they entende to theyr
synguler wele and prouffyt and not to the comyn.

342 **ensewe**, ensue; **domage**, damage. 343 **corumpe**, corrupt. 344 **forsworne**, perjured. 345 **amendis**, amends; **endomaged**, harmed. 346 **rede**, read; **visite**, examine. 349 **contraire**, contrary (to right and reason); **admoneste**, admonish. 356 **put aback**, receded. 357 **deceyve**, deceive; **disordenatly**, unnecessarily. 358 **covenable**, appropriate. 359 **mo traysons**, more treasons. 360 **alyaunces**, alliances or unities. 362–63 **of one accorde**, of unified purpose. 365 **as wel**, as much. 366 **ete**, despoil. 367 **enpovere**, impoverish; **comynté**, community. 368 **pletars**, pleaders or advocates. 369 **longe**, belong; **chaunserye**, chauncery or high court. 369–70 **kynge's benche**, supreme court of common law. 370 **comyn place**, lower courts; **cheker**, exchequer or treasury; **ressayt**, revenue office; **helle**, hall of justice; **bagge berars**, wallet carriers. 372 **entende to**, attend to. 373 **synguler wele**, personal good.

375 How wel they ought to be of good wyl togyder, and admoneste and warne the cytees, eche in his right in suche wyse that they myght have pees and love, one wyth another. And Tullyus saith that frendshyp and good wylle that one ought to have ayenst another for the wele of hym that he loveth, with the semblable wylle of hym, ought to be put forth tofore al other thynges. And ther is nothyng so resemblyng and lyke to the bees that maken hony ne so covenable in prosperité and in

380 adversité, as is love. For by love, gladly the bees holden them togyder, and yf ony trespace to that other, anone they renne upon the malefactour for to punysshe hym.

And veray trewe love faylleth never for wele ne for evyl. And the most swete and the most comfortyng thyng is for to have a frend to whom a man may say his secret,

385 as wel as to hymself. But verayly, amytye and frendshyp is somtyme founded upon somme thyng delectable. And this amytie cometh of yongthe, in the which dwellith a disordynate hete. And otherwhile, amytie is founded upon honesté. And this amytie is vertuous, of the whiche Tullyus saith that there is an amytie vertuous by the whiche a man ought to do to his frende al that he requyreth by reason. For for

390 to do to hym a thyng dishonest, it is ayenst the nature of veray frendshyp and amytye. And thus for frendshyp ne for favour a man ought not to doo onythyng unresonable ayenst the comyn prouffyt, ner agaynst his fayth, ne ageynst his othe. For yf alle tho thynges that the frendes desyre and requyre were accomplisshed and doon, hyt shold seme that they shold be dyshoneste conivracions, and they

395 myght otherwhyle more greve and hurte than proffyte and ayde.

And herof sayth Seneque that amytye is of suche wylle as the frende wylle, and to refuse that ought to be refused by reason. And yet he saith more, that a man ought to alowe and preise his frend tofore the peple, and to correcte and to chastyse hym pryvely, for the lawe of amytie is suche. For a man ought not to demaunde ner do

400 to be doon to hys frende no vylayns thyng that ought to be kept secrete.

And Valerian sayth that it is a foule thynge and an evyl excusasion yf a man confesse that he hath doon ony evyl for his frende ayenst right and reason. And sayth that there was a good man named Taffyle, whiche herde one his frende requyre of hym a thynge dishoneste, whiche he denyed and wold not do. And than

405 his frende said to hym in grete despyte, "What nede have I of thy frendship and amytee whan thou wilt not do that thyng that I requyre of thee?"

And Taffile answerd to hym, "What nede have I of the frendship and of the amyte of thee, yf I shold do for thee thyng dishonest?"

And thus love is founded otherwhile upon good prouffytable, and this love

410 endureth as longe as he seeth his prouffyt. And herof men say a comyn proverbe in Englond, that love lasteth as longe as the money endurith, and whan the money failleth than there is no love.

---

374 **admoneste**, admonish. 377 **semblable**, same. 379 **convenable**, consistent. 381 **renne**, run. 383 **faylleth**, fails. 385 **verayly**, truly; **amytye**, amity. 386 **delectable**, pleasant; **yongthe**, youth. 387 **disordynate hete**, excessive passion. 389 **For for**, Because. 390 **veray**, true. 393 **alle tho thynges**, all those things. 394 **conivracions**, contrivances. 396 **wylle₂**, desires. 398 **alowe and preise**, commend and praise. 399–400 **ner do to be doon**, nor cause to be done. 401 **excusasion**, defense. 403 **one his frende**, one of his friends. 409 **prouffytable**, profit.

And Varro rehercith in his sommes that the riche men ben al lovyd by this love, for their frendes ben like as the huske whiche is about the grayn. And no man may 415 prove his frende so wel as in adversité or whan he is poure, for the veray trewe frende fayleth at no nede.

And Seneque saith that somme folowe the emperour for riches, and so don the flies the hony for the swetenes, and the wolf the carayn. And thyse companye folowe the praye and not the man.

420 And Tullyus sayth that Tarquyn the Proud had a nevewe of his suster, whiche was named Brutus, and this nevewe had banysshed Tarquin out of Rome and had sent hym in exyle. And than sayd he fyrst that he parceyved and knewe his frendes whyche were trewe and untrewe, and that he never perceyved afore tyme whan he was puyssaunt for to do theyr wylle, and sayd wel that the love that they had to hym 425 endured not but as longe as hit was to them prouffytable. And therfore ought al the riche men of the world take hede, be they kynges, prynces, or duckes, to what people they doo prouffyt and how they may and ought be lovyd of theyr peple.

For Cathon sayth in his book, "See to whom thou gevest. And thys love whiche is founded upon theyr prouffit, whiche fayleth and endureth not, may better be 430 callid and sayd 'marchaundyse' than love. For yf we repute this love to our prouffyt onely, and nothyng to the prouffyt of hym that we love, it is more marchaundyse than love, for he byeth our love for the prouffyt that he doth to us."

And therfore sayth the versefier thyse two versis: "*Tempore felici multi numerantur amici / Cum fortuna perit nullus amicus erit,*" whiche is to say in Englissh that "as longe 435 as a man is ewrous and fortunat, he hath many frendes, but whan fortune torneth and perissheth, there abydeth not to hym one frende." And of thys love ben loved the medowes, feldes, trees, and the bestys for the prouffyt that men take of them. But the love of the men ought to be charité, veray gracious and pure by good fayth. And the veray trewe frendes ben knowen in pure adversité.

440 And Piers Alphons sayth in his *Book of Moralité* that there was a phylosophre in Arabye that had an onely sone, of whom he demaunded what frendes he had goten hym in his lyf. And he answerd that he had many. And his fader sayd to hym, "I am an olde man, and yet coude I never fynde but one frende in al my lyf. And I trowe verely that it is no lytyl thyng for to have a frende, and hit is wel gretter and more 445 a man to have many. And hit apperteyneth and behoveth a man to assaye and preve his frende or he have nede."

And thenne commaunded the philosopher his sone that he shold goo and slee a swyne and put hit in a sacke, and fayne that it were a man dede that he had slayn, and bere hit to his frendes for to burye hit secretly. And whan the sone had don as 450 his fader commaunded hym, and had requyred his frendes one after another as

---

413 sommes, summary treatise. **418 hony,** honey; **carayn,** carrion. **419 praye,** prey. **420 nevewe,** nephew. **422 parceyvd,** recognized. **423 never perceyvyd afore tyme,** never before had perceived a time. **424 puyssaunt,** empowered. **426 duckes,** dukes. **428 gevest,** give. **429 endureth not,** does not endure. **430 repute,** esteem. **432 byeth,** buys. **435 ewrous,** prosperous or profitable; **torneth,** turns. **436 medowes,** meadows; **feldes,** fields; **bestys,** beasts. **441 Arabye,** Arabia. **443–44 trowe verely,** truly believe. **445 apperteyneth and behoveth,** is fitting and behooves. **445–46 assaye and preve,** test and try. **446 or,** before. **448 fayne,** pretend. **450 requyred,** requested.

afore is sayd, they denyed hym and answerd to hym that he was a vylayne to requyre and desire of them thyng that was so perilous. And than he came agayn to his fader and sayd to hym how he had requyred al his frendes, and that he had not founden one that wold helpe hym in his nede.

455   And than his fader sayd to hym that he shold goo and requyre his frende, whyche had but one, and requyre hym that he shold helpe hym in his nede. And whan he had requyred hym, anone he put out al his mayné out of hys hows. And whan they were out of the waye or aslepe, he dyd do make secretly a pytte in the grounde. And whan hit was redy and wold have buryed the body, he founde hit an
460   hogge or a swyne, and not a man. And thus this sone prevyd this man to be a veray, trewe frende of his fader, and prevyd that his frendes were fals frendes of fortune.

       And yet reherceth the sayd Piers Alphons that there were two marchauntes, one of Bandach and that other of Egypt, whiche were so joyned togeder by so grete frendshyp that he of Bandache cam on a tyme for to se hys frende in Egypt, of
465   whom he was receyvyd right honuurably. And this marchaunt of Egypt had in his hows a fayre yonge mayden whom he shold have had in mariage to hymself, of the whiche mayde thys marchaunt of Bandach was esprised with her love so ardantly that he was right seek, and that men supposid hym to dye. And than the other dyd do come the phisisiens, whiche sayd that in hym was no sekenes sauf passyon of
470   love. Thenne he axyd of the seek man yf there were ony woman in hys hows that he loved and maad al the women of his hows to come tofore hym. And than he chees her that shold have ben that other's wyf and sayd that he was seek for her. Than his frende sayd to hym, "Frende, comforte yourself. For trewly I gyve her to you to wyf with alle the dowaire that is gyven to me wyth her." And had lever to
475   suffre to be wythout wyf than to lese the body of his frende. And than he of Bandach wedded the mayde and went with his wyf and with his richesse ageyn in to his contré.

       And after this, anone after, hit happend that the marchaunt of Egypt became so poure by evyl fortune that he was constreyned to seche and begge his breed by the
480   contray, in so moche that he cam to Bandach. And whan he entrid in to the toun, hit was derk nyght that he coude not fynde the hows of his frende but went and lay thys nyght in an olde temple. And on the morne, whan he shold yssue out of the temple, the offycers of the toun arestyd hym and sayd that he was an homycide and had slayn a man whiche lay there dede. And anone he confessid hyt wyth a good
485   wylle, and had lever to ben hangyd than to dye in that myserable and pour lyf that he suffryd. And thus whan he was brought to jugement, and sentence shold have ben gyven ayenst hym as an homycide, his frend of Bandach cam and sawe hym, and anone knewe that thys was his good frende of Egypte. And forthwyth stepte in and sayd that he hymself was culpable of the deth of this man and not that other,
490   and enforcid hym in alle maners for to delyver and excuse that other.

457 **mayné**, people. 460 **prevyd**, proved; **veray**, faithful. 463 **Bandach**, Babylon. 467 **esprised**, enamoured (eprisé). 468–69 **dyd do come**, summoned; **sekenes**, sickness; **sauf**, except. 472 **chees**, chose. 474 **to wyf**, to marry; **dowaire**, dowry; **lever**, rather. 475 **lese**, lose. 479 **seche**, seek; **breed**, bread. 483 **arestyd**, arrested; **homycide**, murderer. 490 **enforcid**, encouraged (the judge).

And than whan that he that had doon the feet and had slayne the man sawe this thyng, he considerid in hymself that these two men were innocent of thys feet. And doubtyng the dyvyne jugement, he came tofore the juge and confessyd al the feet by ordre. And whan the juge sawe and herde al thys mater, and also the causes, he

495 considered the ferme and trewe love that was betwene the two frendes, and understood the cause why that one wold save that other, and the trouth of the fayte of the homycide. And than he pardoned al the feet hooly and entierly. And after, the marchaunt of Bandach brought hym of Egipt wyth hym in to his hows, and gaf to hym his sister in mariage, and departed to hym half his goodes. And so bothe of

500 hem were riche, and thus were they bothe veray faythful and trewe frendes.

Furthermore, notaries, men of lawe, and crafty men shold and ought to love eche other, and also ought to be contynent, chaste, and honeste. For by theyr craftes they ought so to be by necessyté. For they converse and accompanye them ofte tyme wyth women. And therfore hit apperteyneth to them to be chaste and

505 honeste. And that they meve not the women, nor entyse them to lawghe and jape by ony dysordynate ensignes or tokenes.

Titus Livius reherceth that the philosopher Democreon dyd doo put out his eyen for as moche as he myght not beholde the women wythoute flesshly desyre. And how wel it is sayd before that he dyd hit for other certeyn cause. Yet was this

510 one of the pryncipal causes.

And Valerian tellyth that there was a yong man of Rome of right excellent beaulté. And how wel that he was right chaste, for as moche as his beaulté mevyd many women to desire hym, insomoche that he understood that the parentes and frendes of them had suspecion in hym, he dyd his vysage to be kutte wyth a knyf

515 and lancettis, endlong and everthwart for to deforme his vysage, and had lever have a fowle vysage and disformed than the beaulté of his vysage shold meve other to synne.

And also we rede that there was a nonne, a virgyne, dyd do put out bothe her eyen, for as moche as the beaulté of her eyen mevyd a kyng to love her, whyche eyen

520 she sente to the kyng in a present.

And also we rede that Plato, the right ryche phylosopher, lefte his owne lande and contré, and chase his mansion and dwellyng in Achadomye, a toun whiche was not onely destroyed but also was ful of pestelence, so that by the cure and charge and customaunce of sorowe that he there suffrid myght eschewe the hetes and

525 occasions of lecherye. And many of hys dysciples dyd in lyke wyse.

Helemand reherceth that Demostenes the philosopher laye ones by a noble woman for his dysporte, and playeng wyth her, he demaunded of her what he shold geve to have to doo wyth her. And she answerd to hym, "A thousand pens."

---

491 **he that had doon the feet**, he who had done the deed (i.e., the real murderer). 493 **doubtyng**, fearing; **dyvyne**, divine. 494 **by ordre**, in sequence. 496 **fayte**, act. 497 **And after**, And after this. 502 **contynent**, self-restrained. 503 **converse and accompanye them**, talk and have dealings with. 505 **meve**, excite; **entyse**, entice; **jape**, seduce. 512 **beaulté**, beauty; **mevyd**, moved or excited. 515 **lancettis**, lancets (surgical instruments usually with two edges and a point); **endlong and everthwart**, from end to end and across. 516 **fowle**, foul. 522 **chase**, chose. 523 **pestelence**, disease. 524 **customaunce**, customary practice; **hetes**, heat. 526 **ones**, once. 527 **dysporte**, amusement or diversion.

530

And he sayd ageyn to her, "I shold repente me to bye hit so dere." And whan he advysed hym that, he was so sore chauffyd to speke to her for to accomplisshe his flesshly desyre, he despoyled hym al nakyd and wente and put hym in the myddes of the snowe.

And Ovyde rehercith that thys thynge is the leste that maye helpe and most greve the lovers.

535

And therfore Saynt Augustyn rehercith in his book, *De civitate dei*, that there was a right noble Romayn named Marculian that wan and took the noble cité of Siracuse. And tofore, er he dyd doo assayle hit or befight hit, and or he had do beshedde ony blood, he wepte and shedde many teeris tofore the cité. And that was for the cause that he doubted that his peple shold defoule and corumpe to moche

540

dishonestly the chastyté of the toun, and ordeyned upon payn of deth that no man shold be so hardy to take and defoyle ony woman by force what that ever she were.

After thys, the crafty men ought to understonde for to be trewe and to have trouth in her mouthes, and that theyr dedes folowe theyr wordes. For he that sayth one thyng and doth another, he condempneth hymself by his word. Also, they

545

ought to see wel to that they be of one accorde in good, by entente, by word, and by dede, so that they be not discordaunt in no caas, but that every man have pure verité and trouth in hymself. For God Hymself is pure verité. And men say comynly that trouth seketh none hernes, ne corners. And trouth is a vertu by the whiche alle drede and fraude is put awey. Men saye trewly whan they saye that they knowe, and

550

they that knowe not trouthe ought to knowe hyt and alwey use trouthe.

For Saynt Austyn sayth that they that wene to knowe trouth and lyveth evyl and vyciously, it is folye yf he knoweth hit not. And also, he sayth in another place that it is better to suffre payn for trouth than for to have a benefete by falsnes or by flaterye. And man that is callyd a beste resonable, and doth not his werkys after

555

reson and trouthe, is more bestyal than ony beste brute. And knowe ye that for to come to the trouthe hit cometh of a resonable forsight in his mynde. And lyeng cometh of an oultrageous and contrarie thought in hys mynde. For he that lyeth wittyngly knoweth wel that hit is ageynst the trouthe that he thynketh.

And herof speketh Saynt Bernard and sayth that the mouth that lyeth destroyeth

560

the sowle.

And yet sayth Saynt Austyn in another place, "For to say one thynge and do the contrarye maketh doctryne suspecious."

And knowe ye verily that for to lye is a right perilous thynge to body and sowle. For the lye that the auncient enemye maad Eve and Adam to beleve hym, made hem

565

for to be dampned with alle their lignage to the deth pardurable, and made hem to be cast out of paradyse terrestre. For he maad them to beleve that God had not

---

529 repente me, regret; **bye**, buy; **dere**, expensively. **530 advysed hym**, considered to himself; **sore chauffyd**, sorely inflamed. **534 greve**, vex. **536 wan**, won. **539 doubted**, feared; **corumpe**, spoil. **541 defoyle**, violate or rape. **544 condempneth**, condemns; **545 of one accorde**, of one will. **548 hernes**, nooks or corners. **551 wene**, think. **554 beste**, beast; **werkys**, duties. **555 bestyal**, bestial. **556 lyeng**, lying. **557 oultrageous**, outrageous (in the sense of evil). **558 wittyngly**, knowingly. **565 lignage**, descendants; **pardurable**, perdurable or existing for all time. **566 paradyse terrestre**, the earthly paradise (i.e., Eden).

forboden them the fruyt but onely bycause they shold not knowe that her Mayster
knewe. But how wel that the devyl sayd thyse wordes yet had he double entente to
hem bothe. For they knewe anone as they had tastyd of the fruyt that they were
570   dampned to the deth pardurable. And God knewe hit wel tofore. But they supposid
wel to have knowen many other thynges and to be lyke unto his knowleche and
science.

And therfore saith Saynt Poule in a pistyl: "Hit ne apperteyneth to saver or
knowe more than behoveth to saver or knowe, but to saver or knowe by mesure or
575   sobrenes."

And Valerian rehercith that there was a good woman of Siracusane that wold
not lye unto the Kyng of Secille, whyche was named Dyonyse. And this kyng was
so ful of tyrannye and so cruel that alle the world desired his deth and cursid hym,
sauf this woman onely, whiche was so olde that she had seen three or four kynges
580   reignyng in the contré. And every mornyng, as sone as she was rysen, she prayed
to God that he wold gyve unto the tyraunt good lyf and longe and that she myght
never see his deth. And whan the Kyng Dyonyse knewe this, he sent for her and
mervaylled moche herof, for he knewe wel that he was sore behated, and demaunded
her what cause mevyd hyr to praye for hym. And she answerd and sayd to hym,
585   "Sir, whan I was a mayde, we had a right evyl tyraunt to our kyng, of whom we
coveyted sore the deth. And whan he was dede, there came after hym a werse, of
whom we coveyted also the deth. And whan we were delyveryd of hym, thou camest
to be our lord, which art worst of al other. And now I doubte yf we have one after
thee he shal be worse than thou art. And therfore I shal praye for thee."
590   And whan Dyonyse understood that she was so hardy in sayeng the trouth, he
durst not do torment her for shame by cause she was so olde.

---

567 **but onely bycause**, only to the end that. **567–68 that her Mayster knewe**, that which
their Master knew. **568 double entente**, deceitful purpose. **569 anone**, immediately. **573
pistyl**, epistle; **saver**, learn. **575 sobrenes**, moderation. **576 Siracusane**, Syracuse. **577
Secille**, Sicily. **579 sauf**, except. **585 to our kyng**, as our king. **586 coveyted**, desired;
werse, worse (king). **588 doubte**, fear.

The fourth chappitre of the third book tretith of the maner of the fourth pawn and of the marchauntis or chaungers.   **Capitulo quarto.**

595

600

The fourth pawn is sette tofore the kyng and is formed in the forme of a man holdyng in his right hand a balaunce and the weyght in the lyft hand, and tofore hym a table, and at his gurdel a purse ful of money redy for to geve to them that requyred hit. And by thys peple ben signefyed the marchauntes of cloth, lynnen, and wollen, and of al other marchaundyses. And by the table that is tofore hym is signefyed the chaungers and they that lene money. And they that bye and selle by the weyght ben signefyed by the balaunces and weyghtes. And the customers, tollars, and receyvours of rentes and of money ben signefyed by the purse. And knowe ye that alle they that ben signefied by this peple ought to flee avarice and covetyse, and eschewe brekyng of the dayes of payment, and ought to holde and kepe theyr promyses, and ought also to rendre and restore that that is gyven to them to kepe.

605

And therfore hit is reson that this peple be set tofore the kyng, for as moche as they signefye the receyvours of the tresours ryal that ought alwey to be redy tofore the kyng, and to answer for hym to the knyghtes and to other persones for theyr wages and souldyes.

610

And therfore have I said that they ought to flee avarice, for avarice is as moche to say as an adourer or as worshypar of fals ymages. And herof sayth Tullyus that avarice is a covetise to gete that thyng that is above necessité. And it is a love disordynate to have onythyng, and it is one of the werst thynges that is, and specially to prynces and to them that governe the thynges of the comuneté. And this vyce causeth a man to do evyll, and thys doyng evyl is whan hit reygneth in olde men.

Title **chaungers**, money changers.   **593 balaunce**, set of scales; **weyght**, weight.   **594 gurdel**, belt.   **595 lynnen**, linen.   **596 wollen**, wool.   **597 lene**, loan.   **598 customers**, custom or dues takers; **tollars**, toll takers.   **599 receyvours of rentes**, tax collectors.   **600 covetyse**, covetousness.   **601 eschewe brekyng of the dayes of payment**, avoid missing payment deadlines.   **606 souldyes**, Italian coins.   **610 disordynate**, immoderate.   **612 hit reygneth in olde men** (avarice was usually associated with age).

And herof sayth Seneque that all worldly thynges ben mortefyed and appetissed in olde men, reservyd avarice onely, whyche alwey abydeth wyth hym and dyeth
615   with hym. But I understonde not wel the cause wherof this cometh ne wherfore hit may be. And hit is a fowle thyng and contrarye to reson that whan a man is at the ende of his journey for to lengthe his viage and to ordeyne more vitayl than hym behoveth. And this may wel be likned to the avaricious wolf, for the wolf doth never good tyl he be dede.

620   And thus it is sayd in the proverbys of the wyse men that the avaricious man doth no good tyl that he be deed, and he desireth nothynge but to lyve long in thys synne. For the covetous man certeynly is not good for onythyng, for he is evyl to hymself and to the riche and to the poure, and fyndeth cause to gaynsay theyr desire.

625   And herof rehercith Seneque, and sayth that Antigonus was a covetous prynce. And whan Tynque, whiche was his frende, requyred of hym a besaunt, he answerd to hym that he demaunded more than hyt apperteyned to hym. And than Tynque, constrayned by grete necessité, axid and requyred of hym a peny. And he answerd to hym that it was no yefte covenable for a kyng. And so he was alwey redy to fynde
630   a cause nought to geve, for he myght have gyven to hym a besaunt as a kynge to his frende and the peny as to a poure man. And ther is nothyng so litil but that the humanyté of a kyng may geve hyt. Avarice ful of covetise is a maner of al vices of luxurye.

And Josephus rehercith in the *Book of Auncient Histories* that ther was in Rome
635   a right noble lady named Paulyne, and was of the most noble of Rome, right honest for the noblesse of chastité, whiche was maryed in the tyme that the wommen glorefyed them in theyr chastyté unto a yonge man, fayr, noble, and riche above al other, and was lyke and semblable to his wyf in al caasis. And thys Pawlyne was belovyd of a knyght namyd Enymerancian and was so ardantly esprised in her love
640   that he sent to her many right riche yeftes and made to her many grete promyses. But he myght never torne the herte of her, which was on her syde also colde and harde as marbyll. But she had lever to refuse his yeftes and hys promyses than to entende to covetyse and to lose her chastyté.

And we rede also in the *Histories of Rome* that there was a noble lady of Rome
645   whiche lyved a solytarye lyf and was chaste and honeste, and had gadrid togeder a grete somme of golde, and had hyd hit in the erthe in a pytte wythin her hows. And whan she was deed, the bisshop dyd do burye her in the chirche wel and honestly. And anone after, this gold was founden and born to the bysshop. And the bisshop had to caste hit in to the pytte where she was buryed. And thre dayes men
650   herd her crye and make grete noyse, and say that she brenned in grete payn, and they herd her ofte tymes thus tormentid in the chirche. The neyghbours went unto the bysshop and tolde hym therof, and the bisshop gaf hem leve to open the

---

613 **mortefyed and appetissed**, deadened and lessened. 614 **reservyd**, except; **onely**, alone. 617 **lengthe his viage**, lengthen his trip (i.e., by sinning); **vitayl**, provisions. 619 **tyl**, until. 626 **besaunt**, a gold coin. 627 **apperteyned**, was appropriate. 628 **axid**, asked. 629 **convenable**, suitable. 638 **semblable to**, similar to; **caasis**, instances. 639 **esprised in her love**, taken with love for her. 642 **lever**, rather. 643 **entende to**, incline towards. 650 **brenned**, burned. 652 **hem**, them.

sepulcre. And whan they had openyd hit, they fonde al the golde molten with fire
ful of sulphre, and was poured and put in her mouth. And they herd one say,
655 "Thou desiredest this gold by covetyse! Take hyt and drynke hyt!" And thenne they
took the body out of the tombe. And hit was cast out in a prevy place.

Seneque rehercith in the *Book of the Cryes of Women* that avaryce is foundement
of alle vyces.

And Valerian rehercith that avarice is a ferdful garde or kepar of richessis, for
660 he that hath on hym or in his kepyng moche money or other richessis is alwey
aferd to lose hit or to be robbid or to be slayn therfore. And he is not ewrous ner
happy that by covetise getith hit.

And al the evyls of this vice of avarice had a man of Rome named Septenulle,
for he was a frend of one named Tarchus. And this Septenulle brent so sore and
665 so cruelly in this synne of covetise that he had no shame to smyte of the hede of hys
frend by trayson, for as moche as one Framosian had promysed to hym as moche
weyght of pure gold as the heed wayed. And he bare the said heed upon a staf
thrugh the cité of Rome, and he voyded the brayn out therof and filled hyt ful of
leed for to weye the hevyar. This was a right horrible and cruel avarice.

670 Ptolomé, Kyng of Egipciens, poursewed avarice in another manere. For whan
Anthonie, Emperour of Rome, sawe that he was right riche of gold and silver, he
had hym in grete hate and tormentid hym right cruelly. And whan he shold perissh
bycause of his richessis, he toke al his havoir and put hyt in a shippe, and went
withalle into the hye see to the ende for to drowne and perissh there the shippe
675 and his richesses bycause Anthonye, his enemye, shold not have hit. And whan he
was there, he durst not perisshe hit, ner myght not fynde in hys herte to departe
from hit, but cam and brought hit agayn into his hows, where he receyvyd the
rewarde of deth therfore. And without doubte he was not lord of the richesse, but
the richesse was lady over hym.

680 And therfore hit is said in proverbe that a man ought to seignorie over the
riches, and not for to serve hit. And yf thou canst dewly use thy richesse, than she
is thy chamberer. And yf thou cannot departe from hit and use hit honestly at thy
plesure, knowe verily that she is thy lady. For the riches never satisfyeth the covetous,
but the more he hath, the more he desireth.

685 And Saluste saith that avarice destroubleth fayth, poesté, honesté, and al thise
other good vertues, and taketh for thyse vertues pryde, cruelté, and to forgete God,
and sayth that al thynges be vendable.

And after this, they ought to be ware that they lene not to moche, ner make so
grete creaunces by whiche they may falle in poverté. For Saynt Ambrose saith upon
690 Thoby: "Poverté hath no lawe, for to owe, hit is a shame, and to owe and not paye
is a more shame. Yf thou be poure, beware how thou borowest and thynke how

---

656 prevy, hidden. **657 foundement**, foundation. **659 ferdful**, fearful; **kepar**, keeper. **661
ewrous**, lucky or prosperous. **665 smyte of**, cut off. **667 wayed**, weighed; **bare**, carried.
668 voyded, emptied. **669 leed**, lead. **673 havoir**, possessions. **674 hye see**, high sea. **675
bycause**, in order that. **676 perisshe it**, destroy it. **680 seignorie**, rule. **681 dewly**, duly.
682 chamberer, handmaid. **685 destroubleth**, disturbed; **poesté**, strength. **687 vendable**,
capable of being sold. **688 lene**, borrow. **689 creaunces**, buying things on credit.

thou mayst paye and rendre agayn. Yf thou be riche, thou hast no nede to borowe and axe."

695   And it is said in the proverbis that hit is fraude to take that thou wylt not ner mayst [not] rendre and paye agayn.

And also, hit is sayd in reproche: "Whan I lene, I am thy frende, and whan I axe, I am thyn enemye," as who saith God at the lenyng and the devyll atte rendryng. And Seneke saith in his auctorités that they that gladly borowe ought gladly to paye, and ought to surmounte in corage to love hem the better bycause they lene
700   hem and ayde hem in her nede. For benefetes and good tornes don to a man ought to gyve hym thankynges therfore, and moche more ought a man to repaye that is lent hym in his nede. But now in these dayes many men by lenyng of their money have made of their frendes enemyes.

And herof speketh Domas the philosopher and saith that, "My frende borowed
705   money of me, and I have lost my frende and my money."

There was a marchaunt of Gene and also a chaungeour whos name was Albert Ganor. And this Albert was a man of grete trouth and loyalté. For on a tyme there was a man cam to hym and sayd and affermyd that he had delyveryd into his banke five honderd floryns of gold to kepe, whiche was not trouth, for he lyed, whiche
710   five honderd floryns the sayd Albert knewe not of, ner coude fynde in al his bookes ony suche money to hym due. And this lyar coude brynge no wytnes, but began to braye, crye, and deffame the said Albert. And than this Albert callyd to hym this marchaunt and sayd, "Dere frende, take here five honderd florens whiche thou affermest and sayest that thou hast delyverd to me." And forthwyth tolde hem and
715   toke hem to hym. And lo this good man had lever to lose his good than his good name and renome.

And this other marchaunt toke these florens that he had wrongfully receyvyd and enployed them in dyverse marchaundyse, in so moche that he gate and encresid and wan with them fifteen thousand florens. And whan he sawe that he approched
720   toward his deth, and that he had no children, he establisshed Albert his heyr in al thynges, and sayd that with the five honderd florens that he had receyvyd of Albert falsely, he had goten alle that he had in the world. And thus by devyne purveaunce, he that had be a theef fraudelent was maad afterward a trewe procurour and atorney of the sayd Albert.

725   But now in thyse dayes there be marchauntis that do marchaundise with other menny's money whiche is taken to hem to kepe. And whan they ben requyred to repaye hyt, they have no shame to denye hit apperty.

Wherof hit happend that ther was a marchaunt which had a good and a grete name and renome of kepyng wel suche thynges as was delyveryd to hym to kepe.
730   But whan he sawe place and tyme, he reteyned hit lyke a theef. So hit befel that a marchaunt of without forth herd the good reporte and fame of this man, cam to

---

693 axe, ask. **694 wylt**, will; **ner**, nor. **696 reproche**, reproach; **lene**, lend. **699 surmounte**, surmount. **700 tornes**, turns. **702 lenyng**, loaning. **706 Gene**, Genoa; **chaungeour**, money changer. **708 affermyd**, confirmed. **709 floryns**, gold coins. **714 tolde hem**, counted them out. **716 renome**, reputation. **718 gate**, gained. **719 wan**, earned. **722 devyne purveaunce**, divine providence. **725 do marchaundise**, engage in trade. **726 menny's**, men's. **727 apperty**, publicly. **731 of without**, from elsewhere.

hym, and delyverd hym grete tresour to kepe. And thys tresour abode three yere in his kepyng. And after this thre yere, thys marchaunt came and requyred to have his good delyverd to hym agayn. And thys man knewe wel that he had no recorde ne witnes to preve on hym this dueté, nor he had no obligacion ne wrytyng of hym therof, in suche wyse that he denyed al entierly and sayd playnly he knewe hym not. And whan this good man herd and understood this, he went sorowfully and wepyng from hym so ferre and longe that an olde woman mette wyth hym and demaunded of hym the cause of his wepyng. And he sayd to her, "Woman hit aperteyneth nothyng to thee! Goo thy waye!"

And she prayed hym that he wold telle her the cause of his sorowe, for paraventure she myght geve hym counceyl good and proffytable. And thenne this man tolde to her by ordre the caas of his fortune. And the olde woman, that was wyse and subtil, demaunded of hym yf he had in that cité ony frende whiche wold be faythful and trewe to hym. And he sayd "ye," that he had dyverse frendes. Than sayd she, "Goo thou to them and saye to them that they doo ordeyne and bye dyverce cofres and chestes, and that they doo fylle them wyth somme olde thynges of no value, and that they fayne and say that they be ful of golde, silver, and other jewels, and of moche grete tresour. And thenne that they brynge them to thys sayd marchaunt, and to say to hym that he wold kepe them, for as moche as they had grete trust in hym, and also that they have herd of his grete trouth and good renome, and also they wold go into fer contré and shold be longe er they retorned agayn. And whilis they speke to hym of this mater, thou shalt come upon them and requyre hym that he doo delyver to thee that thou tokest to hym. And I trowe, bycause of tho good men that than shal proffre to hym the sayd tresour and for the covetise to have hit, he shal delyver to thee thy good agayn. But beware! Late hym not knowe they ben thy good frendes ner of thy knowleche."

This was a grete and good counceyl of a woman. And verily it cometh of nature often tymes to women to geve counceyl shortly and unadvysedly to thynges that ben in doubte or perilous and nedeth hasty remedye. And as ye have herd, this good man dyd, and did after her counceyl, and came upon them whan they spack of the mater to the marchaunt for to delyver to hym the sayd cofres to kepe, whiche his frendes had fayned, and requyred of hym that he had taken to hym to kepe. And than anone the sayd marchaunt sayd to hym, "I knowe thee now wel. For I have advysed me that thou art suche a man, and camest to me suche a tyme, and delyvered to me suche a thynge whyche I have wel kept."

And thenne callyd his clerk and bad hym goo fetche suche a thyng in suche a place and delyver hit to that good man, "for he delyverd hit to me." And than the good man receyvyd his good and went his waye right joyously and glad. And this marchaunt trichour and deceyvour was defrauded from his evyl malice. And he ne had neyther that one ne that other onythyng that was of value.

---

735 wrytyng, record. **738 so ferre and longe**, for such a long time. **742 paraventure**, perchance. **746 ordeyne and bye**, arrange and buy. **748 fayne**, feign. **752 fer contré**, distant lands. **753 whilis**, while. **754 tho**, those. **756 Late**, Let. **759 unadvysedly**, unexpectedly. **761 did after her**, sought their. **765 advysed me**, considered to myself. **770 trichour**, cheat.

And therfore hit is sayd in proverbe, "To defraude the begiler is no fraude."
And he that doth wel foloweth our Lord.

775 And Seneke sayth that charité enseigneth and techeth that men shold paye wel,
for good payement is somtyme good confessyon.

And this marchaunt trichour and deceyvour resemblith and is lyke to an hound
that bereth a chese in his mouth whan he swymmeth over a water. For whan he is
on the watre, he seeth the shadowe of the chese in the watre, and than he weneth
hit be another chese. And for covetyse to have that, he openyth his mouth to catche
780 that. And than the chese that he bare fallith doun into the watre, and thus he loseth
bothe two. And in the same wyse was servyd thys marchaunt deceyvour. For for to
have the cofres whiche he had not seen, he delyverd agayn that he wold have
holden wrongfully, and thus by his covetise and propre malyce he was deceyved.

And therfore hit apperteyneth to every good and wyse man to knowe and
785 considere in hymself how moche he hath receyved of other men. And upon what
condycion hit was delyverd to hym. And it is to wete that thys thyng apperteyneth to
receyvours and to chaungeours, and to alle trewe marchauntis and other, what that
somever they be, and ought to kepe theyr bookes of resaytes and of payementes of
whom and to whom, and what tyme and day. And yf ye demaunde what thyng
790 makyth them to forgete suche thynges as ben taken to them to kepe, I answer and
say that it is grete covetise for to have tho thynges to themself and never to departe
from them. And hit is alle her thought and desire to assemble alle the goodes that
they may gete, for they beleve on none other god, but on her richesses theyr hertes
ben so obstynat.

795 And this suffyseth of the marchauntes.

---

772 begiler, cheater. **774 enseigneth,** instructs. **777 bereth,** carries; **chese,** cheese. **778
weneth,** believes. **781 For for,** Because in order to. **787–88 what that somever,**
whatsoever. **788 resaytes,** receipts. **791 tho,** those. **794 obstynat,** resolute.

The fifthe chappitre of the thyrd book treteth of physiciens, medecynes, spycers, and appotiquaries. **Capitulo five.**

The pawn that is sette tofore the quene signefyeth the physicien, spicer, apotiquare, and is formed in the fygure of a man. And he is sette in a chayer as a maistre, and holdeth in his right hand a book, and an ample or a boxe with oynementis in his lyft hand. And at his gurdel his instrumentis of yron and of silver
800 for to make incisions and to serche woundes and hurtes, and to cutte apostumes. And by thyse thynges ben knowen the surgyens. By the book ben understonden the phisiciens and all gramariens, logyciens, maystres of lawe, of geometrye, arsmetrique, musique, and of astronomye. And by the ampole ben signefyed the makers of pygmentaries, spicers, and apotiquaries, and they that make confeccions, and
805 confites, and medecynes maad wyth precious spyce. And by the ferremens and instrumentis that hangen on the gurdel ben signefyed the surgyens and the maysters.
And knowe ye for certeyn that a maystre and physicyen ought to knowe the proporcions of lettres of gramayre, the monemens, the conclucions, and the sophyms of logique, the gracious speche and utteraunce of rethorique, the mesures of the
810 houres and dayes, and of the cours of astronomye, the nombre of arsmetrique, and the joyous songes of musique. And of al thyse tofore named, the maysters of

Title **medecynes**, medical practitioners; **spycers**, spice dealers; **appotiquaries**, apothecaries. **798 maistre**, teacher; **ample**, ampule or a small container. **799 oynementis**, ointments. **800 serche**, probe; **apostumes**, apostems or abscesses. **802 gramariens**, teachers of grammar; **logyciens**, teachers of logic; **maystres of lawe**, teachers of law; **arsmetrique**, arithmetic. **804 pygmentaries**, makers of ointments and drugs; **confeccions**, medical compounds. **805 confites**, preserves; **ferremens**, possibly "ferments" or organic material that causes yeast. **808 proporcions of lettres of gramayre**, harmonious arrangement of words; **monemens**, movements (Caxton has put an "n" in the place of a "v"); **sophyms**, sophisms.

rethorique ben the chyef maysters in speculatyf. And the two last that ben practiciens and werkes ben callyd physiciens and surgyens, how wel they ben sage and curious in thyse sciences, and how wel that manny's lyf is otherwhyle put in the ordonaunce of the physicien or surgyen. Yf he have not sagesse and wysedom in hymself of dyverce wrytynges and is not expert, and medlyth hym in the craft of physique, he ought better be callyd a slear of peple than a phisicien or surgyen. For he may not be a maystre but yf he be sewre and expert in the craft of phisike that he slee not moo than he cureth and maketh hoole.

And therfore sayth Avycenne in an *Anforysme:* "Yf thou curest the seek man and knowest not the cause wherof the maladye ought to be cured, hit ought to be sayd that thou hast cured hym by fortune and happe more than by ony kunnyng." And in al thyse maner of people, ther ought to be meurté of good maners, curtosie of wordes, chastité of the body, promysse of helthe, and, as to them that been seek, contynuel vysitacion of them. And they ought to enquere the cause of theyr sekenessys and the sygnes and tokens of theyr maladyes, as is rehercid in the bokes of the auctours by right grete dyligence, and specially in the bookes of Ypocras, Galiene, and of Avycene.

And whan many maysters and phisiciens ben assemblid tofore the pacient or seke man, they ought not there to argue and dispute, one agaynst another. But they ought to make good and symple colacion togeder in suche wyse as they be not seen in theyr dysputyng one agaynst another for to encroche and gete more glory of the world to them self than to trete the salute and helthe of the pacient and seek man. I mervaylle why that, whan they see and knowe that whan the seek man hath grete nede of helthe, wherfore than they make gretter objeccion of contrariousnes, for as moche as the lyf of man is demened and put amonge them. But hit is by cause that he is reputed most sage and wyse that argueth and bryngeth in most subtiltees. And alle this maner is amonge doctours of lawe that tretith nothyng of manne's lyf but of temporel thynges that he is holden most wyse and best lerned, that by hys counceyl can best accorde the contencions and dyssencions of men. And therfore ought the phisiciens and surgyens leve, whan they be tofore the seek men, al discencions and contrariousnes of wordes, in suche wyse that hit appere that they studye more for to cure the seek men than for to despute.

And therfore is the phisicien duly sette tofore the quene, so that it is figured that he ought to have in hymself chastyté and contynence of body. For hit apperteyneth som tyme unto the phisicien to vysite and cure quenes, duchesses and countesses, and alle other ladyes, and see and beholde somme secrete sekenessis that falle and

815

820

825

830

835

840

845

---

812 rethorique, rhetoric or the art of persuasion; **speculatyf**, speculative thinking.   **813 how wel**, because; **curious**, studious; **814 otherwhyle**, sometimes; **ordonaunce**, care.   **815 sagesse**, wisdom or knowledge.   **816 medlyth**, meddles.   **817 slear**, slayer.   **818 but yf**, unless; **sewre**, sure; **slee**, slay.   **819 moo**, more.   **822 happe**, luck; **kunnyng**, knowledge or skill.   **823 meurté**, maturity; **825 contynuel**, continual.   **826 tokens**, symptoms.   **827–28 Ypocras, Galiene, and of Avycene** (see note).   **831 colacion**, consultation; **in suche wyse**, in such a way.   **832 encroche**, encroach or seize.   **833 salute**, well-being or safety.   **833–34 seek man**, sick man.   **836 demened**, controled.   **840 dyssencions**, dissent.   **841 leve**, leave.   **842 discencions**, dissent.   **844 figured**, represented.   **845 contynence**, continence or self-restraint.

850

come otherwhile in the secretis of nature. And therfore hit aperteyneth to them that they be chaste and folowe honesté and chastyté, and that they be ensaumple to other of good contynence.

For Valerian rehercith that Ypocras was of mervayllous contynence of his body. For whan he was in the scoles of Athenes, he had by hym a right fayr woman, whiche was comyn. And the yong scolers and the joly felawes that were students promysed to the woman a besaunte yf she myght or coude torne the corage of

855

Ypocras for to have to doon wyth her. And she came to hym by nyght and dyd so moche by her craft that she laye wyth hym in his bedde. But she coude never do so moche that she myght corumpe his chaste lvyyng ne defoule the crowne of his conscience. And whan the yonge men knewe that she had ben wyth hym al the nyght and coude not chaunge his contynence, they began to mocque her and to axe

860

and demaunde of her the besaunt that they had geven to her. And she answerd that hit was holden and gaged upon an ymage. For as moche as she myght not chaunge hys contynence, she callyd hym an ymage.

And in semblable wyse rehercith Valeryan of Scenocrates, phylosopher, that there laye wyth hym a woman alle nyght and tempted hym dysordonatly. But that

865

right chaste man made never semblaunt to her, ner he never remevyd from hys ferme purpoos, in suche wyse as she departed from hym al confused and shamed. Cornelius Scipion, that was sent by the Romayns for to governe Spayn, as sone as he entrid in to the castellys and into the townes of that londe, he began to take aweye al tho thynges that myght stere or meve his men to lecherye, wherfore men

870

sayd that he drof and chased out of the hoost moo than two thousand bourdellys. And he that was wyse knewe wel that delyte of lecherye corupted and apayred the corages of tho men that ben abandoned to the same delyte.

And herof it is sayd in the fables of the poetes in the first book of the *Truphes of the Philosophres* by figure that they that entrid in to the fonteyne of the sirenes or

875

mermaydens were corumped, and they took them awey wyth hem.

And also ye ought to knowe that they ought to entende dylygently to the cures of the infirmytees in cyrurgerye. They ought to make theyr plaisters accordyng to the woundes or soores. Yf the wounde be rounde, the enplastre must be rounde. And yf hit be longe, hit must be longe. And otherwhyle hit must be cured by his

880

contrarye, lyke as it apperteyneth to phisique. For the hete is cured by colde, and the colde by hete, and joye by sorowe and sorowe by joye. And hit happeth ofte tymes that moche peple be in grete parille in takyng to moche joye and lese her membris, and become half benomen in the sodeyn joye. And joye is a repleccion of thynge that is delectable, sprad abrode in alle the membres wyth right grete

---

853 comyn (i.e., a prostitute). **854 besaunte**, a gold coin; **torne the corage of**, seduce. **855 for to have to doon wyth her**, to have sex with her. **859 axe**, ask for. **861 holden and gaged**, held and fastened on. **863 in semblable wyse**, in a similar way. **865 made never semblaunt**, never made a welcome. **869 stere**, stir. **870 hoost**, army; **bourdellys**, prostitutes. **871 apayred**, weakened. **872 corages**, strength. **873 Truphes**, Frivolties. **874 by figure**, figuratively; **fonteyne**, fountain. **875 corumped**, corrupted. **877 cyrurgerye**, surgery; **plaisters**, plasters or dressings. **878 enplastre**, dressing. **879 otherwhyle**, sometimes. **879–80 by his contrarye**, by its opposite. **880 phisique**, medical treatments. **882–83 lese her membris**, lose their body parts. **883 benomen**, ravished; **repleccion**, filling up.

885   gladnes. And al men entende and desyre to have the sayd right grete joye naturelly, but they knowe not what may ensue and come therof. And this joye cometh otherwhile of vertue of conscience, and the wise man is not wythout this joye. And thys joye is never interrupt ne in defaulte at no tyme, for hit cometh of nature. And fortune may not take awey that nature geveth.

890   And Marcial sayth that joyes fugetyves abyde not long, but fle awey anone.

And Valerian rehercith that he that hath force and strengthe resonable hath hit of veray matier of complecconn, and that cometh of love. And this joye hath as moche power to departe the sowle fro the body as hath the thondre. Wherof hit happend that there was a woman named Lyna, whiche had her husbond in the

895   warre in the shyppys of the Romayns, and she supposid verayly that he was deed. But hit happend that he came agayn home, and as he entrid into his yate, his wyf mette wyth hym sodaynly, not warned of his comyng, whiche was so gladde and joyous that in enbracyng hym she fyl doun deed.

Also, of another woman to whom was reported by a fals messanger that her

900   sone was deed, whiche went hoom soroufully to her hows. And afterward, when her sone came to her, as sone as she sawe hym, she was so esmoved wyth joye that she deyde tofore hym. But this is not so grete mervayle of women as is of the men.

For the women ben lykened unto softe waxe or softe ayer, and therfore she is callyd *mulier*, whiche is as moche to saye in Latyn as *mollis aer* and in Englissh "softe

905   ayer." And hit happeth ofte tymes that the nature of them that ben softe and mole taketh sonner inpressyon than the nature of men that be rude and stronge.

Valerie rehercith that a knyght of Rome named Instavlosus that had newly conquerid and subdued the Yle of Corsika. And as he sacrefyed his goodes, he receyvyd lettres from the senate of Rome in whiche were conteyned dyverce

910   supplicacions, the whiche whan he understood, he was so glad and so enterprised wyth joye that he knewe not what to do. And than a grete fume or smoke yssued out of the fire, in whiche he dispayrid and fyl into the fyre, where he was anone deed.

And also it is sayd that Phylomenus lawghed so sore and distemperatly that he

915   dyed al lawghyng.

And we rede that Ypocras, the phisicien, fond remedye for thys joye. For whan he had long dwellyd out of hys contrey for to lerne kunnyng and wysedom, and shold retorne unto his parentis and frendes, whan he approchyd nygh them, he sent a messanger tofore for to telle them his comyng and commaunded hym to

920   saye that he cam. For they had not longe tofore seen hym, and that they shold attempre them in that joye or they shold see hym.

---

888 **in defaulte**, wanting. 890 **joyes fugetyves**, fleeting pleasures. 892 **veray matier of complecconn**, true matter of temperament. 893 **thondre**, thunder. 898 **enbracyng**, embracing. 901 **esmoved**, moved. 904 *mulier*, as Caxton notes, is the Latin word for woman. 905 **mole**, without perception. 906 **sonner**, more quickly. 908 **Yle of Corsika**, Island of Corsica; **sacrefyed his goodes**, made sacrifices to his gods. 910 **enterprised**, taken. 914 **distemperatly**, excessively. 917 **kunnyng**, knowledge or skill. 918 **nygh**, near to. 920 **had not longe tofore seen hym**, had not seen him for a while. 921 **attempre them**, moderate themselves; **or**, before.

And also, we rede that Titus, the sone of Vaspasian, whan he had conquerd
Jherusalem and abode in the contrees by, he herde that his fader, Vaspasian, was
chosen by al the Senate for to governe the Empyre of Rome. Wherfore he had so
925   right grete joye that sodeynly he lost the strength of al his membris and became
al inpotent. And whan Josephus, that made the historye of the Romayns ayenst the
Jewys, whiche was a right wyse phisicien, sawe and knewe the cause of this sekenes
of the sayd Titus, he enquyred of his folke yf he had in hate ony man gretely so
moche that he myght not here speke of hym ne wel se hym. And one of the
930   servauntes of Tytus sayd that he had one persone in hate so moche that ther was
no man in his courte so hardy that durst name hym in hys presence.

And than Josephus assigned a day whan this man shold come and ordeyned a
table to be sette in the sight of Titus, and did hit to be replenysshed plentously
wyth al dayntees. And ordeyned men to be armed to kepe hym in suche wise that no
935   man shold hurt hym by the commaundement of Titus, and ordeyned boutelers,
cokes, and other officers for to serve hym worshipfully like an emperour. And
whan al this was redy, Josephus brought in this man that Titus hated, and sette
hym at the table tofore his eyen, and was servyd of yong men with grete reverence
right curtoisly. And whan Titus behelde his enemye sette tofore hym wyth so grete
940   honour, he began to chauffe hymself by grete felonye, and commaunded his men
that this man shold be slayn. And whan he sawe that none wold obeye hym, but
that they alwey servyd hym reverently, he waxe so ardant and enbracid wyth so
grete yre that he, that had lost al the force and strengthe of his body and was al
impotent in alle his membrys, recoverd the helth agayn and strengthe of hys
945   membris by the hete that entryd into the vaynes and synewes. And Josephus dyd
so moche that he was recoveryd and hoole, and that he helde that man no more
for hys enemye but helde hym for a veray trewe frende, and afterward maad hym
his loyal felowe and companyoun.

And the espycers and apoticaries ought to make trewly suche thynges as is
950   commaunded to them by the phisiciens. And they ought to accomplisshe their billes
and charge curiously with grete diligence, that for none other cause they shold be
ocupied but in makyng medecynes or confecconns trewly. And that they ought,
upon paryl of their sowle, not to forgete by neglygence ne rechelesnes to gyve one
medecyne for another, in suche wyse that they be not slears of men, and that they
955   doo put no false thynges in her spices for to enpayre, or encrecyng the weyght. For
yf they so do, they may better be callyd thevys than espycers or apoticaries. And
they that ben acustumed to make oynementis, they ought to make it proprely of
trewe stuffe and of good odoure after the receptes of the auncient doctours, and
after the forme that the phisiciens and surgiens devyse unto them.

---

925 al his membris, all his body parts. **928 folke,** people; **had in hate,** despised. **929 here
speke of,** hear any talk of; **se,** see. **932 ordeyned,** commanded. **935 boutelers,** servants.
936 cokes, cooks. **939 curtoisly,** graciously. **940 chauffe,** fume; **felonye,** anger. **942 waxe
so ardant,** became so fired up. **942–43 enbracid wyth so grete yre,** was taken with such
anger. **945 hete,** heat; **synewes,** sinews. **946 hoole,** whole. **949 espycers,** spice sellers.
950 billes, orders. **951 charge curiously,** fill [them] skillfully. **952 confecconns,** medicinal
compounds. **953 rechelesnes,** carelessness. **955 enpayre,** worsen; **encrecyng,** increasing.
956 thevys, thieves. **958 stuffe,** ingredients; **odoure,** fragrance; **receptes,** formulae.

960   Also, they ought to be ware that for none avayle ne gyfte that they ought have, that they put in their medecynes nothyng venemous ne doyng hurte or scathe to ony persone of whom they have no good ne veray knowleche, to the ende that they to whom the medecynes shold be geven torne not to them hurt, ne domage, ne in destrucconns of their neyghbours. And also that they that have mynystrid tho

965   thynges to them been not taken for parteners of the blame and of the synne of them.

The surgyens ought also to be debonayr, amyable, and to have pyté of theyr pacients. And also, they ought not be hasty to launce and cutte apostumes and soores, ne open the heedes, ner to arrache bones broken, but yf the cause be apparant. For they myght ellys lose theyr good renomee, and myght better be

970   callyd bouchers thenne helars or guarysshours of woundes and sores. And also hit behoveth that alle thys maner of peple aforesayd, that have the charge for to make hoole and guarisshe alle maner of maladyes and infirmytees, that they first have the cure of themself. And they ought to purge themself from alle apostumes and alle vyces, in suche wyse that they be net and honeste and enformed in al good

975   maners. And that they shewe hem hole and pure and redy for to hele other.

And herof sayth Boecius [in] *De consolacisone*, in his first booke that the sterres that ben hyd under the clowdes may gyve no light. And therfore, yf ony man wyl beholde clerely the verité, late hym withdrawe hym fro the obscureté and derknes of the cloudes of ygnoraunce. For whan the engyne of a man sheweth in joye or in

980   sorow, the pensee or thought is envoluped in obscureté and under the clowdes.

960 avayle, profit.   **961 scathe**, damage.   **963 domage**, harm.   **964 destrucconns**, destructions.   **966 debonayr**, gracious.   **967 launce**, pierce; **apostumes**, abscesses.   **968 arrache**, tear; **but yf**, unless.   **969 renomee**, reputation.   **970 bouchers**, butchers; **helars or guarysshours**, healers or guarishers (curers).   **973 cure**, care.   **974 net**, clean.   **976 sterres**, stars.   **479 engyne**, intelligence.

The sixte chappitre of the thyrd book treteth of the sixte pawn, whiche is lykenyd to taverners, hostelers, and vytayllers.   **Capitulo six.**

The sixte pawn, whiche stondeth tofore the alphyn on the lyfte syde, is made in this forme, for hit is a man that hath the right hond stratched out as for to calle men, and holdeth in his lift honde a loof of breed and a cuppe of wyn, and on his gurdel hangyng a bondel of keyes. And this resemblith the taverners, hostelers,

985 and sellars of vytayl. And thyse ought properly to be sette tofore the alphyn, as tofore a juge. For there sourdeth oft tymes amonge hem contencion, noyse, and stryf, whyche behoveth to be determyned and trayted by the alphyn, whiche is juge of the kyng. And hit apperteyneth to them for to seke and enquere for good wynes and good vytayl for to gyve and selle to the byars, and to them that they herberowe.

990 And hit apperteyneth to them wel to kepe theyr herberowes and innes, and alle tho thynges that they brynge into theyr lodgyng, and for to putte hyt in seure and sauf warde and kepyng.

And the first of them is signefyed by the lyfte hand in whyche he bereth breed and wyn. And the second is signefyed by the right hand whiche is stratched out to

995 calle men. And the thyrd is representyd by the keyes hangyng on the gurdel.

And thyse maner of peple ought to eschewe the synne of glotonye. For moche people come into theyr howses for to drynke and for to ete, for whyche cause they ought resonably to rewle themself and to refrayne them from to moche mete and drynke, to the ende that they myght the more honestly delyver thynges nedeful

1000 unto the peple that come unto them, and nothyng by outrage that myght noye the body.

Title **taverners**, tavern-keepers; **hostelers**, innkeepers; **vytayllers**, purveyors of victuals or provisions. **981 alphyn**, chess bishop or judge. **982 stratched**, stretched. **983 loof of breed**, loaf of bread. **984 gurdel**, belt; **bondel**, bunch. **986 sourdeth**, arises; **noyse**, contention or strife. **987 stryf**, strife; **trayted**, settled. **988 enquere**, inquire. **989 vytayl**, food; **byars**, buyers. **990 herberowes**, lodgings. **991 seure and sauf**, secure and safe. **992 warde**, care. **1000 outrage**, excess; **noye**, disturb.

For hit happeth oft tymes that there cometh of glotonye, tencions, stryfs, riottes, wronges, and molestaconns, by whiche men lese otherwhyle their handes, theyr eyen, and other of theyr membris, and somtyme ben slayn or hurte unto the

1005   deth as it is wreton in *Vitas Patrum*, as on a tyme an hermyte went for to vysite his gossibs. And the devyl apperid to hym on the wey in likenes of another hermyte for to tempte hym, and said: "Thou hast left thyn hermytage and goest to visite thy gossibs. Thee behoveth by force to do one of the three thynges that I shal say to thee. Thou shalt chese whether thou wolt be dronk, or ellys have to do flesshlye

1010   with thy gossyb, or ellis thou shalt slee her husbond, whiche is thy gossib also."

And the hermyte, that thought for to chese the leste evyl, chase for to be dronke. And whan he cam unto them, he drank so moche that he was veray dronk. And whan he was dronke and eschauffyd with the wyn, he wold have a doo with his gossyb. And her husbond withstood hym. And than the hermyte slewe hym and

1015   after that laye by his gossyb and knewe her flesshly. And thus by this synne of dronkenshyp, he accomplisshed the two other synnes.

By whiche thyng ye may understonde and knowe that whan the devyl wyl take one of the castellys of Jhesu Cryst, that is to wete the body of a man or of a woman, he doth as a prynce that setteth a siege tofore a castel that he wold wynne, whyche

1020   entendeth to wynne the gate. For he knoweth wel whan he hath wonne the gate he may sone doo his wylle wyth the castel. And in lyke wyse doth the devyl wyth every man and womman. For whan he hath wonne the gate, that is to wete the gate of the mouthe by glotonye or by ony other synne, he may do wyth the offyces of the body al his wylle as ye have herd tofore. And therfore ought every man ete and

1025   drynke sobrely in suche wyse as he may lyve, and not lyve to ete glotonsly and for to drynke dronk. Ye se comunely that a grete bole is suffisid with right a litil pasture, and that one wode suffiseth to many olephauntes. And hit behoveth a man to be fedde by the erthe or by the see. Nevertheles, it is no grete thynge to fede the bely, nothyng so grete as is the desire of many metes.

1030   Wherof Quyntilian saith that hit happeth ofte tymes in grete festes and dyners that we be fylled with the sight of the noble and lichorous metis, and whan we wold ete, we ben saciat and fylled.

And therfore it is sayd in proverbe: "Hit is better to fille the belye than the eye."

And Lucan saith that "glotony is the moder of al vices, and especial of lecherye,

1035   and also is destroyar of al goodes, and may not have suffysaunce of lytil thynge, a covetous honger, what sekest thou mete and vytayllis on the lande and in the see. And thy joye is nothyng ellis but to have playnteuous dysshes and wel filled at thy table. Lerne how men may demene theyr lyf with litil thynge."

1003 **molestaconns**, injuries; **lese**, lose; **otherwhyle**, sometimes. 1004 **eyen**, eyes; **membris**, body parts. 1005 **on a tyme**, one time; **hermyte**, hermit. 1006 **gossibs**, a gossip is a godfather, godmother, close friend, soulmate (sibling in God), or sponsor at baptism; it also refers to the people who are sponsored. 1008 **behoveth by force**, are compelled. 1009 **chese**, choose; **have to do flesshlye**, have sex with. 1013 **eschauffyd**, heated; **have a doo with**, have sexual relations with. 1014 **withstood**, resisted. 1026 **se comunely**, see frequently; **bole**, bull; **suffisid**, satisfied. 1027 **wode**, forest; **suffiseth to**, is sufficient for; **olephauntes**, elephants. 1031 **lichorous metis**, rich foods. 1032 **saciat**, sated. 1036 **vytayllis**, food. 1038 **Lerne**, Know; **demene**, conduct.

And Cathon saith, "In no wyse obeye to glotonye, whiche is frende to lecherye."

1040 And the holy doctour Saynt Augustyn saith, "The wyn eschauffith the bely that falleth anone to lecherye." The bely and the membris ben neighbours to lecherie, and thus the vice of glotonye provoketh lecherye, wherof cometh forgetenes of his mynde and destruccion of alle quyck and sharpe reason, and is cause of distemperaunce of his wyttes. What synne is fowler than this synne and more

1045 stynkyng, ne more dommageous? For this synne hath taken awey the vertu of man. His prowesse languyssheth, his vertue is torned to diffame, the strengthe of body and of corage is torned by thee.

And therfore saith Vasilly la Graunt: "Late us take hede howe we serve the bely and the throte by glotonye like as we were dombe bestys. And we studye for to be

1050 lyke unto belues of the see, to whom nature hath gyven to be alwey enclyned toward the erthe, and therto loke for to serve their belyes."

And herof sayth Boecius [in] *De consolacione* in his fourth book, that a man that lyveth and doth not the condicions of a man may never be in good condicion. Than must hit nedes be that he be transported in nature of a beste or of a belue of

1055 the see. How wel that right grete men and women, ful of mervayllous sciences and noble counceyl in thyse dayes in the world, be norisshed in this glotonye of wynes and metes, and ofte tymes ben overseen. How suppose ye is hit not right a perilous thyng that a lord or governour of the peple and comyn wele, how wel that he be wyse, yf he eschauffe hym sone, so that the wyn or other drynke surprise hym and

1060 overcome his brayn? His wisedom is lost.

For as Cathon sayth: "Ire enpessheth the corage in suche as he may not kepe verité and trouth." And anone as he is chauffid, lecherye is mevyd in hym in suche wyse that the lecherye makyth hym to meddle in dyverse vylayns dedes, for than his wysedom is a slepe and goon.

1065 And therfore saith Ovyde in his book *De remedio amoris*: "Yf thou take many and dyverce wynes, they apparayle and enforce the corages to lecherye."

And Thobye wytnessyth in his book that luxurie destroyeth the body and mynyssheth rychessys. She loseth the sowle, she febleth the strengthe, she blyndeth the syght, and maketh the voys hoors and rawe. A right evyl and foule synne of

1070 dronkenshyp, by thee perisshith virgynyté, whiche is suster of aungellis, possedyng al goodnes and seurté of al joyes pardurable.

Noe was one tyme so chauffyd wyth wyn that he discoverd and shewid to hys sones his prevy membris in suche wyse as one of his sones mocqued hym, and that other coverd hem. And Loth, whiche was a man right chaste, was so assoted by

---

1042 **forgetenes**, forgetfulness. 1044 **distemperaunce**, imbalance or disturbance. 1045 **dommageous**, damaging. 1049 **dombe bestys**, insensible animals. 1050 **belues**, monsters (whales). 1051 **belyes**, bellies. 1053 **doth not the condicions**, does not live in the manner appropriate to. 1059 **eschauffe hym sone**, drinks alcohol quickly. 1061 **enpessheth**, impedes. 1062 **chauffid**, heated (with drink). 1063 **vylayns dedes**, villainous deeds. 1066 **apparayle**, enhance. 1068 **mynyssheth**, diminishes; **febleth**, weakens. 1069 **voys hoors and rawe**, voice hoarse and ragged. 1070 **aungellis**, angels; **possedyng**, possessing. 1071 **seurté**, surety; **pardurable**, lasting. 1072 **Noe**, Noah; **discoverd**, exposed. 1073 **prevy membris**, sexual organs; **mocqued**, mocked. 1074 **assoted**, infatuated.

1075   moche drynkyng of wyn that on a mounteyn he knewe hys doughters carnelly, and
had to doo wyth them as they had ben his propre wyves.

And Crete rehercith that Boece, whiche was flour of the men, tresour of richesses,
synguler hous of sapyence, myrrour of the world, odour of good renomee, and
glorie of his subgettis, lost al thise thynges by his luxurie. We have seen that dyverce
1080   that were joyned by grete amytie to geder whiles they were sobre, that that one
wold put his body in parell of deth for that other, and whan they were eschauffid
with wyn and dronke, they have ronne eche upon other for to slee hem. And
somme have ben that have slayn so his frende.

Herodes Antipas had not doon Saynt John Baptist to ben beheded, ne had the
1085   dyner ben ful of glotonye and dronkship. Balthazar, kyng of Babylone, had not
been chaced out of his kyngdom, ne be slayn, yf he had be sobre emonge hys
peple, whom Tyrus and Dares fond dronken and slewe hym.

The hostelers ought to be wel bespoken and curtoys of wordes to them that they
receyve in to theyr lodgyng. For fayr speche, and joyous chiere and debonayr, cause
1090   men to gyve the hosteler a good name. And therfore hit is sayd in a comyn
proverbe: "Curtoyse langage and wel sayeng is moche worth and coste lytyl." And
in another place it is sayd that curtosye passeth beaulté.

Also, for as moche as many pareylls and adventures may happen on the wayes
and passages to hem that been herberowed wyth in theyr innes, therfore they ought
1095   to accompanye them whan they departe, and enseigne them the weyes and telle to
them the parilles, to the ende that they may surely goo theyr vyage and journey.
And also they ought to kepe theyr bodyes, theyr goodes, and the good fame and
renomee of theyr innes.

We rede that Loth, whan he had receyvyd the aungellys into his hows right
1100   debonayrly, whiche he had supposid had ben mortal men and straungers, to the
ende that they shold eskape the disordynate and unnaturel synne of lecherye of the
Sodomytes, by the vertu of good fayth, he sette a part the naturel love of a fader
and proferd to them his doughters, whiche were vyrgyns, to the ende that they
shold kepe them and defende them fro that villayn and horrible synne.

1105   And knowe ye for certeyn that al tho thynges that been taken and delyverd to
kepe to the hoste or hostessis, they ought to be sauf and yelden ageyn without
appayryng. For the hoste ought to knowe who that entrith in to hys hous for to be
herberowed takith hit for his habitacion for the tyme he hymself, and alle suche
thynges as he bryngeth wyth hym, ben commysed of right in the warde and kepyng
1110   of the hoste or hosteler, and ought to be as sauf as they were put in his owne
propre hows.

1077 tresour, treasure.   **1078 hous of sapyence**, source of wisdom; **odour of good renomee**, imbued with the very essence of good fame. **1079 dyverce**, diverse men. **1080 amytie**, friendship. **1081 parell**, peril; **eschauffid**, heated. **1082 ronne eche upon other**, attacked each other. **1085 dyner**, dinner. **1086 chaced**, chased; **emonge**, among. **1087 fond**, found. **1088 wel bespoken**, well-spoken; **curtoys**, polite. **1089 debonayr**, used as an adjective modifying *chere*, in the sense of "graciousness." **1092 passeth**, surpasses. **1094 herberowed**, lodged. **1095 enseigne**, teach. **1104 defende them**, protect themselves. **1106 yelden**, yielded. **1107 appayryng**, appairing or damage. **1108 herberowed**, lodged. **1109 commysed**, entrusted; **warde**, care.

And also suche hostes ought to holde servauntes in theyr hows whiche shold be trewe and without avarice, in suche wyse that they coveyte not to have the goodes of theyr ghestes, and that they take not awey the provender fro theyr horses whan
1115 hit is gyven to them, that by the occasion therof, their horses perisshe not, ne faylle theyr maister whan they have nede, and myght falle in the handes of theyr enemyes. For than shold the servauntes be cause of that evyl wherfore their maysters shold see to. For without doubte, this thyng is worse than thefte.

Hit happend on a tyme in the parties of Lombardye in the cyté of Jene that a
1120 noble man was lodgyd in an hostelrye wyth moche companye. And whan they had gyven provendour to theyr horses, in the first oure of the nyght, the servaunt of the hows came secretly tofore the horses for to stele awey theyr provender. And whan he came to the lorde's hors, the hors caught with his teth his arme and helde hit fast that he myght not escape. And whan the theef sawe that he was so strongly holden,
1125 he began to crye for the grete payn that he suffrid and felte, in suche wyse that the noble manny's meyné cam wyth the hoste. But in no maner, ner for ought they coude doo, they coude not take the theef out of the horse's mouth unto the tyme that the neyghbours, whiche were noyed wyth the noyse, came and sawe hit. And the theef was knowen and taken and brought tofore the juge, and confessyd the
1130 feet, and by sentence diffynytyf was hanged and lost his lyf. And in the same wyse was another that dyd so. And the hors smote hym in the vysage that the prynte of the hors shoo and nayles abode ever in his vysage.

Another caas right cruel and vilaynous fyl at Tholouse. Hit happend a yong man and his fader went a pylgremage to Saynt James in Galice and were lodgyd in an
1135 hostelrye of an evyl hoost, and ful of right grete covetyse, inso moche that he desired and coveyted the goodes of the two pylgrymes. And here upon advysed hym, and put a cuppe of silver secretly in the male that the yonge man bare. And whan they departed out of theyr lodgyng, he folowed after hem and sayd tofore the peple of the court that they had stolen and borne awey his cuppe. And the yong man
1140 excused hymself and his fader and sayd they were innocent of that caas. And thenne they serchyd hem, and the cuppe was founden in the male of the yonge man. And forthwyth he was dampned to deth and hanged as a theef. And thys feet doon, al the goodes that longed to the pylgrym were delyverd to the hoste as confisqued.

And than the fader went forth for to do his pylgremage. And whan he came
1145 ageyn, he must nedes come and passe by the place where his sone hynge on the gybet. And as he came he complayned to God and to Saynt James how they myght suffre this adventure to come unto hys sone. Anone his sone that hyng spake to his fader and said how that Saynt James had kept hym wythout harme, and bad his fader goo to the juge and shewe to hym the myracle, and how he was innocent of
1150 that fait. And whan this thyng was knowen, the sone of the pylgrym was taken doun

---

1114 **ghestes**, guests; **provender**, fodder. 1119 **parties**, regions. 1121 **oure**, hour. 1126 **meyné**, company of men. 1128 **noyed wyth**, disturbed by. 1129 **knowen**, exposed. 1130 **feet**, act; **sentence diffynytyf**, final verdict. 1131 **vysage**, face. 1132 **abode**, remained. 1133 **caas**, case; **Tholouse**, Toulouse. 1134 **Galice**, Galicia. 1136 **advysed hym**, considered to himself. 1137 **male**, purse or sack; **bare**, carried. 1140 **excused**, maintained the innocence of. 1142 **feet**, deed. 1143 **confisqued**, confiscated. 1145 **must nedes**, had to; **hynge**, hung. 1146 **gybet**, gibbet or gallows. 1150 **fait**, act.

fro the gybet, and the cause was brought tofore the juge, and the hoost was accused of the trayson. And he confessyd his trespaas and sayd he dyd hit for covetyse to have his good. And than the juge dampned hym for to be hanged on the same gybet where as the yonge pylgrym was hanged.

1155   And that I have sayd of the servauntes beyng men, the same I say of the women as chaumberers and tapsters. For semblable caas fyl in Spayn at Saynt Donne of a chaumberer that put a cuppe in lyke wyse in the scrippe of a pylgryme bycause he wold not have a do wyth her in the synne of lecherye, wherfore he was hanged. And his fader and moder that were there wyth hym went and dyd her pylgremage. And 1160 whan they came agayn, they fonde her sone lyvyng. And than they went and tolde the juge, whiche juge sayd that he wold not beleve hit til a cok and an henne, whiche rosted on the fyre, were a lyve, and the cok crewe. And anone they began to wexe a lyve, and the cok crewe and began to crowe and to pasture. And whan the juge sawe this myracle, he went and toke doun the sone, and made the chaumberer 1165 to be taken and to be hanged. Wherfore I say that the hostes ought to holde no tapsters ne chaumberers but yf they were good, meure, and honeste. For many harmes may befalle and come by the disordenate rewle of servauntes.

The seventh chappitre of the thyrd tractate treteth of kepars of townes, customers, and tolle gaderers.   **Capitulo seven.**

1151 **cause**, case. 1152 **trayson**, treason. 1156 **chaumberers and tapsters**, chambermaids and barmaids; **semblable**, a similar. 1157 **scrippe**, small bag or wallet. 1162 **crewe**, crowed. 1162–63 **began to wexe a lyve**, there seems to be something missing here, although the sense is clear: the couple kills a rooster by burning it. 1163 **pasture**, feed. 1166 **meure**, careful. *Title* **customers**, officials who collect customs.

The gardes and kepars of citees ben signefyed by the seventh pawn, whiche stondeth in the lyft side tofore the knyght, and is formed in the semblaunce of a man holdyng in his lyft hond grete keyes and in hys right hand a potte and an elle for to mesure wyth, and ought to have on his gurdel a purse open. And by the keyes ben signefied the kepars of the citees and townes and comyn offyces. And by the potte and elle ben signefyed them that have the charge to weye and mete and mesure trewly. And by the purse been signefyed them that receyve the costumes, tolles, scawage, peages, and duetees of the cytees and townes.

And thyse peple ben sette by right tofore the knyght. And hit behoveth that the gardes and offycers of the townes be taught and ensigned by the knyghtes, and that they knowe and enquyre how the citees and townes ben governed, whiche aperteyneth to be kept and defended by the knyghtes. And first hit aperteyneth that the kepars of the cyté be dyligent, besy, clere sayeng, and lovers of the comyn prouffyt and wele, as wel in the tyme of pees as in the tyme of warre. They ought alwey to goo in the cyté and enquyre of al thynges and ought reporte to the governours of the cyté suche thyng as they fynde and knowe, and suche thynge as aperteyneth and to the seurté of the same, and to denounce and telle the defaultes and parellys that there be. And yf hit be in tyme of warre, they ought not to open the gates by nyght to no man.

And suche men as ben put in this offyce ought to be of renome and fame, trewe, and of good conscience, in suche manere that they love them of the cyté or towne, and that they put to no man ony blame or vylanye with out cause by envye, covetyse, ne by hate, but they ought to be sory and hevy whan they see that ony man shold be compleyned on for ony cause. For hit happeth ofte tymes that dyverce offycers accuse the good peple fraudulently, to the ende that they myght have a thanke and ben praysed, and to abyde stylle in theyr offyces. And trewly hit is a grete and hye maner of malice to be in wylle to doo evyl and dyffame other wythout cause to grete glorye to hymself.

Also, the kepars and offycers of cytees ought to be suche that they suffre no wronegs ne vylonyes tofore the juges and governours of citees wythout cause to be doon to them that ben innocentes, but they ought to have theyr eyen and regarde unto hym that knoweth the hertes and thoughtes of al men. And they ought to drede and doubte Hym with out whos grace theyr watche and kepyng is nought, and that promyseth to them that doubte Hym shal be ewrous and happy. And by Hym ben al thynges accomplisshed in good.

Hit is founden in the histories of Rome that the Emperour Frederik the Second dyd doo make a gate of marble of mervayllous werk and enteyle in the cyté of

1170 elle, measuring rod. **1171 gurdel**, belt. **1173 mete**, take measurements. **1174 receyve**, receive; **costumes**, customs. **1175 scawage**, a "scavage" or special toll imposed by the mayor of a town; **peages**, tolls paid for passing through a place; **duetees**, duties or taxes. **1177 ensigned**, trained. **1180 besy**, active; **clere sayeng**, of clear speech. **1184 seurté**, security; **denounce**, make known; **defaultes**, failures or shortcomings. **1185 parellys**, perils. **1187 renome**, reputation. **1190 sory and hevy**, sad and dispirited. **1191 compleyned on**, cried out upon. **1192 have a thanke**, receive thanks. **1200 doubte**, fear. **1201 ewrous**, prosperous. **1204 enteyle**, carving or sculpture.

1205   Capuane upon the watre that renneth about the same. And upon this gate he made an ymage lyke hymself sittyng in his magesté and two juges, whiche were sette one on the right side and that other on the lift side. And upon the sercle above the hede of the juge on the right side was wreton: "Al they entre seurely that wyl lyve purely." And upon the sercle of the juge on the lift side was wreton: "The untrewe

1210   man ought to doubte to doo thyng that he be put to pryson fore." And on the sercle above the emperour was wreton: "I make them lyve in mysery that I see lyve dysmesurably." And therfore hit aperteyneth to a juge to shewe to the peple for to drede and doubte to do evyl. And hyt aperteyneth to the gardes and offycers to doubte the juges and to doo trewly theyr servyces and offyces. And hit aperteyneth

1215   to a prynce to menace the traytours and the malefactours of right grevous paynes.

    And herof we fynde in the auncient histories of Cecille that the Kyng Denys had a broder whom he lovyd sore wel. But alwey where he went, he made hevy and triste semblaunt. And thus as they went bothe to gyder on a tyme in a chare, ther cam agayn hem two poure men with glad vysage but in foule habyte. And the kyng,

1220   anone as he sawe them, sprange out of his chare and receyvyd them worshipfully with grete reverence, wherfore his barons were not onely amervaylled but also angry in their corages. Notwithstondyng, fere and drede letted them to demaunde hym the cause, but they made his broder to demaunde the cause and to knowe the certeynté. And whan he had herde his broder say to hym the demaunde, that he

1225   was blessyd and also a kyng whiche was riche and ful of delytes and worshyppes, he demaunded hym yf he wold assaye and knowe the grace and beneurté of a kyng. And his broder answerd "ye," and that he desired and requyred hit of hym. And than the kyng commaunded unto alle hys subgettis that they shold obeye in al thynges onely unto his broder. And than, whan the oure of dyner cam and al

1230   thynge was redy, the broder was sette at the table of the kyng. And whan he sawe that he was servyd with right noble botelers and other offycers, and he herde the sownes of musique right melodyous, the kyng demaunded hym than yf he supposid that he were benerous and blessyd. And he answerd, "I wene wel that I am right blessyd and fortunat, and that I have wel proved and fele, and am expert therof."

1235   And than the kyng secretly made to be hanged over hys heed a sharpe cuttyng swerde, hangyng by an hors here or a sylken threde so smale that no man myght see hit where by hit henge. And whan he sawe his broder put no more his hand to the table, ne had no more regarde unto his servauntes, he sayd to hym: "Why ete ye not? Ar ye not blessid? Say yf ye fele onythyng otherwyse than blessid and wel."

1240   And he answerd, "For as moche as I see thys sharpe swerde hangyng so subtilly and parilously over myn hede, I fele wel that I am not blessyd, for I drede that hit shold falle on my hede."

1205 **Capuane**, Capua, a city in the southwest region of Campania, Italy. **1207 sercle**, circle. **1212 dysmesurably**, without measure. **1216 Cecille**, Sicily. **1217–18 triste semblaunt**, sad expression. **1218 chare**, chariot. **1219 agayn**, in the opposite direction of; **vysage**, demeanor; **habyte**, clothing. **1222 corages**, hearts; **Notwithstondyng**, Nevertheless; **letted**, prevented. **1224 certeynté**, state of affairs; **he**, i.e., Dionysus; **demaunde**, inquiry. **1226 assaye**, put to the test;. **beneurté**, blessedness. **1227 "ye,"** yes; **requyred**, requested. **1233 benerous**, blessed; **wene**, believe. **1236 hors here**, horse hair.

And thenne dyscoverd the kyng unto hem al wherfore he was alwey so hevy, cherid, and tryste. For where he was, he thought alwey on the swerde of the secrete
1245 vengaunce of God, whyche he behelde alwey in his herte, wherfore he had alwey in hymself grete drede. And therfore he worshyppyd gladly the poure peple with glad vysage and good conscience. And by this sheweth the kyng wel that what man that is alwey in drede is not alwey mery or blessyd.

And herof sayth Quyntilian that thys drede surmounteth alle other maleurtees
1250 and evylles, for it is maleurté of drede nyght and day. And it is verité that to hym that is doubted of moche peple, so muste he doubte moche. And that lorde is lasse thenne his servauntes that dredyeth his servauntes. And truly hit is a right sure thyng to drede nothyng but God. And somtyme, right hardy men ben constrayned to lyve in drede. Drede causith a man to be besy to kepe the thynges that be
1255 commysed to hym that they perisshe not. But to be to moche hardy and to moche ferdful, bothe two ben vices.

The comyn officers ought to be wyse and wel advysed in suche wise that they take not of the peple ne requyre no more than they ought to have by reson, ne that they take of the sellars ne of the byars no more than the right custume, for they bere
1260 the name of a persone, and therfore ought they to shewe them comune to alle men. And for as moche as the byars and sellars have somtyme moche langage, they ought to have wyth them these vertues, that is to wete pacience and good corage wyth honesté. For they that ben despytous to the comune been otherwhile had in vylayns despite. Therfore, beware that thou have no despyte unto the poure mendycants,
1265 yf thou wylt come and atteyne to thynges soverayn, for the injurye that is doon wythout cause torneth to diffame hym that doth hit.

A jogheler on a tyme behelde Socrates and sayd to hym: "Thou hast the eyen of corumpour of children and art as a traytre." And whan his dysciples herde hym, they wold avengyd theyr maister. But he reprevyd hem by suche sentence sayeng:
1270 "Suffre my felawes, for I am he and suche one as he sayth by the sight of my vysage. But I refrayne and kepe me wel from suche thyng."

This same Socrates hymself was chidde and right foul spoken to of hys wyf, and she imposid to hym many grete injuries wythout nombre. And she was in a place above over his heed. And whan she had brawled ynough, she made her water and
1275 poured hit on his heed. And he answerd to her nothyng agayn, sauf whan he had dryed and wyped his heed, he said he knewe wel that after suche wynde and thondre shold come rayne and watre. And the philosophers blamed hym that he coude not governe two women, that was his wyf and his chaumberer, and shewyd hym that one cokke governed wel fifteen hennes. He answerd to them that he was
1280 so used and acustumed with theyr chidyng that the chidyngis of them ne of

1243 dyscoverd, showed. **1243–44 hevy, cherid, and tryste**, burdened, preoccupied, and sad. **1244 For where**, For wherever. **1249 maleurtees**, misfortunes. **1251 doubted**, feared. **1255 commysed**, entrusted. **1261 byars**, buyers; **langage**, conversation or words. **1263 despytous**, pitiless. **1263 vylayns**, vile. **1264 mendycants**, beggars. **1265 wylt**, wish. **1267 jogheler**, jester; **eyen**, eyes. **1268 corumpour**, corrupter. **1272 chidde**, chided. **1273 imposid to hym**, imputed to him. **1274 brawled**, quarreled; **made her water**, urinated. **1275 agayn**, in return; **sauf**, except. **1278 chaumberer**, chamber maid; **shewyd**, demonstrated to. **1279 cokke**, rooster. **1280 acustumed with**, accustomed to.

straungers dyd hym no greef ne harme: "Gyve thou place to hym that brawleth or chideth, and in suffryng hym thou shalt be his vaynquysshour."

And Cathon saith: "Whan thou lyvest rightfully, retche thee not of the wordes of evyl peple."

1285 And therfore hit is sayd in a comyn proverbe: "He that wel doth retcheth not who seeth hit, and hit is not in our power to lette men to speke."

And Prosper sayth that to good men lacketh no goodnes, ner to evyl men tencions, stryves, and blames.

And pacience is a right noble vertu, as a noble versefier saith that pacience is 1290 a right noble maner to vaynquysshe. For he that suffreth overcometh. And yf thou wylt vaynquysshe and overcome, lerne to suffre.

The peagers, ner they that kepe passages, ought not to take other peage ne passage money but suche as the prynce or the lawe have establisshed, so that they be not more robbours of money than receyvours of peage and passage. And hit 1295 aperteyneth to them to goo out of the perelous weyes and doubteuous for to kepe theyr offyce. And they ought to requyre theyr passage of them that owe to paye hit wythout noyeng and contencion. And they ought not to love the comyn prouffyt so moche that they falle in the hurtyng of theyr conscience, for that shold be a maner of robberye.

1300 And herof saith Ysaye: "Woo to thee that robbest! For thou, thyself, shalt be robbyd."

The gardes or porters of the gates of citees and of the comyn good ought to be good and honeste. And al trouth ought to be in them, and they ought not to take ne withdrawe the goodes of the comyn that they have in kepyng more than 1305 aperteyneth to them for their pencion or fee, so that they that ben made tresorers and kepars ben not named thevys. For who that taketh more than his, he shal never thryve with al, ner shal not enjoye hit longe. For of evyl goten good, the third heyre shal never rejoyse.

And thys suffyseth.

1283 retche, heed. **1286 lette**, prevent. **1292 peagers**, toll takers; **kepe passages**, guard the ways. **1294 peage**, tolls. **1295 perelous**, perilous; **doubteuous**, fearful. **1297 noyeng**, harming or vexing. **1305 pencion**, payment. **1308 heyre**, heir

This eyght chappytre of the third book treteth of ribauldes, players of dyse, and of messagers and currours. **Capitulo eight.**

1310   The ribauldes, players at dyse, and the messagers and currours ought to be sette tofore the rook, for hit apperteyneth to the rook, whiche is vicayr of the kyng to have men covenable for to renne here and there for to enquyre and espye the places and citees that myght be contrarie to the kyng. And thys pawn that representeth this peple ought to be formyd in this maner: he must have the forme of a man that

1315 hath long heeris and black, and holdeth in his ryght hand a litil money, and in his lift hand thre dyse, and aboute hym a corde in stede of a gurdel, and [he] ought to have a boxe ful of lettres.

    And by the first, whiche is money, is understonde they that be fole large and wastours of theyr goodes. And by the second, whiche is the dyse, ben represented

1320 the playes at dyse, ribauldes, and butters. And by the thyrd, whyche is the boxe ful of lettris, ben represented the messagers, currours, and berars of lettres. And ye shal understonde that the rooke, whiche is vycayre of the kyng, whan he seeth tofore hym suche peple as ben fole large and wastours, he is bounden to constitute and ordeygne upon them tutours and curatours to see that they ete not ne waste in

1325 suche maner their goodes ne their heritages, that poverté constrayne hem not to stele. For he that of custume hath had habundaunce of money, and goeth and dispendeth hit folily, and wasteth hit awey, whan he cometh to poverté and hath nought, he must nedes begge and axe his breed, or ellis he must be a theef. For suche maner of peple, yf they have been delycious, they wyl not laboure, for they

1330 have not lernyd hit. And yf they be noble and comen of gentylmen, they be

1310 **ribauldes**, ribald or dissolute characters; **currours**, couriers.   **1312 covenable**, suitable; **enquyre and espye**, seek out and find.   **1315 heeris**, hair.   **1316 gurdel**, belt.   **1318 fole large**, foolishly liberal with money.   **1320 playes**, players; **butters**, betters.   **1321 berars**, bearers.   **1323 bounden**, under obligation; **constitute**, appoint.   **1324 curatours**, guardians.   **1325 heritages**, inheritances.   **1327 dispendeth**, spends.   **1328 axe**, ask for; **breed**, bread.   **1329 delycious**, addicted to indulgence.

ashamyd to axe and begge, and thus must they by force, whan they have wasted theyr owne propre goodes, yf they wyl lyve, they must stele and robbe the goodes of other. And ye shalle understonde that fole large is a ryght evyl vyce. For how wel that she doeth good and prouffyt somtyme to other, yet she doth harme and

1335   dommage to hym that so wasteth.

Cassiodore admonesteth the fole larges to kepe their thynges that by no necessité they falle in poverté and that they be not constrayned to begge ne to stele of other men. For he sayth that hit is gretter subtilté to kepe wel his owne goodes than to fynde straunge thynges, and that it is gretter vertue to kepe that is goten than to

1340   gete and wynne more.

And Claudyan saith in like wyse in his book that hyt is a gretter thynge and better to kepe that is goten than to gete more. And therfor hit is sayd that the poure demaundeth and beggith or he felith. And also hit is said that he that dispendeth more than he hath without stroke, he is smyton to the deth.

1345   There was a noble man named John de Ganazath, whiche was right riche. And this man had but two doughters, whom he maried to two noble men. And whan he had maried them, he loved so wel his sones-in-lawe, theyr husbondes, that in space and successyon of tyme, he departed to them al his goodes temporel. And as longe as he gaf to them, they obeyed hym and were right dyligent to plese and serve

1350   hym.

So hit befel that on a tyme that he had alle gyven in so moche that he had right nought. Than hit happend that they to whom he had gyven his goodes, whiche were wont to be amyable and obeysaunt to hym as longe as he gaf, whan the tyme came that he was poure and knewe that he had nought, they became unkynde,

1355   dysagreable, and dysobeysaunt. And whan the fader sawe that he was deceyvyd by his debonayrté and love of his doughters, he desyred and coveyted sore to eschewe hys poverté.

Atte laste he went to a marcheunt that he knewe of olde tyme and requyrid him to lene to hym ten thousand pound for to paye and rendre agayn wythin thre dayes.

1360   And he lente hit hym. And whan he had brought hit into hys hous, hit happend that hit was a day of a solempne feste, on whiche day he gaf to his doughters and her husbond a right noble dyner. And after dyner he entrid into his chaumbre secretly wyth them, and drewe out of a coffre that he had do make al newe shittyng wyth thre lockes, the money that the marchaunt had lente hym, and poured hit out

1365   upon a tapite that his doughtres and their husbondes myght see hit. And whan he had shewyd hit unto them, he put hit up ageyn and put hit into the cheste, faynyng that hit had been al his. And whan they were departed, he bare the money home to the marchaunt that he had borowed hit of.

1331 by force, necessarily. **1333 fole large**, foolish generosity. **1335 dommage**, damage. **1336 admonesteth**, admonishes. **1339 straunge thynges**, things that belong to others. **1343 felith**, falls; **dispendeth**, dispenses. **1344 stroke**, a blow; **smyton**, smitten. **1348 departed**, gave; **goodes temporel**, worldly goods. **1353 amyable and obeysaunt**, pleasant and obedient. **1356 sore**, sorely; **eschewe**, escape. **1358 requyrid**, requested. **1361 solempne feste**, religious feast. **1362 her husbond**, their husbands. **1363 had do make**, had made; **shittyng**, shutting. **1365 tapite**, tapet or table cover.

1370 And the next day after, his doughters and their husbondes axyd of hym how moche money was in the cheste that was shette wyth thre lockis. And than he fayned and sayd that he had therin twenty-five thousand pounde, whiche he kept for to make his testament and for to leve to his doughters and hem yf they wold bere hem as wel to hym afterward as they did whan they were maried. And than whan they herde that, they were right joyous and glad. And they thought and concluded

1375 to serve hym honourably as wel in clothyng as in mete and drynke, and of alle other thynges necessarye to hym unto hys ende. And after this, whan the ende of hym began to approche, he callyd his doughters and their husbondes, and sayd to hem in this manere: "Ye shalle understonde that the money that is in the cheste shette under thre lockes I wyl leve to you, savyng I wyl that ye geve in my presence,

1380 er I dye whiles I lyve, to the frere prechours an hondred pounde, and to the frere menours an hondred pounde, and to the heremytes of Saynt Austyn fifty pound to the ende that whan I am buryed and put in the erthe, ye may demaunde of them the keyes of the chest where my tresour is inne, whiche keyes they kepe. And I have put on eche keye a bylle and writyng in witnessyng of the thynges above sayd."

1385 And also ye shal understonde that he dyd to be gyven, whiles he lay in his deth bedde, to eche chirche and recluse and to pour peple, a certeyn quantité of money by the handes of his doughter's husbondes, whiche they dyd gladly in hope to have shortly the money that they supposid in the cheste. And whan hit came to the last day that he dyed, he was borne to chirche and his exequye doon and was buried

1390 solempnly. And the seventh day, the servyse worshypfully accomplisshed, they went for to demaunde the keyes of the religyous men that they had kept, whiche were delyverd to them. And than they went and opend the coffre where they supposid the money had ben inne. And there they fond nothyng but a grete clubbe. And on the handlyng was wreton: "I, John of Canazath, make this testament: that he be slayn

1395 wyth thys clubbe that leveth his owne prouffyt and gyveth hit to other, as who sayth hit is no wysedom for a man to gyve his good to his chyldren and kepe none for hymself."

And ye shal understonde that hit is a grete folye to dyspende and waste his good in hope for to recover hit of other, be hit of sone or doughter, or right nygh

1400 kynne. For a man ought to kepe in his hand in dispendyng his owne goodes tofore he see that he dispende other mennys. And he ought not to be holden for a good man that hath litil renomee and spendeth many thynges. And I trowe that suche persones wold gladly make noveltees as for to noye and greve seignories and meve warres and tencions ageynst them that habounde in richessis and goodes, and also

1405 make extorcions, clamours, and tribulaconns agenst their lordes to the ende to

1370 **shette**, shut. 1372–73 **bere hem as wel to hym**, conduct themselves as nicely to him. 1379 **savyng**, except that. 1380 **er I dye**, before I die; **frere prechours**, preaching friars or Dominicans. 1380–81 **frere menours**, minor friars or Franciscans. 1381 **heremytes of Saynt Austyn**, the Augustinians. 1384 **bylle**, a formal document of deed. 1385 **dyd to be gyven**, commanded to be given. 1386 **recluse**, place of seclusion (for those of religious orders). 1389 **exequye**, funeral rites. 1391 **demaunde**, ask for. 1394 **handlyng**, handle. 1399–1400 **nygh kynne**, near relatives. 1403 **make noveltees**, generate news or tidings; **noye and greve**, annoy and vex; **seignories**, feudal lords. 1404 **habounde**, abound. 1405 **clamours**, outcrys.

waste the goodes of the peple, lyke as they have wasted theyres. And suche a wastour of goodes may never be good for the comyn prouffyt.

And ye shal understonde that after these wastours of goodes we saye that the players of dyse and they that use bordellys ben worst of al other. For whan the hete of playeng at the dyse and the covetise of theyr stynkyng lecherye hath brought hem to poverté, hit foloweth by force that they must ben thevys and robbours. And also dronkenshyp, glotenye, and alle maner of evyls folowe them and myschyef. And they folowe gladly the companyes of knyghtes and of noble men whan they goon unto the warre or batáylles. And they coveyte not so moche the victorye as they doo the robberye. And they doo moche harme as they goo, and they brynge lityl gayn or wynnyng.

Wherof hit happend on a tyme that Saynt Bernard rode on an hors about the contrey and mette wyth an hasardour, or dyse player, which sayd to hym: "Thou, Goddes man, wylt thou playe at dyse with me, thyn hors agenst my sowle?"

To whom Saint Bernard answerd: "Yf thou wylt oblyge thy sowle to me agenst my hors, I wyl alyght doun and playe wyth thee. And yf thou have mo poyntes than I on thre dyse, I promyse thee thou shalt have myn hors."

And thenne he was glad, and anone caste thre dyse. And on eche dyse was a sise, whiche made eighteen poyntes. And anone he took the hors by the brydel, as he that was seure that he had wonne, and sayd that the hors was his. And than Saynt Bernard sayd: "Abyde my sone, for there be mo poyntes on the dyse than eighteen." And than he cast the dyse in suche wyse that one of the three dyse clefte a sondre in the myddes. And on that one parte was six, and on that other side an aas, and eche of that other was a sise. And than Saynt Bernard sayd that he had wonne his sowle for as moche as he had cast on thre dyse nineteen poyntes. And than whan this player sawe and aperceyvyd thys myracle, he gaf his sowle to Saynt Bernard and became a monke and finysshed his lyf in good werkys.

The currours and berars of lettres ought hastely and spedely doo her vyage that is commaunded hem without taryeng. For theyr taryeng myght noye and greve them that sende hem forth, or ellis them to whom they be sent to, and torne hem to right grete dommage or vylonye, for whiche cause every noble man ought wel to take hede to whom he delyver his lettres and his maundementis.

And otherwhiles suche peple ben joghelers and dronklewe, and goon out of their weye for to see abbayes and noble men for to have avauntage. And hit happeth ofte tymes that whan suche messagers or currours ben enpesshid by ony taryeng, that other currours bere letters contrarye to hys and come tofore hym, of whiche thynges ofte tymes cometh many thynges discovenable of losse of frendes, of castellys, and of lande and many other thynges as in the feet of marchaundyses. And

---

1409 bordellys, prostitutes. **1420 oblyge**, bet or pledge. **1421 alyght**, dismount. **1424 sise**, six. **1425 seure**, sure. **1427–28 clefte a sondre**, broke apart. **1429 aas**, an ace or the side of a die with one point. **1433 spedely**, expeditously; **vyage**, voyage. **1434 taryeng**, delay. **1436 dommage**, harm. **1437 maundementis**, commands. **1438 otherwhiles**, sometimes; **joghelers and dronklewe**, jesters and given to drunkenness. **1440 enpesshid**, impeded. **1442 discovenable**, unsuitable. **1443 feet of marchaundyses**, mercantile transactions.

otherwhile hit happeth that a prynce, for the faulte of suche messangers, leseth to
1445   have victorye upon his enemyes.

And also, there be somme that, whan they come in a cité where they have not
ben tofore, they ben more besy to visite the cyté and the noble men that dwelle
therin than they ben to do theyr voyage, whiche thyng they ought not to do, but yf
they had special charge of them that sent hem forth so to doo. And also whan they
1450   be sent forth of ony lordes or marchauntes, they ought to be wel ware that they
charge hem not wyth over moche mete on mornynges ne wyth to moche wyne on
evenynges, wherby her sinewes and vaynes myght be grevyd that they must for
faute of good rewle tarye. But they ought to goo and come hastely for to reporte
to their maysters answers as hit aperteyneth.
1455   And thise suffysen of the thynges above sayd.

1444 leseth, fails. **1448 but yf**, unless. **1450 wel ware**, well aware. **1452 grevyd**, taxed.
1452–53 for faute of good rewle tarye, on account of their lack of self-control. **1453**
hastely, quickly.

BOOK FOUR

The fourth tractate and the last: of the progressyon and draughtes of the forsayd playe of the chesse.

The first chappitre of the fourth tractate of the chesse borde, in genere how it is maad.

Capitulo primo.

We have devysed above the thynges that apperteyne unto the formes of the chesse men and of their offices that is to wete as wel of noble men as of the comyn peple. Than hit aperteyneth that we shold devyse shortly how they yssue and goon out of the places where they be sette. And first we ought to speke of the forme and of the facion of the chequer, after that hit representeth and was made after. For hit was made after the forme of the cyté of Babyloyne, in the whiche this same playe was founden, as hit is sayd afore.

5

And ye shal understonde that ye ought to considere here in foure thynges. The first is wherfore that sixty-four poyntes been sette in the eschequer, whyche ben al square. The second is wherfore the bordeure about is hygher than the squarenes of the poyntes. The thyrd is wherfore the comyn peple ben sette tofore the nobles. The fourth is wherfore the nobles and the peple been sette in theyr propre places.

10

Title **draughtes**, moves; **in genere**, universally. **2 to wete**, to say. **3 yssue**, first advance. **5 facion**, fashion or shape; **chequer**, chessboard. **9 wherfore**, to what purpose; **poyntes**, spaces. **10 bordeure**, border; **squarenes**, squareness (i.e., the square parts).

Ther ben as many poyntes in the eschequer voyde as fulle. And ye shal first understonde wherfore that there ben sixty-four poyntes in the eschequyer. For as the blessyd Saynt Jherome sayth, the cité of Babylone was right grete and was maad al square. And in every quarter was sixteen myle by nombre and mesure, the whiche nombre four tymes tolde was sixty-four myles. After the maner of Lombardye, they be callyd myles, and in Fraunce leukes, and in Englond they be callyd myles also. And for to represente the mesure of this cyté, in whiche this playe or game was founden, the philosopher that fonde hit first ordeyned a tablier conteynyng sixty-four poyntes square, the whiche ben comprised wyth in the bordeur of the tablyer. There ben thirty-two on that one side and thirty-two on that other side, whiche ben ordeygned for the beaulté of the playe and for to shewe the maner and drawyng of the chesse, as hit shal appere in the chappytres folowyng.

And as to the second, wherfore the bordeure of the eschequyer is hygher than the table wyth in, hit is to be understonde that the bordeur about representeth the walle of the cyté, whyche is right hygh. And therfore made the philosopher the bordeur more hygh than the tablier. And as the blessyd Saynt Jherome sayth, upon the prophesie of Ysaye, that is to wete upon a mounteyn of obscureté, whiche wordes were sayd of Babylone, whiche standeth in Caldee, and nothyng of that Babylone that stondeth in Egypt. For it is so that Babilone, whiche stondeth in Caldee, was sette in a right grete playn, and had so hygh walles that by the heyght of them was contynuel derknes envyronned and obscureté that none erthly man myght beholde and see the ende of the highnes of the walle, and therfore Ysaye callyd hit "The Montaigne Obscure." And Saynt Jherome saith that the mesure of the heyght of this walle was thre thousand paas, whiche extendeth unto the lengthe of thre myle Lombardes. Hit is to wete that Lombarde mylis and Englissh myles ben of one lengthe. And in one of the corners of thys cyté was made a tour treangle as a shelde, wherof the heyght extended unto the lengthe of [seven] thousand paas, whiche is seven myle Englissh. And thys toure was called the tour of Babel. The walles about the toure made a woman whos name was Semyramis, as sayth Virgilius.

As to the thyrd, wherfore the comyn peple ben sette tofore the nobles in the felde of the batayl in one renge: first for as moche as they ben necessarye to al nobles. For the rook, whiche stondeth on the right side and is vycayr of the kyng, what may he doo yf the labourer were not sette tofore hym and laboured to mynystre to hym suche temporel thynges as be necessarie for hym? And what may the knyght do yf he ne had tofore hym the smyth for to forge his armours, sadellys, axys, and speres, and suche thynges as aperteyneth to hym? And what is a knyght worth wythout hors and armes? Certeynly nothyng more than one of the peple or lasse, peraventure. And in what maner shold the nobles lyve yf no man made cloth and bought and solde marchandyse? And what shold kynges and quenes and the other lordes doo yf they had no physiciens ne surgyens? Than I say that the peple

---

13 **voyde**, empty.   17 **Lombardye**, the Lombard region in northern Italy.   18 **leukes**, leagues.   20 **ordeyned**, arranged; **tablier**, chessboard.   23 **drawyng**, motion.   29 **Ysaye**, Isaiah; **wete**, know; **obscureté**, obscurity.   30 **Caldee**, Chaldea.   31 **For it is so**, For it is the case.   35 **Montaigne**, Mountain.   36 **paas**, paces (each roughly equal to a step of a flight of stairs).   38 **tour treangle**, triangular tower.   43 **renge**, row.   47–48 **sadellys, axys, and speres**, saddles, axes, and spears.   50 **peraventure**, perchance.

ben the glorye of the crowne and susteyne the lyf of the nobles. And therfore thou
that art a lord or a noble man or knyght, despyse not the comyn people, for as
55   moche as they ben sette tofore thee in the playe.

The second cause is why the peple ben sette tofore the nobles and have the
table voyde tofore them is because they begynne the bataylle. They ought to take
hede and entende to do theyr offyces and theyr craftes, in suche wyse that they suffre
the noble men to governe the cytees and to counceylle and make ordenaunces of
60   the peple and of the bataylle. How shold a labourer, a plow man, or a crafty man
counceyl and make ordenaunce of suche thynges as he never lerned, and wote ne
knoweth the mater upon what thyng the counceyl ought to be taken? Certes the
comyn peple ought not to entende to none other thyng but for to do their servyce
and the offyce whiche is covenable unto hem. And hit apperteyneth not to hem to
65   be of counceyls, ne at the advocacions, ne to menace, ne to threte no man. For ofte
tymes by menaces and by force, good counceyl is destroubled. And where good
counceyl faylleth, there ofte tymes the cytees ben betrayed and destroyed.

And Plato sayth that the comyn thynges and the cytees ben blessyd whan they
ben governed by wyse men, or whan the governours studye in wysedom. And so hit
70   aperteyneth to the comyn to lerne to uttre the maters and the maner of procuracion
tofore they be counceyllours. For hyt happeth often tymes that he that makyth hym
wyser that he understandeth is made more foole than he is.

And the fourth cause wherfore that there ben in tablier as many poyntes voyde
as been fulle, hit is to wete for that they, whatever they be that have peple to governe,
75   ought to enforce to have citees and castellys and possessyons for to sette his peple
therin, and for to laboure and do their ocupacion. For to have the name of a kyng
wythout a royame is a name voyde and honour without prouffyt. And al noblesse
without good maners, and wythout suche thynges as noblesse may be maynteyned,
ought better be callyd folye than noblesse. And shameful poverté is the more grevous
80   whan hyt cometh by nature of an hygh and noble byrth or hous. For no man gladly
wyl repreve a poure man of the comyn peple, but every man hath in despyte a noble
man that is poure, yf he have not in hym good maners and vertuous, by whiche his
poverté is forgoten. And truly, a royame without habundaunce of goodes by whyche
hyt may be governed and prospere may better be callyd a latrocynye or a nest of
85   thevys than a royame.

Alas, what habundaunce was somme tymes in the royames, and what prosperité
in whiche was justyce and every man in his offyce contente! How stood the cytees
that tyme in worship and renome! How was renomed the noble royame of Englond!
Alle the world dradde hit and spake worshyp of hit. How hit now standeth and in
90   what habundaunce I reporte me to them that knowe hit. Yf there ben thevys wyth
in the royame or on the see, they knowe that laboure in the royame and sayle on
the see. I wote wel the fame is grete therof. I praye God save that noble royame
and sende good, trewe, and polletique counceyllours to the governours of the

---

59 **counceylle**, rule or direct; **ordenaunces of**, decrees for. **61–62 wote ne knoweth**, doesn't
understand or know. **63 servyce**, jobs. **64 covenable**, appropriate. **65 advocacions**, the
callings of people to council. **66 destroubled**, thwarted. **70 procuracion**, management. **77
royame**, kingdom. **79 grevous**, grievous. **84 latrocynye**, band of robbers. **86 somme
tymes**, formerly. **88 renome**, renown **90 reporte me**, appeal. **92 wote**, believe.

95   same. And noblesse of lignage wythout puyssaunce and myght is but vanyté and
dyspyte.

And hit is so, as we have sayd tofore, that the schequer whiche the phylosopher
ordeyned represented and figured the said cité of Babylone. And in like wyse may
hit figure a royame and signefye alle the world. And yf men regarde and take heed
unto the poyntes unto the myddes of every quadrante, and so to double every
100   quadrant to other, the myles of this cité alwey doublyng unto the nombre of sixty-
four, the nombre of the same shold surmounte al the world. And not onely the
world, but many worldes by the doublyng of myles, whiche doublyng so as afore is
sayd shold surmounte all thynges.

And thus endeth the first chappytre of the fourth booke.

*The second chappitre of the fourth tractate treteth of the draught of the kyng and how he
mevyth in the chequer.*   **Capitulo secundo.**

105   We ought to knowe that in thys world the kynges seygnourie and reygne eche
in his royame. And in this play we ought to knowe by the nature of hit how the kyng
meveth hym and yssueth out of his place. For ye shal understonde that he is sette
in the fourth quadrante or poynt of the eschequer. And whan he is black, he
standeth in the whyt, and the knyght on his right side in whyt, and the alphyn and
110   the rook in black. And on the lift side the four holden the places apposite. And the
reason may be suche: for bycause that the knyghtes been the glorie and the crowne
of the kyng, they ensiewe in semblable residence that they do whan they be sette
semblaby on the right side of the kyng and on the lift side of the quene. And for
as moche as the rook on the right side is vicayr of the kyng, he accompanyeth the

---

96 schequer, chessboard.   **107 meveth hym,** moves himself; **yssueth out,** advances out.
109 alphyn, bishop or judge.   **110 apposite,** opposite.   **112 ensiewe,** ensue or follow;
semblable, similar.   **114 vicayr,** representative.

115   quene in semblable siege that the alphyn doth, whiche is juge of the kyng. And in
       like wyse, the lift rook and the lift alphyn accompanye the kyng in semblable siege.
            In suche wyse as they ben sette about the kyng in bothe sides with the quene in
       maner of a crowne that they may seurely kepe the royame that reluyseth and
       shyneth in the kyng and in the quene. In suche wyse as they may conferme and
120   diffende hym in their sieges and in theyr places, and the more hastely renne upon
       his enemyes. And for as moche as the juge, the knyght, and the vicayr kepe and
       garnysshe the kyng on that one side, they that been sette on the other side kepe
       the quene, and thus kepe they al the strength and fermete of the royame, and
       semblably otherwhile for to ordeigne the thynges that aperteyne to the counceyl
125   and to the besoyngue of the royame. For yf eche man shold entende to his owne
       proper thynges, and that they deffendyd not ner toke hede unto the thynges that
       apperteynen to the kynge, to the comyn, and to the royame, the royame shold
       anone be devyded in parties. And thus myght the juge reygne, and the name of the
       dygnyté ryall shold be loste.
130   And trewly, for as moche as the kynge holdeth the dygnyté above alle other and
       the seignorye royall, therfore hit apperteyneth not that he absente hym long, ne
       wythdrawe hym ferre by space of tyme from the maister siege of his royame. For
       whan he wyl meve hym, he ought not to passe at the first draught the nombre of
       three poyntes. And whan he begynneth thus to meve from his whyt poynt, he hath
135   the nature of the rookes of the right side and of the lift for to goo black or whyt.
       And also he may goo unto the whyt poynt where the gardes of the cyté ben sette.
       And in this poynt he hath the nature of a knyght. And thise two maners of mevyng
       aperteyneth otherwhile to the quene. And for as moche as the kyng and the quene
       that be conjoyned togeder by mariage ben one thyng as one flesshe and blood,
140   therfore may the kyng meve on the lift side of his propre poynt also wel as he were
       sette in the place of the quene, whiche is black, and whan he goeth right, in maner
       of the rook onely. And hit happen that the adversary be not coverd in ony poynte
       in the second ligne, the kyng may not passe from his black poynt unto the thyrd
       ligne. And thus he sortiseth the nature of the rook on the right side and lift side
145   unto the place of the knyghtes, and for to goo right tofore into the whyt poynt
       tofore the marchaunt. And the kyng also sortist the nature of the knyghtes whan
       he goeth on the right side in two maners. For he may put hym in the voyde space
       tofore the phisicien and in the black space tofore the taverner. And on the other
       side he goeth into other two places in like wyse, that is tofore the smyth and the
150   notarye. And thus as in goyng out first into four poyntes, he sorteth the nature of
       knyghtes. And also, the kyng sortyseth the nature of the alphyns at hys fyrst yssue
       into two places. And he may goo on boothe sydes unto the whyte place voyde, that
       one tofore the smyth on that one side and that other tofore the taverner on that
       other side.

115 **siege**, seat or place. 118 **seurely**, surely; **reluyseth**, shines forth. 119–20 **conferme
and diffende**, add strength to and defend. 120 **renne upon**, attack. 122 **garnysshe**,
garrison. 123 **fermete**, integrity. 124 **semblably otherwhile**, similarly sometimes. 125
besoyngue, business. 129 **ryall**, royal. 132 **ferre**, far. 134 **poyntes**, spaces. 139 **conjoyned
togeder**, conjoined together. 140 **also wel as**, in the same way as. 142 **And**, If; **coverd**,
defended against. 144 **sortiseth**, acquires. 148 **taverner**, tavern keeper.

155   Al these yssues hath the kyng out of his propre place of his owne vertu whan he
        begynneth to meve. But whan he is ones mevyd fro his propre place, he may not
        meve but into one space or poynt, and so from one to another. And than he
        sortiseth the nature of the comyn peple, and thus by good right he hath in hymself
        the nature of al. For al the vertue that is in the membris comyth of the heed and
160   al mevyng of the body, the begynnyng, and lyf cometh from the herte. And al the
        dygnyté that the subgettis have by execusion and continuel apparence of theyr
        mevyng and yssue, the kyng deteyneth hit, and is attributed to hym the victorye of
        the knyghtes, the prudence of the juges, the auctorité of the vycayrs or legates, the
        contynence of the quene, the concorde and unyté of the people. So ben alle thise
165   thynges ascribed unto the honour and worshyp of the kyng in his yssue, whan he
        mevyth first.
            The third ligne tofore the peple he never excedyth, for in the third nombre alle
        maner of states begynne to meve. For the trynary nombre conteyneth thre parties,
        whyche make a perfect nombre. For a trynarye nombre hath one, two, three,
170   whiche joyned togider maketh six, which is the first parfit nombre, and signefieth
        in this place six persones named that constitute the perfeccion of a royame, that
        is to wete the kyng, the quene, juges, knyghtes, vicairs or legates, and the comyn
        peple. And therfore the kyng ought to begynne in his first mevyng of three poyntes
        that he shewe perfeccion of lyf as wel in hymself as in other.
175   After the kyng begynneth to meve, he may lede with hym the quene, after the
        maner of his issue. For why the quene foloweth unto two angularye places after the
        maner of the alphyn, and to a place indyrecte in the maner of a rook into the
        blacke poynt tofore the phisicien, herin is signefyed that the women may not meve
        nether make vowes of pylgremage ner of viage without the wylle of theyr
180   husbondes. For yf a woman had avowed onythyng, her husbond lyvyng and agayn
        sayeng, she may not yelde ner accomplisshe her vowe. Yf the husbond wyl goo ony
        where, he may wel goo wythout her. And yf so be that the husbond wyl have her
        wyth hym, she is bounden to folowe hym. And by reson, for a man is the heed of
        a woman and not econverso. For as to suche thynges as longe to patrymonye, they
185   ben like. But the man hath power over her body, and so hath not the woman over
        his. And therfore, whan the kyng begynneth to meve, the quene may folowe, and
        not alwey whan she mevyth it is no nede the kyng to meve.
            For why: four [of] the first lignes be wyth in the lymytes and space of the royame,
        and unto the thyrd poynt the kynge may meve at his first mevyng out of his propre
190   place. And whan he passyth the fourth ligne, he goeth out of his royame. And yf he
        passe one poynt, lete hym bewaar! For the persone of a kyng is acounted more than
        a thousand of other. For whan he exposith hym unto the parilles of bataylle, hit is
        necessarye that he goo attemporatly and slily. For yf he be taken or deed, or ellys

---

161 execusion, the act of doing or moving.   **162 deteyneth**, holds or restrains.   **164
contynence**, self-restraint.   **167–68 alle maner of states**, (i.e., all the pieces).   **168 trynary**,
ternary.   **174 perfeccion**, perfection.   **176 angularye**, diagonal.   **179 nether . . . ner**, neither
. . . nor; **viage**, voyage.   **181 yelde ner accomplisshe**, break or hold.   **184 econverso**,
conversely; **longe to**, belong to.   **188 For why**, The reason for this is; **lignes**, lines.   **191
acounted more**, worth more.   **193 attemporatly and slily**, with moderation and stealthily.

inclusid and shette up, alle the strengthes of al other faylle, and al is finysshed and
195   lost. And therfore he hath nede to goo and meve wysely.

And also, therfore, he may not meve but one poynt after hys first mevyng, but
where that ever he goo, foreward or bacward, or on that one side or on that other,
or ellis cornerwyse, he may never approche his adversarye the kyng nerrer than in
the thyrd poynt. And therfore, the kynges in bataylle ought never to approche one
200   nygh that other. And also, whan the kyng hath goon so ferre that al hys men be
lost, than he is sole, and than he may not endure long whan he is brought to that
extremyté. And also, he ought to take hede that he stonde not so that a knyght or
another sayth "chek rook." Than the kyng loseth the rook. That kynge is not wel
fortunat that lesith hym to whom his auctorité delegate aperteyneth, who may do
205   the nedes of the royame yf he be pryvyd, taken, or deed, that was provysour of al
the royame. He shal bere a sacke on his heed that is shette in a cité, and al they
that were therin ben taken in captyvyté and shette up.

The third chappitre of the fourth book: of the quene and how she yssueth out of her place.
Capitulo tercio.

Whan the quene, whiche is accompanyed unto the kyng, begynneth to meve
from her propre place, she goeth in double manere, that is to wete as an alphyn.
210   Whan she is black, she may goo on the right side and come into the poynt tofore

---

194 **inclusid and shette up**, captured. 197 **where that ever he goo**, wherever he goes. 198
cornerwyse, diagonally; **nerrer**, nearer. 203 **"chek rook,"** the call of check at the same
time that one of the rooks is threatened with capture. 204 **lesith**, loses; **auctorité delegate**,
delegated authority. 205 **pryvyd**, taken away or captured; **provysour**, the manager or
head. 206 **bere a sacke on his heed** (i.e., all the pieces will be tossed back in a bag once the
king is mated and the game ends). *Title* **yssueth**, issues. 209 **wete**, understand; **alphyn**,
judge or chess bishop.

the notarye, and on the lift side in the black poynt and come tofore the gardes of the cyté. And hit is to wete that she sortiseth in herself the nature in three maners: first on the right side tofore the alphyn, secondly on the lift side where the knyght is, and thirdly indirectly unto the black poynt tofore the phisicien.

215   And the reason why is for as moche as she hath in herself by grace the auctorité that the rookes have by commyscion. For she may gyve and graunte many thynges to her subgettis graciously. And thus also ought she to have parfyt wysedom as the alphyns have, whiche ben juges, as hit sayd above in the chappytre of the quene. And she hath not the nature of knyghtes, and hit is not fittyng ne covenable thyng 220 for a woman to goo to bataylle for the fragylité and feblenes of her. And therfore holdeth she not the waye in her draught as the knyghtes doon. And whan she is mevyd ones out of her place, she may not goo but fro one poynte to another, and yet covertly, whether hit be forwarde or bacward, takyng or to be taken.

    And here may be axyd why the quene goeth to the bataylle wyth the kyng. 225 Certeynly, it is for the solace of hym and ostencion of love. And also, the peple desire to have successyon of the kyng. And therfore the Tartaris have their wyves into the felde with hem. Yet hit is not good that men have theyr wyves wyth hem, but that they abyde in the cytees or wythin theyr owne termys. For whan they been out of theyr cytees and lymytes, they ben not sure but holden suspecte. They shold 230 be shamefast and holde al men suspect.

    For Dyna, Jacob's doughter, as longe as she was in the hows of her brethern, she kept her vyrgynyté. But assone as she wente for to see the straunge regyons, anone she was corupt and defowled of the sone of Sichem.

    Seneka sayth that the women that have evyl vysages ben gladly not chaste, but 235 theyr corage desyreth gladly the companye of men.

    And Solinus sayth that no bestys femeles desire to be touched of their males whan they have conceyvyd, except woman whiche ought to be a beste resonable, and in this caas she lesith her rayson. And Sidrac witnessith the same.

    And therfore, in the olde lawe the faders had dyverse wyves and ancellis to the 240 ende whan one was with childe, they myght take another.

    They ought to have the vysage enclyned for to eschewe the sight of the men, that by the sight they be not mevyd with incontynence and dyffame of other.

    And Ovyde sayth that there ben somme that, how wel that they eschewe the dede, yet have they grete joye when they be prayed. And therfore ought the good 245 women fle the curiositees and places where they myght falle in blame and noyse of the peple.

---

211 notarye, personal secretary or clerk. **212 sortiseth,** acquires. **216 commyscion,** commission. **219 covenable,** suitable. **224 axyd,** asked. **225 ostencion,** manifestation or display. **226 Tartaris,** Tartars or inhabitants of Central Asia. **229 holden,** held. **235 corage,** disposition. **236 bestys femeles,** female animals. **238 lesith,** loses. **239 ancellis,** female servants or concubines. **242 incontynence,** lack of self-restraint; **dyffame,** disfame. **243 how wel,** however well. **244 prayed,** sexually solicited. **245 fle,** flee.

The fourth chappytre of the fourth book: of the issuyng of the alphyn.   **Capitulo quarto.**

The manere and nature of the draught of the alphyn is suche that he that is black in his propre siege is sette on the right side of the kyng and he that is whyt is sette on the lift side, and ben callyd and named "black" and "whyt," but for no
250 cause that they be so in substaunce of her propre colour, but for the colour of the places in whiche they ben sette. And alwey be they black or whyt whan they ben sette in theyr places.

The alphyn on the right side goyng out of his place to the right sydeward cometh tofore the labourer. And hit is reason that the juge ought to deffende and
255 kepe the labourers and possessyons whiche ben in his jurisdyccion by al right and lawe. And also, he may goo on the lift side to the voyde place tofore the phisicien. For like as the physiciens have the charge to hele the infirmytees of a man, in like wise have the juges charge to appese alle stryves and contencions, and reduse unto unyté, and to punysshe and correcte causes crymynels.

260 The lift alphyn hath also two wayes fro his owne place, one toward the right side unto the black space voyde tofore the marchaunt, for the marchauntes nede ofte tymes counceyl and been in debate of questyons whiche must nedes be determyned by the juges, and that other yssue is unto the place tofore the rybauldes. And that is bycause that ofte tymes among them falle noyses, dyscencions, thefte, and
265 manslaughter, wherfore they ought to be punysshed by the juges.

And ye shal understonde that the alphyn goeth alwey cornerwyse fro the thyrd poynt to the thyrd poynt, kepyng alwey his owne siege. For yf he be black, he goeth alwey black. And yf he be whyt, he goeth alwey whyte. The yssue or goyng cornerly or angularly signefyeth cautele or subtilyté, whiche juges ought to have. The thre
270 poyntes betoken thre thynges that the juge ought to attende. A juge ought to

---

248 siege, seat or place.   **258 stryves**, discords.   **258–59 reduse unto unyté**, bring them back to one accord.   **259 causes crymynels**, criminal cases.   **263 rybauldes**, ribald or dissolute characters.   **264 noyses**, troubles; **dyscencions**, disagreements.   **269 cautele**, craftiness; **subtilyté**, shrewdness.

further rightful and trewe causes. Secondly, he ought to geve trewe counceyl. And thyrdly, he ought to geve and juge rightful sentences after the alegeaunces, and never to goo fro the rightwysnes of the lawe.

275 And it is to wete that the alphyn goeth in six draughtes al the tablier rounde about, and that he cometh agayn into his owne place. And how be hit that al reason and good perfeccion shold be in a kyng, yet ought hit also specially be in them that ben counceyllours of the kyng and the quene. And the kyng ought not to do onythyng doubtouse til he have axyd counceyl of his juges and of the sages of the royame. And therfore ought the juge to be parfaytly wyse and sage as wel in science 280 as in good maners. And that is signefyed whan they meve from thre poyntes into thre. For the sixte nombre by whiche they goo al the eschequer and brynge hem agayn into her propre place, in suche wyse that the ende of her moevyng is conjoyned agayn to the begynnyng of the place fro whens they departed. And therfore hit is callyd a parfayt moevyng.

The fifthe chappytre of the fourth tractate: of the mevyng of the knyghtes. **Capitulo quinto.**

285 After the issue of the alphyns we shal devyse to you the yssue and the moevyng of the knyghtes. And we say that the knyght on the right side is whyt and on the lift side black. And the yssue and moevyng of hem bothe is in one maner, whan so is that the knyght on the right side is whyt, the lift knyght is black. The moevyng of hem is suche: that the whyt may goo into the space of the alphyn as hyt apperyth 290 of the knyght on the ryght syde that is whyt, and hath thre yssues from his propre

---

272 sentences, verdicts; **alegeaunces**, duties (to the law).   **273 rightwysnes**, rule.   **274 draughtes**, moves; **tablier**, chessboard.   **278 doubtouse**, uncertain.   **281 goo al the eschequer**, complete the circuit of the board; **hem**, themselves. **283 conjoyned**, conjoined. *Title* **mevyng**, moves.   **285 alphyns**, judges or chess bishops; **devyse**, explain.   **287–88 whan so is that**, although.   **289 apperyth**, is expected.

place, one on his right side in the place tofore the labourer. And hit is wel reson that whan the labourer and husbond man hath laboured the feldes, the knyghtes ought to kepe them to the entente that they have vitailles for themself and theyr horses.

295   The second yssue is that he may meve hym unto the black space tofore the notarye or draper, for he is bounden to deffende and kepe them that make hys vestementes and covertours necessarye unto hys body.

     The thyrd yssue is that he may goo on the lift side into the place tofore the marchaunt whiche is sette tofore the kyng, the whiche is black. And the reson is for 300 as moche as he ought and is holden to deffende the kyng, as wel as his owne persone, whan he passyth the first draught, he may goo four weyes. And whan he is in the myddes of the tablier, he may goo into eight places sondry, to whiche he may renne. And in like wyse may the lift knyght goo, whiche is black, and goeth out of his place into whyt. And in that maner goeth the knyght fightyng by his myght, 305 and groweth and multeplyeth in his poyntes. And ofte tymes by them the felde is wonne or lost.

     A knyghte's vertue and myght is not knowen but by his fightyng. And in his fightyng he doeth moche harme, for as moche as his myght extendeth into so many poyntes, they ben in many parellis in theyr fightyng. And whan they escape, 310 they have the honour of the game. And thus is hit of every man the more vayllyant and the more honoured, and he that meketh hymself ofte tymes shyneth clerest.

---

292 husbond man, one who practices husbandry or a farmer. **293 to the entente**, for the purpose; **vitailles**, food or provisions. **296 notarye or draper**, clerk or dealers in cloth. **297 vestementes and covertours**, clothes and coverings (either for beds or in the sense of garments). **302 myddes**, middle; **tablier**, chessboard; **sondry**, individually or separately. **303 renne**, run. **305 and groweth and multeplyeth in his poyntes** (i.e., after the first move, the knight increases the spaces to which he is able to move). **309 parellis**, risks. **311 he that meketh hymself**, he who makes himself humble.

The sixte chappytre of the fourth tractate treteth of the yssue of the rookes and of her progressyon.   **Capitulo sexto.**

        The moevyng and yssue of the rookes, whiche ben vycayrs of the kynge, is
        suche: that the right rook is black and the lift rook is whyt. And whan the chesse
        ben sette, as wel the nobles as the comyn peple first in theyr propre places, the
315   rookes by theyr propre vertu have no waye to yssue but yf hit be maad to them by
        the nobles or comyn peple. For they been enclosid in theyr propre sieges. And the
        reson why is suche: that for as moche as they ben vycayrs, lieuetenauntes, or
        commyssyoners of the kyng, theyr auctorité is of none effect tofore they yssue out.
        And that they have begonne to enhaunce their offyce, for as longe as they be wythin
320   the palays of the kyng, so longe may they not use ne execute theyr commyssyon.
        But anone as they yssue they may use theyr auctorité.
        And ye shal understonde that theyr auctorité is grete, for they represente the
        persone of the kyng. And therfore, where the tablier is voyde, they may renne alle
        the tablier, in lyke wyse as they goon thrugh the royame. And they may goo as wel
325   whyt as black, as wel on the right side and lifte, as foreward and bacward. And as fer
        may they renne as they fynde the tablier voyde, whether hit be of his adversaries
        as of his owen felawshyp. And whan the rook is in the myddel of the tablier, he may
        goo whiche way he wyl into four right lignes on every syde. And it is to wete that
        he may in no wyse goo cornerwyse, but alwey right forth, goyng and comyng as
330   afore is sayd, wherfore al the subgettis of the kyng, as wel good as evyl, ought to
        knowe by theyr moevyng that the auctorité of the vycayrs and commyssyoners
        ought to be veray trewe, rightwys, and juste. And ye shal understande that they ben
        stronge and vertuous in bataylle. For the two rookes onely may vaynquysshe a kyng,
        theyr adversarye, and take hym, and take from hym his lyf and his royame.

        312 vycayrs, representatives. **314 propre**, own. **316 sieges**, places. **318 commyssyoners**,
        commissioners. **325 fer**, far. **328 it is to wete**, this is to say. **329 cornerwyse**, diagonally.
        332 rightwys, forthright. **333 onely**, alone.

335   And this was doon whan Cirus, kyng of Perse, and Darius, kyng of Medes, slewe Balthazar and took his royame from hym, whiche was nevewe to Evylmoradach under whom thys game was founden.

The seventh chappytre of the fourth book: of the yssue of the comyn peple.

Capitulo septimo.

One yssue and one moevyng apperteyneth unto all the comyn peple. For they may goo fro the poynt they stande in at the first mevyng unto the third poynt ryght
340 forth tofore them. And whan they have so doon, they may afterward meve nomore but fro one poynt right forth into another. And they may never retorne bacward. And thus, goyng forth fro poynt to poynt, they may gete by vertue and strengthe that thynge that the other nobles fynde by dygnyté. And yf the knyghtes and other nobles helpe hem, that they come to the ferthest ligne tofore them where theyr
345 adversaryes were sette, they acquyre the dignyté that the quene hath graunted to her by grace. For yf ony of them may come to thys sayd ligne, yf he be whyt as labourer, draper, phisicien, or kepar of the cité been, they reteyne suche dignyté as the quene hath, for they have goten hit. And than retornyng agayn homeward, they may go like as it is sayd in the chappitre of the quene. And yf ony of the
350 pawnes that be black, as the smyth, the marchaunt, the taverner, and ribaulde, may come without dommage into the same utterest ligne, he shal gete by his vertu the dygnyté of the black quene.

    And ye shal understonde, whan thyse comune peple meve right forth in her ligne and fynde ony noble persone or of the peple of their adversaries sette in the
355 poynt on ony side tofore hym, in that corner poynte he may take his adversarye,

343 **dygnyté**, nobility. 344 **that**, so that; **ferthest ligne**, farthest row. 348 **have goten**, have earned. 350 **smyth**, blacksmith; **taverner**, tavern keeper; **ribaulde**, ribald. 351 **dommage**, harm; **utterest**, farthest. 354–55 **in the poynt on ony side tofore hym**, in any diagonal square in front of him.

whether hit be on the right side or on the lift. And the cause is that the adversaries ben suspecious that the comyn peple lye in a wayte to robbe her goodes or to take her persones whan they go upward right forth. And therfore he may take in the right angle tofore hym one of his adversaryes, as he had espied his persone, and

360 in the right angle as robber of his goodes. And whether hit be goyng forward, or retornyng fro black to whyt, or whyt to black, the pawne must alwey goo in his right ligne, and alwey take in the corner that he fyndeth in his waye. But he may not goo on neyther side til he hath been in the fardest ligne of the eschequer and that he hath taken the nature of the draughtes of the quene. And than he is a "fiers." And

365 than he may goo on al sides cornerwyse fro poynt to poynt onely as the quene, both fightyng and takyng whom he fyndeth in his waye. And whan he is thus comen unto the place where the nobles, his adversaries, were sette, he shal be made "whit fiers" and "black fiers" after the poynte that he is in. And there taketh he the dygnyté of the quene.

370 And alle these thynges may appere to them that beholden the playe of the chesse. And ye shal understonde that no noble man ought to have despyte of the comyn peple. For hit hath been ofte tymes seen that by their vertu and wytte, dyverce of them have comen to right hygh and grete astate as poopes, bysshops, emperours, and kynges, as we have in the historye of Davyd, that was made kyng

375 of a shepeherd and one of the comyn peple and of many other. And in lyke wise we rede of the contrarye, that many noble men have been brought to myserye by theyr defaulte, as of Gyges, whiche was right riche of landes and of richessis, and was so proud that he went and demaunded of the god Appollo yf there were ony in the world more riche and more heppy than he was. And than he herde a voys

380 that yssued out of the fosse or pitte of the sacrefises that a peple named Agalans Sophide, whiche were poure of goodes and riche of corage, was more acceptable than he whiche was kyng. And thus the god Appollo alowed more the sapyence and the sureté of the poure man and of his litel meyne than he dyd the astate and the persone of Gyges, ne of his riche mayne. And hit is more to alowe a lytyl thyng

385 seurly poursewed thenne moche good taken in fere and drede. And for as moche as a man of lowe lignage is by his vertue enhaunsed, so moche the more he ought to be glorious and of good renomee.

Virgyle, that was borne in Lombardye of the nacion of Mantua and was of lowe and symple lignage, yet he was soverayn in wysedom and science, and the most

390 noble of al the poyntes, of whom the renomee was, is, and shal be duryng the world. So hit happend that another poete axyd and demaunded of hym wherfore he sette not the versis of Homere in his book. And he answerd that he shold be of right grete strengthe and force that shold plucke the clubbe out of Hercules handes.

And thys suffiseth the state and draughtis of the comyn peple.

363 on neyther side, backwards; **fardest,** farthest. **364 "fiers,"** the name for a promoted pawn. **371 have despyte of,** look down on. **373 astate,** estate or social standing; **poopes,** popes. **375 of a shepeherd and one of the comyn peple,** after being a shepherd and common. **379 heppy,** happy. **380 fosse,** pit. **380–81 Agalans Sophide,** Aglaus of Psophis. **382 alowed more,** praised more. **383 meyne,** means. **384 mayne,** means. **385 poursewed,** pursued.

The eighth chappytre and the last of the fourth book: of the epylogacion and recapytulacion of thys book.

                                                                                        Capitulo octavus.

395   For as moche as we see and knowe that the memorye of the peple is not retentyf but right forgeteful, whan somme here longe talis and historyes whiche they can not al reteyne in her mynde or recorde. Therfore I have put in thys present chappytre al the thynges abovesayd as shortly as I have conne.

400   First, this playe or game was founden in the tyme of Evylmerodach, kyng of Babylone, and Excerses the philosopher, otherwyse named Philometer, founde hit. And the cause why was for the correccion of the kyng, lyke as hit apperith in thre [of] the first chappytres. For the sayd kyng was so tyrannous and feloun that he myght suffre no correcion but slewe them and dyd do put hem to deth that correctid hym, and had than doo put to deth many right wyse men. Than the peple, beyng sorouful

405   and right evyl plesid of this evyl lyf of the kyng, prayed and requyred the phylo-sopher that he wold reprise and telle the kyng of his folye. And than the philosopher answerd that he shold be dede yf he so dyde. And the peple sayd to hym: "Certes, thou oughtest sonner wylle to dye to the ende that thy renome myght come to the peple than the lyf of the kyng shold contynue in evyl for lacke of thy counceil, or by

410   faulte of reprehension of thee, or thou darist not doo and shewe that thou sayest."

      And whan the philosopher herde thys, he promysid to the peple that he wold put hym in devoyr to correct hym. And thenne he began to thynke hym in what maner he myght escape the deth and kepe to the people his promesse. And thenne thus he maad in thys maner and ordeygned the eschequer of sixty-four poyntes,

415   as is afore sayde. And dyd do make the forme of chequers of gold and silver in humayn figure after the facions and formes as we have dyvysid and shewid to you

---

Title **epylogacion**, conclusion. **396 talis**, stories. **398 abovesayd**, aforementioned; **shortly**, briefly; **have conne**, am able. **402 feloun**, felonious. **405 evyl plesid**, displeased; **requyred**, requested. **407 Certes**, Certainly. **408 sonner**, sooner. **412 put hym in devoyr**, do what he could. **414 ordeygned**, arranged; **eschequer**, chessboard.

tofore in theyr chappytres, and ordeyned the moevyng and the estate after that it is sayd in the chappitres of the eschessys.

420 And whan the pyhlosophre had thus ordeyned the playe or game, and that hit plesid alle them that sawe hit, on a tyme, as the philosopher played on hit, the kyng came and sawe hit, and desired to playe at this game. And thenne the phylosopher began to ensigne and teche the kyng the science of the playe and the draughtes, sayeng to hym first how the kyng ought to have in hymself pyté, debonayrté, and rightwysnes, as hit is sayd tofore in the chappytre of the kyng. And he enseygned 425 to hym the astate of the quene and what maners she ought to have. And thenne of the alphyns as counceyllours and juges of the royame. And after the nature of the knyghtes, how they ought to be wyse, trewe, and curtoys, and al the ordre of knyghthode. And than after the nature of the vycayrs and rookes, as hit apperyth in theyr chappytre. And after thys how the comyn people ought to goo eche in his 430 offyce, and how they ought to serve the nobles.

And whan the phylosopher had thus taught and enseygned the kynge and his nobles by the maner of the playe, and had reprehendyd hym of his evyl maners, the kyng demaunded hym upon payn of deth to telle hym the cause why and wherfore he had made and founden thys playe and game, and what thyng mevyd hym therto. 435 And than the phylosopher, constrayned by fere and drede, answerd that he had promysed to the people, whyche had requyryd hym that he shold correcte and reprise the kyng of his evyl vices. But for as moche as he doubted the deth and had seen that the kyng dyd do slee the sages and wyse men that were so hardy to blame hym of his vyces, he was in grete anguysshe and sorowe how he myght fynde a 440 maner to correcte and reprehende the kyng and to save his owen lyf. And thus he thought longe and studyed that he fond this game or playe, whiche he hath do sette forth for to amende and correcte the lyf of the kyng and to chaunge his maners. And he adjoustyd, wyth al that he had founden, thys game for so moche as the lordes and nobles haboundyng in delices and richessis, and enjoyeng temporel 445 pees, shold eshewe ydelnes by playeng of thys game, and for to gyve hem cause to leve her pensifnes and sorowes in avysyng and studyeng this game.

And whan the kyng had herde al thyse causes, he thought that the philosopher had founde a good maner of correccion. And than he thankyd hym gretely. And thus by the ensignement and lernyng of the philosopher, he chaunged his lyf, his 450 maners, and alle his evyll condicions. And by this maner hit happend that the kyng that tofore tyme had ben vycious and disordynate in hys lyvyng was made juste and vertuous, debonayr, gracious, and ful of vertues unto al peple. And a man that lyvyth in thys world without vertues lyveth not as a man but as a beste. Thenne late every man of what condycion he be that redyth or herith this litel book redde, take 455 therby ensaumple to amende hym.

417–18 after that it is sayd, after the rules that are stated. **422 ensigne**, instruct. **423–24 pyté, debonayrté, and rightwysnes**, pity, graciousness, and honesty. **427 curtoys**, courteous. **437 reprise**, reprove; **doubted the deth**, feared death. **438 hardy**, brave. **440 reprehende**, rebuke. **443 adjoustyd**, composed. **444 haboundyng**, abounding; **delices**, delights. **446 pensifnes**, pensiveness or worries; **avysyng**, considering. **451 tofore tyme**, before; **disordynate**, unchecked or immoderate.

❦ Explanatory Notes

Abbreviations: *CA*: Gower, *Confessio Amantis*; *CT*: Chaucer, *Canterbury Tales*; *LGW*: Chaucer, *Legend of Good Women*; *OED*: *Oxford English Dictionary*; *PL*: Migne, *Patrologiae cursus completus, series Latina*; **Whiting**: Whiting, *Proverbs, Sentences, and Proverbial Phrases*.

The two best sources for identifying the *Game and Playe*'s various *exempla* are Alain Collet's *Le Jeu des Éschaz Moralisé*, a modern edition of Jean de Ferron's mid-fourteenth-century French translation of Jacobus' *Liber*, and William E. A. Axon's introduction to *Caxton's Game and Playe of the Chesse, 1474*. I have used Axon and Collet as the base for my notes, adding a few additional sources that they did not find. I have also included modern editions and translations of these sources so that readers can easily locate them. In the notes I cite these editions by page numbers, or, in instances where the title of the work is unclear, by the title followed by the page numbers. Complete citations of these sources appear in the Bibliography. All citations from the Bible are from the Douay-Rheims translation of the Vulgate.

When comparing Caxton's *Game and Playe* to Jacobus' *Liber*, I have used Marie Anita Burt's edition of the *Liber*. When comparing Caxton's text to French translations of Jacobus' *Liber*, I have used Collet's edition (above) and have also consulted MS 392 at the Regenstein Library, the University of Chicago. This manuscript, a hybrid of translations done by Jean de Ferron and Jean de Vignay, was the most likely base text for Caxton's translation.

Preface and Table of Contents

Caxton's French manuscript copy may or may not have contained a prologue or preface. If it did not have one, Caxton might have returned to the *Recuyell* for a model.[1] If it did include a prologue or preface, it was most likely from Jean de Vignay, who dedicated his French translation to Prince John of France.[2] The parallels between Jean's prologue and

---

[1] Arguing this point is Blake, who claims that as in the *Recuyell*, Caxton uses his preface to the *Game and Playe* to launch into "a rather extravagant praise of [his patron], which is expressed in laudatory platitudes" ("Continuity and Change," pp. 75–76).

[2] In the introduction to his reprint of Caxton's 1474 printing of the *Game and Playe*, Axon posits that the printer borrowed heavily from Jean de Vignay's preface: "The bulk of Caxton's work is undoubtedly from the French translation of Jehan de Vignay, whose dedication to Prince John of France has simply been transformed into a similar address to the Duke of Clarence" (*Caxton's Game and Playe of the Chesse, 1474*, pp. xxiii–xxiv). Jean de Vignay's preface reads: "A Tres noble & excellent prince Jehan de france duc de normendie & auisne filz de philipe par le grace de dieu Roy de france.

that of Caxton are striking. Yet it is not clear that Caxton had access to one of Jean de Vignay's manuscripts for his translation. It is also worthwhile to note that Jean de Ferron's translation of the *Liber* is prefaced by remarks that resemble Caxton's 1483 prologue.[3]

1   *The holy appostle and doctour of the peple, Saynt Poule, sayth in his Epystle.* This saying from Romans 15:4 was a popular one both with Caxton and with earlier medieval writers, e.g., Chaucer in The Nun's Priest's Tale (*CT* VII[B²]3441–42).

5–6   *And accordyng to the same saith Salamon, that the nombre of foles is infenyte.* This saying is from Ecclesiastes 1:15.

9–11   *Thenne emonge whom there was an excellent doctour of dyvynyté in the royame of Fraunce of the ordre of the Hospytal of Saynt John's of Jherusalem.* This is apparently a reference to Jean de Vignay, although as Axon notes this is the only reference that would place the French translator at the Order of the Hospital of St. John's

---

Frere Jehan de vignay vostre petit Religieux entre les autres de vostre seignorie / paix sante Joie & victoire sur vos ennemis. Treschier & redoubte seign'r / pour ce que Jay entendu et scay que vous veez & ouez volentiers choses proffitables & honestes et qui tendent al informacion de bonne meur ay Je mis vn petit liuret de latin en francois le quel mest venuz a la main nouuellement / ou quel plussieurs auctoritez et dis de docteurs & de philosophes & de poetes & des anciens sages / sont Racontez & sont appliquiez a la moralite des nobles hommes et des gens de peuple selon le gieu des eschez le quel livre Tres puissant et tres redoubte seigneur jay fait ou nom & soubz umbre de vous pour laquelle chose treschr seign'r Je vous suppli & requier de bonne voulente de cuer que il vostre daigne plaire a receuvoir ce livre en gre aussi bien que de un greign'r maistre de moy / car la tres bonne voulente que Jay de mielx faire se je pouoie me doit estre reputee pour le fait / Et po'r plus clerement proceder en ceste ouvre / Jay ordene que les chappitres du liure soient escrips & mis au commencement afin de veoir plus plainement la matiere de quoy le dit liure pole" ["To the very noble and excellent Prince John of France, duke of Normandy and oldest son of Philippe, by the grace of God, king of France. Brother John de Vignay, an unworthy monk amongst the others in your realm, [wishes you] peace, health, joy, and victory over your enemies. Very dear and feared sir, because I heard and know that you see and listen willingly to things [that are] profitable and honest and lend themselves to the formation of good morals, I have translated a little book out of Latin into French that recently came into my possession in which several true stories and sayings of doctors, philosophers, poets, and wise men of old are narrated and applied to the morals of noble men and of commoners according to the game of chess. Very powerful and feared sir, I have completed this book in your name and under your shadow. Very dear sir, I beg and pray with all my heart that you deign to receive this book as willingly as if [it came] from a greater scholar than me, for the very great desire that I have to do better if I could must outweigh the deed. In order to proceed more clearly with this work, I have commanded that the book's chapters be written and set at the beginning in order to see more clearly the matter for which this said book speaks"].

[3] Ferron writes: "Le Sainte Escripture dit que Dieux a fait a chascun commandement de pourchassier a tous nos prochains leur sauvement. Or est-il ainsi que nos prochains ne sont pas tout un, ains sont de diverses condicions, estas et manieres, sy comme il appert. Car les uns sont nobles; les aultres non: les aultres sont de cler engin; les aultres, non: les aultres sont enclins a devocion; les aultres, non" ["Holy Scripture says that God gave each [of us] the commandment to obtain the salvation of all our neighbors. Now our neighbors are not all one, but are of diverse conditions, estates, and classes, as it appears. For some are noble, others not. Some are of honest intent, others not. Some are bent to devotion, others not"] (qtd. Axon, *Caxton's Game and Playe of the Chesse, 1474,* p. xx). Many thanks to Meriem Pages for help with both of these translations.

of Jerusalem. Axon also notes that Jean de Vignay "styles himself 'hospitaller de l'ordre de haut pas,' which was situated in the Faubourg St. Jacques of Paris" (*Caxton's Game and Playe of the Chesse, 1474*, p. xxiv).

36   *alphyns*. bishops. In 4.2 the *alphyn* is defined as "juge of the kyng" and 4.4 indicates that he sits on the right side of the king. According to the *OED*, the term "alfin" derives from Arabic *al-fil*, meaning elephant; the chess piece still bears the figure and name of an elephant among the Chinese, Persians, and Indians.

BOOK ONE

Chapter 1

4–5   *in suche wyse as did the emperour Nero, whiche did do slee his mayster, Seneque.* Lucius Annaeus Seneca (4 B.C.E.–65 C.E.) was a philosopher, statesman, and advisor to the Emperor Nero. When he fell out of favor with Nero, the emperor ordered him to commit suicide. The account of his death was popularized by the *Roman de la Rose* where he is said to have bled himself to death in a warm bath (Guillaume de Lorris and Jean de Meun, *Romance of the Rose*, lines 6211–22, pp. 122–24).

7   *Evylmerodach*. In many places Caxton substitutes an "n" for a "v," thus "Enylmerodach" rather than "Evylmerodach." A scriptural mention of Evilmerodach appears in 4 Kings 25:27: "And it came to pass in the seven and thirtieth year of the captivity of Joachin, king of Juda, in the twelfth month, the seven and twentieth day of the month: Evilmerodach, king of Babylon, in the year that he began to reign, lifted up the head of Joachin, king of Juda, out of prison." D. J. Wiseman describes Evil-merodach (Amēl-Marduk) as the son of Nebuchadnezzar, who took over his father's throne in 562. Wiseman adds that Amēl-Marduk's "reign was marred by intrigues, some possibly directed against his father." See Wiseman's *Nebuchadnezzar and Babylon*, p. 9. The historical Nebuchadnezzar, who was the king of Babylon in the sixth century B.C.E., is famous for his immense building in the city.

11   *Nabugodonosor*. In Daniel 2:12, Nebuchadnezzar [Nabuchodonsar] orders his wise men to be slain after they are unable to interpret his dream.

17   *Caldees*. Also called the Chaldeans, they were the inhabitants of the region in which Babylon was the main city.

       Diomedes the Greek. This is most likely a reference to Diomedes, a Latin grammarian and author of *Ars grammatica*, who was writing at the end of the fourth century C.E. See *The Oxford Classical Dictionary*, p. 476.

19   *Alixander the Grete*. Alexander (356–323 B.C.E.) conquered much of Persia and the Middle East. Legends of his rule, along with those of Charlemagne and King Arthur, enjoyed tremendous popularity throughout the Middle Ages.

Chapter 2

23   *"Exerses," or in Greke "Philemetor."* Jacobus initially refers to Philometer as
      "Xerxes" but then reverts to his "Greek" name for most of the rest of the *Liber*.
      This historical Xerxes was the king of Persia and the son of Darius of Persia. In
      Book 7 of his *Histories* Herodotus describes Xerxes' attacks on Egypt and Greece.

33–34 *And therfore reherceth Valerius that there was a wyse man named Theodore Cerem.* The
      Valerius here is Valerius Maximus, author of *Factorum ac dictorum memorabilium,*
      or the *Book of Memorable Doings and Sayings*, which he wrote in the first century.
      This was one of the primary sources for Jacobus de Cessolis, author of the *Liber
      de ludo scacchorum,* and it also served as a sourcebook for many other authors
      throughout the Middle Ages. A brief version of the story of Theodorus of Cyrene
      (Theodore Cerem) is recounted in Book 6.2. See *Memorable Doings and Sayings*,
      2:29. In the introduction to his 1883 transcription of the 1474 *Game and Playe*,
      Axon writes: "[Theodorus] was banished from the (supposed) place of his birth,
      and was shielded at Athens by Demetrius Phalerus, whose exile he is assumed to
      have shared. Whilst in the service of Egypt he was sent as an ambassador to
      Lysimachus, whom he offended by the directness and plainness of his speech.
      The offended monarch threatened him with crucifixion, and he replied in a
      phrase which became famous, 'Threaten thus your courtiers, for it matters not
      to me whether I rot on the ground or in the air.' The king's threat was not
      executed, as Theodorus was afterwards at Corinth, and is believed to have died
      at Cyrene" (*Caxton's Game and Playe of the Chesse, 1474*, pp. lxvi–lxvii). The life
      of Theodorus is described in more detail in Diogenes Laertius' third-century
      Lives and Opinions of the Eminent Philosophers, 1:224–33.

41   *In like wyse as Democreon the philosopher.* The story of Democritus is recounted by
      Aulus Gellius in Book 10.18 of his second-century *Noctes Atticae.* See *Attic Nights*,
      2:258–61.

43   *And also Desortes the philosophre.* This story of Socrates, here called "Desortes,"
      comes from Book 7.2 of Valerius, *Memorable Doings and Sayings* (2:114–17). Axon
      notes: "The transformations of some of the names are peculiar. At p. 12 we read
      of Desortes. The philosopher disguised under this strange name appears to be
      Socrates. The story is told in the *Apology of Socrates* attributed to Xenophon. The
      person to whom the saying was addressed was not Xanthippe, but was a disciple
      named Apollodorus, whose understanding was not equal to his admiration"
      (*Caxton's Game and Playe of the Chesse, 1474*, pp. lxvii–lxviii).

Chapter 3

73–74 *In like wyse, as Valerius reherceth, that the kyng Alixandre had a noble and renomed
      knyght that sayd in reprevyng of Alixandre.* Although this is credited to Valerius
      Maximus, such an episode does not appear in his *Memorable Doings and Sayings.*
      However, it does appear in a modified form in Gautier de Châtillon's twelfth-
      century *Gesta Alexandri Magni,* Book 8, lines 434–64 and lines 536–41. (Gautier
      de Châtillon is also known as Gaultier de Lille, Gautier de Ronchin, Gualterus

de Insulis, and, in English, Walter of Châtillon.) Gautier's primary source for the *Gesta* was Quintus Curtius Rufus' *Historia Alexandri Magni.* See *The Alexandreis of Walter of Châtillon,* pp. 142–43 and 145.

86   *Wherof Seneque sayth unto Lucylle.* From Seneca's *Moral Letters,* Number 82.3 (2:242 and 243).

88   *And Varro saith in his Sentences.* This is most likely taken from the *Menippean Satires* of Marcus Terentius Varro (116–27 B.C.E.). Neither Jacobus nor Caxton states which satire is cited.

99   *Therfore we rede that Democrite the philosopher.* As noted above, the source for this reference to Democritus is most like Aulus Gellius' *Attic Nights.* However, there are two other sources that might have contributed to this reference. One is Cicero's *Tusculan Disputations,* or *Tusculanae Quaestiones,* a meditative treatise he wrote in roughly 45 B.C.E. Cicero's mention of Democritus comes in Book 5, chapter 39. See *Tusculan Disputations,* p. 471. The other possible source is Plutarch's first-century *Moralia,* 521(D). In his description Plutarch claims that the story is false but that the sentiment is true. See *Moralia,* vol. 6 (ed. and trans. W. C. Helmbold, 1934), pp. 506(G)–507(E).

101–04   *Didimus, bysshop of Alixandrie . . . Anthonye.* The writer and theologian Didymus the Blind (c. 310–98 C.E.) lost the use of his eyes when he was four years old. (Contrary to popular belief, Didymus always remained a layman.) *Gregore Nazanz* is Gregory of Nazianzus born at Arianzus, in Asia Minor, c. 325. Although he served for awhile as the bishop of Sasima, he eventually quit to become a hermit. *Saynt Jerome,* c. 347–420 C.E., is known primarily for his revisions and translations of the Bible. *Saynt Anthonye* was purportedly the founder of Christian monasticism. This description comes from St. Jerome's *De viris illustribus* CIX: "Didymus of Alexandria, while still quite young, became blind and as as a result never learned the alphabet. He presented to all an extraordinary proof of his talent by acquiring complete mastery of dialectic and geometry, which particularly needs the sight." See St. Jerome, *On Illustrious Men,* pp. 142–44.

BOOK TWO

Chapter 1

12–13   *And for as moche as mysericorde and trouth conserve and kepe the kyng in his trone.* Jean de Ferron's French translation of Jacobus' *Liber* includes an extra sentence, credited to Seneca, that essentially repeats this same idea. See Seneca's *De clementia* [*On Mercy*], Book 1, 11.4, in *Moral Essays* (1:390 and 391).

15   *And Valerius saith that deboneyrté percyth the hertes of straungers.* The story of Pisistratus and his daughter comes from Book 5.1, ext. 2a of *Memorable Doings and Sayings* (1:454 and 455).

24   *This prynce had also a frende that was named Arispe.* The story of Thrasippus comes
            from Book 5.1, ext. 2b of Valerius, *Memorable Doings and Sayings* (1:454–56 and
            455–57).

35   *And in lyke wise rede we of the Kyng Pirre.* The story of Pyrrhus comes from Book
            5.1.3a of Valerius, *Memorable Doings and Sayings* (1:456 and 457).

47–48   *Valerius reherceth that Alyxandre, wyth alle his ooste, rood for to destroye a cyté whiche
            was named Lapsare.* The story of Alexander the Great and Anaximenes is in Book
            7.3, ext. 4 of *Memorable Doings and Sayings* (2:140 and 141). Anaximenes of
            Lampsacus (380–320 B.C.E.), a Greek rhetorician and historian, was a favorite
            of Alexander the Great, whom he accompanied in his Persian campaigns.

58–59   *Quyntilian sayth that no grete man ne lord shold not swere but where as is grete nede.*
            The first part of this quote is a paraphrase of Quintilian, a first-century Roman
            rhetorician whose only extant work is a twelve-volume textbook on rhetoric
            entitled *Institutio oratoria.* The original quote, "Nam et in totum iurare, nisi ubi
            necesse est, gravi viro parum convenit," can be found in Book 9.2.98. See
            Institutio oratoria of Quintilian, 3:436 and 437.

60–62   *Alas, who kepe . . . amende hit.* These last two sentences are additions by Caxton.

64–66   *Therfore recounteth Valerius that there was a man named Therile, a werkman in metalle,
            that maad a boole of coppre.* The story of Perillus and his copper bull comes from
            Book 1, chapter 20 of the *Historiarum adversus paganos libri VII* [*History against the
            Pagans in Seven Books*] by Paulus Orosius (c. 385–420), a historian and theologian.
            See Orosius, *Seven Books of History against the Pagans,* p. 40. The Latin and French
            translations of the *Liber* cite Orosius by name, although Caxton mistakenly attri-
            butes the story to Valerius Maximus. It also appears in Ovid's *Tristia,* III.11, lines
            39–54 (see Ovid, *Tristia,* pp. 144 and 145). Gower tells the story in *CA*
            7.3295–3338, following Godfrey of Viterbo's *Pantheon,* where the craftsman of
            the "bole of bras" is named "Berillus," and the cruel tyrant "Siculus," rather than
            "Philardes." Philarde, or Phalarius, was a ruler in Sicily from about 570–554 B.C.E.

76–77   *Therfore, sayth Ovide, "there is no thyng more resonable thenne that a man dye of suche
            deth as he purchaseth unto other."* This quote comes from Ovid's *Art of Love,* Book
            1, lines 655–56: "Iustus uterque fuit: neque enim lex aequior ulla est, / Quam
            necis artifices arte perire sua" (pp. 56 and 57). Ovid states this maxim right after
            he himself narrates the story of Perillus and the copper bull.

79–81   *Therfore reherceth Saynt Augustyn, in a book whyche is intituled The Cyté of God, that
            there was a theef of the see named Diomedes.* The story of Alexander and Diomedes
            the pirate was extremely popular throughout the Middle Ages. It is found in
            Augustine's fifth-century *City of God,* Book 4, chapter 4 (1:115). It also appears
            in Cicero's first-century *De re publica,* Book 3, chapter 14 (pp. 202–03). The
            pirate is given the name Diomedes in the *Gesta Romanorum,* Tale CXLVI (p.
            293). And it appears in an abbreviated form in John of Salisbury's *Policraticus*
            3.14. See John of Salisbury, *Frivolities of Courtiers,* pp. 204–05. In English, see
            Gower's *CA* 3.2363–2417; Chaucer, too, makes a reference to the story in his
            Manciple's Tale (*CT* IX [H] 223–39). Neither Gower nor Chaucer names the thief.

95   Although University of Chicago Manuscript 392, Caxton's most likely primary source, uses the word *destre*, or *right*, here, other French translations of the *Liber* refer to the king's *senestre*, or *left*, side.

108–09   *Of this chasteté reherceth Valerius an example, and saith that ther was a man of Rome whyche was named Scipio Affrican.* The story of Scipio the African and the woman from Carthage comes from *Memorable Doings and Sayings*, Book 4.1 (1:366–67). It also appears in John of Salisbury's *Policraticus*, Book 5, chapter 7. See John of Salisbury, *Statesman's Book*, p. 97.

Chapter 2

125–26   *like as it is sayd in Scripture in the Canticles.* This phrase appears twice in the Canticles, once at 2:6 and again at 8:3. Axon notes that "the quotation from the Canticles . . . may be compared with the translation in the Wicliffite version made by Nicholas de Hereford, A. D. 1380. This passage is rendered: 'His left hond is undur myn heed; and his right hond shal biclippe me'" (*Caxton's Game and Playe of the Chesse, 1474*, p. lvi).

141–42   *And accordyng therto, Macrobe rehercheth in the Book of the Dremes of Scypyo, that there was a chyld of Rome that was named Papirus.* Macrobius, an early fifth-century grammarian and philosopher known for his *Saturnalia*, was also the author of a influential and popular commentary in two books on the *Dream of Scipio* narrated by Cicero at the end of his *Republic*. Although Caxton, following Jacobus, attributes this story to Macrobius' commentary, it actually comes from *Saturnalia*, Book 1, chapter 6.20–25 (pp. 52–53). This story also appears in the *Gesta Romanorum*, Tale CXXVI (pp. 271–72). In all of these versions, as in most translations of the *Liber*, there is no mention of Papirus becoming a senator, and this seems to have been added by Caxton.

174–75   *Wherof Jerome rehercheth agaynst Jovynyan.* This is a reference to Jerome's treatise *Adversus Jovinianum* [*Against Jovinian*]. The story about Duillius and Bilia is found in Book 1, section 46. For the original quote, see *Adversus Jovinianum* in *PL* 23:0275B.

191   *Also, we rede that there was a wedowe named Anna.* This story also comes from *Adversus Jovinianum*, Book 1, section 46. The name given in Jerome's version is Annia. The last sentence in this story — "And so she concluded that she wold kepe her chasteté" — seems to have been added by Caxton.

198–99   *Saynt Austyn rehercheth in the book De civitate dei that in Rome was a noble lady, gentyl of maners and of hygh kynrede, named Lucrecia.* The story of the rape of Lucretia enjoyed an immense popularity throughout the Middle Ages. Caxton, following Jacobus, credits St. Augustine's *De civitate dei*, Book 1, chapter 18 (1:22–24). But it is earlier found in Ovid's *Fasti* 2.687–852; Valerius, *Memorable Doings and Sayings*, Book 6.1.1 (2:2 and 3); and Livy's early first-century *Ab urbe condita* [*From the Founding of the City*], more commonly know as the *History of Rome* (Book 1, chapters 57–60 in *Ab urbe condita*, 1:196–209). For popular Middle English versions see Gower, *CA* 7.4754–5123, and Chaucer, *LGW* 1680–1895.

243–44   *Wherfore sayth Symachus that they that ben not shamefast have no conscience of luxurye.*
          This reference is either to Symmachus the Ebionite (late second century C.E.),
          the author of one of the Greek versions of the Old Testament, or Pope
          Symmachus (498–514 C.E.)

245–46   *And Saynt Ambrose sayth that one of the best parementes and maketh a womman most fayr
          in her persone is to be shamefast.* This is from Book 1, chapter 18 of St. Ambrose's
          De officiis, a treatise on the office of the clergy that he wrote in roughly 388–89
          C.E. See *De officiis*, 1.156–57.

247   *Seneque reherceth that there was one named Archezylle.* This story is found in Seneca's
          De beneficiis [*On Benefits*] Book 2, 10.1 (*Moral Essays*, 3:64–65). It should be noted
          that in Seneca's version Arcesilaus is male.

257–58   *Wherof Valeryus Maximus sayth that there was one that wold marye.* Although Caxton
          and the French translators of the *Liber* attribute this to Valerius, the Latin ver-
          sions do not, nor does it appear in the *Memorable Doings and Sayings.* I have not
          been able to locate a source for this story.

263–64   *as hit is wryten in Ecclesiastes:* "*Yf thou have sones, enseigne and teche them. And yf thou
          have doughters, kepe wel them in chastyté.*" Although the text credits Ecclesiastes,
          this is from Ecclesiasticus 7:25–26.

265   *For Helemonde reherceth that every kynge and prynce ought to be a clerke.* This
          reference is most likely to Hélinand de Froidmont (c. 1160–1229), a medieval
          poet and chronicler who spent time at the court of Philip Augustus then later
          became a monk at the Cistercian abbey in Froidmont. Although Hélinand com-
          posed most of his poetry in French, he also authored several moral treatises in
          Latin, which include *De reparatione lapsi* [Of the restoration of the fallen], *De
          cognitione sui* [On the knowledge of self], and a mirror of princes *De bono regimine
          principis* [Of the good rule of princes], later collected into his *Chronicon.* This
          quote most likely comes from *De bono regimine principis.*

269   *The Emperour Octovyan maad his sones to be taught.* This is from Suetonius' first-
          century *Lives of Caesars*, Book 2 (Augustus), chapter 64. See Suetonius, *Suetonius*,
          1:218–21.

279–80   *For Poule the Historiagraph of the Lombardes reherceth that ther was a duchesse named
          Remonde.* Paulus Diaconus, or Paul the Deacon, (c. 720–99) wrote the *Historia
          Langobardorum* (*History of the Lombards*), in the late eighth century. His descrip-
          tion of Romilda appears in Book 4, chapter 37. Although incomplete, the
          Historia narrates the history of the Lombards from 568 to the death of King
          Liutprand in 747. See Paul the Deacon, *History of the Langobards*, pp. 179–84.

289–90   *was duc of Boneventan, and sithen kyng of the Lumbardis.* Boneventan, or Benevento,
          is a town and commune northeast of Naples. In the French versions of the *Liber*,
          it is rendered as "Bienventains," and it appears later in Caxton's translations in
          reference to the commune's citizens, the "Buneventayns." The Lombard area lies
          in northwest Italy, encompassing the modern-day city of Milan. The daughters
          become queens of France and Germany respectively.

Chapter 3

316–17   *And as touchyng the first poynt, Seneque saith in the Book of Benefets that the pour Diogenes was more strong than Alixandre.* This derives from Seneca's *De beneficiis* [*On Benefits*] Book 5, chapter 4.4. See *Moral Essays*, 3:298–99.

319   *Marcus Cursus, a Romayn of grete renomee, saith thus.* This story of Marcus Curius comes from Valerius, *Memorable Doings and Sayings*, Book 4.3.5a (1:370–71). As noted above, "Beneuvetans" refers to Benevento. "Samente" refers to the land occupied by the Samnites, in the center-south of Italy.

331–32   *Helymond rercheth that Demostene demaunded of Aristodone how moche he had wonne.* For Helymond, see "Helemonde" or "Hélinand" above, note 265. The story of Demosthenes is also recounted by Aulus Gellius in Book 11, chapter 9.2 of his *Attic Nights* (2:320 and 321). Demosthenes (384–322 B.C.E.) was a Greek statesman of ancient Athens.

338–39   *Valerius rercith that the senatours of Rome took counceil togeder of two persones.* This story of Scipio's advice is from *Memorable Doings and Sayings*, Book 6.4.2b (2:46 and 47).

346–47   *Therfore we rede that as longe as the Romayns lovyd poverté, they were lordys of alle the world.* In the *Liber* Jacobus attributes this quote to the Valerius' chapter "Of Poverty," although the paragraph in Caxton's translation is more of a distillation of what Valerius says there. See Book 4.5 (1:384–96).

356–57   *Valere rercheth that he is not riche that moche hath, but he is riche that hath lityl and coveyteth no thyng.* This saying derives from *Memorable Doings and Sayings*, Book 4.3.6a (1:372 and 373).

359   *For Theofrast saith that all love is blynde.* Theophrastus (371–287 B.C.E.) was a Greek philosopher and the immediate successor to Aristotle at the Lyceum. He is most famous for his *Characters* (brief sketches of negative allegorial character types, such as "Cowardice" and "Grouchiness"), but he also wrote essays about plants, winds, and nature, as well as about poetics, politics, and ethics. These latter exist mostly as fragments, and this quote most likely comes from one of these fragments.

362–63   *And so rercheth Quinte Curse in his first book that the grete Godaches sayth the same to Alyxandre.* Quintus Curtius Rufus, a second-century historian, is the author of the *Historia Alexandri Magni* [*A History of Alexander the Great*], a history of Alexander's wars. This story of Guodares (or Gobares) comes from Book 7, chapter 4.10–12. See Curtius, *Quintus Curtius*, 2:152–55.

366–67   *Tullyus sayth that an angry and yrous persone weneth that for to doo evyl is good counceyl.* Cicero does indeed address the sin of wrath in Book 3, chapter 5 of his *Tusculan Disputations* (pp. 367–68). But this quote, "Iratus etiam facinus consilium putat," in fact has its origin in the *Sententiae* [*Sayings*] of Publius Syrus, a Latin writer of the first century B.C.E. The *Sententiae*, a collection of moral maxims, is his only extant work.

368–69   *And Socrates saith that two thynges ben contrarious to counceyl, and they ben hastynes and wrath.* In Book 2, chapter 7 of *A Treatise of Moral Philosophie Containing the Sayings of the Wise*, written by William Baldwin in 1555, the idea that "Wrath and hastiness are very evyl counsaylours" is attributed to Isocrates, not Socrates. The expression is clearly proverbial. A similar idea is found in Arthur Brooke's *Romeus and Juliet*, a source for Shakespeare's *Romeo and Juliet* (lines 1491–92): "skill-less youth for counsel is unfit, / And anger oft with hastiness are joined to want of wit."

370   *And Galeren sayth in Alexandrye.* Galeren's "Alexandrye" is Gautier de Châtillon's twelfth-century *Gesta Alexandri Magni.* This counsel on judgment is advice given to a young Alexander in Book 1, lines 210–16 (p. 11).

373–74   *Helemond reherceth that Cambyses, kyng of Perce, whiche was a right wis kyng, had an unrightwis juge.* Although Jacobus may have taken this story from Hélinand de Froidmont, it seems more likely that he used Valerius, *Memorable Doings and Sayings*, Book 6.3, ext. 3 (2:42 and 43). The story also appears in Herodotus' *Histories*, Book 5, chapter 25. See Herodotus, *Herodotus*, 2:363. For information about Hélinand, see note 265.

380–81   *Caton saith: "Accomplisshe and do the lawe in suche wyse as thou hast ordeigned and geven."* Marcus Porcius Cato (234–139 B.C.E.) was a famous statesmen and orator. This saying is number 53 of Cato's *Monsticha (One-liners)*, which although attributed to Cato may in fact not be his. The original quote reads: "Pati legem, quam ipse tuleris," or "Keep the law you make yourself."

382   *Valerius reherceth that Calengius.* The story of Zaleucus and his son comes from *Memorable Doings and Sayings*, Book 6.5, ext. 3 (2:64 and 65).

389   *We rede that there was a counceyllour of Rome.* The story of the Roman consul comes from Valerius, *Memorable Doings and Sayings*, Book 6.5, ext. 4 (2:64 and 65).

397–98   *But alas we fynde not many in thyse dayes that so do. But they do lyke as Anastasyus saith.* This quote from Anacharsis is from Valerius, *Memorable Doings and Sayings*, Book 7.2, ext. 14 (2:122–25).

416–17   *Wherfore saith Seneke: "Beleve me that they seme that they do no thyng, they do more than they that laboure, for they do spirituel and also corporal werkis."* This saying is taken from Seneca's *Moral Letters*, Number 8.6 (1:40 and 41).

420   *And therfore Angelius saith in Libro Atticors de Socrate.* Caxton means to refer here to Aulus Gellius' *Attic Nights*, where a slightly different version of this story appears in Book 2, chapter 1 (1:122 and 123). Although Latin versions of the *Liber* refer to "A. Gellius" and give the correct name for his work (*Noctes Atticae*), the French translators often open this section with the name *Socrates*.

425–26   *And Valerius rehercith that Carnardes, a knyght, was so sage, wyse, and laborous in pensifnes of the comyn wele.* The story of Carneades is from *Memorable Doings and Sayings*, Book 8.7, ext. 5 (2:232 and 233). It should be noted that Valerius describes Melissa as a woman that Carneades "had in lieu of a wife."

431 *Didimus sayd to Alixandre.* This story comes from *Collatio Alexandri et Dindimi* [*The Correspondence of Alexander and Dindimus*], one of the many short narratives of Alexander in circulation among medieval authors. See "Correspondence of Alexander and Dindimus" in Stoneman, *Legends of Alexander the Great*, p. 64.

Chapter 4

462 *Therfore saith the philosopher.* Latin versions of the *Liber* do not refer to "the philosopher," although French translations often do. The source is unknown.

464–65 *Alixandre of Macedone vaynquysshed and conquerd Egipte, Judé, Caldee, Affrique, and Assyrie, unto the Marches of Bragmans.* Judea historically refers to the land in the southern part of Israel now divided between Israel and the West Bank. Chaldea, the Western term for the ancient kingdom of Babylonia, usually refers to the region's southern parts. It is now found in Iraq. Assyrie is an ancient kingdom that at its peak spanned much of the modern-day Middle East. The Bragmans are most likely the Brahmans, who would have inhabited modern-day India, although this might also refer to another ascetic group such as the Jains. References to the Bragmans also appear in Mandeville's *Travels* and in Gower's *Confessio Amantis*.

467–68 *We rede in the Historye of Rome that there was a knyght whiche had to name Malechete.* The story of Malecote (also "Mascezel") comes from Book 7, chapter 36 of Orosius' *Historiae adversus Paganos* (pp. 346–49).

488 *In lyke wyse, Judas Machabeus, Jonathas, and Symon, his brethern.* This story comes from 1 Maccabees 3. Judas' inspirational speech before his battle against Apollonius is from 1 Maccabees 3:18–22.

495–96 *Paule the Historiagraph of the Lombardes reherceth that there was a knyght named Enulphus.* The story of the faithful knight Unulf comes from Paul the Deacon's *Historia Langobardorum*, Book 5, chapters 2–4 (pp. 209–16).

534–36 *lyke as were the noble knyghtes Joab and Abysay, that fought ageynst the Syryens and Amonytes, and were so trewe.* The story of Joab and Abisai comes from 2 Kings 10:9–14.

539 *We rede that Damon and Phisias.* The story of Damon and Phisias is taken from Cicero's *De officiis*, Book 3, chapter 10.45 (pp. 312–13). It is also found in Valerius, *Memorable Doings and Sayings*, Book 4.7, ext. 1 (pp. 422–25).

555 *Anthonyus sayth that Julius Cesar.* The Anthonyus here is really Suetonius, who writes about Caesar in Book 2, chapter 72 of his *Lives* (1:234–37). In the Latin *Liber*, as in French translations, this story is correctly attributed to "Suetonius," and the reason Caxton changes this to "Anthonyus" remains unclear.

557 *Scipion of Affrique saith.* Scipio's saying comes from Cicero's *De amictia*, Book 10. (See *On Friendship*, pp. 44–45.)

567–72 *And thus . . . large gevyng.* This passage is found in Latin versions of the *Liber*; most French translations contain only Scipio's quote.

581–82   *And therfore Davyd. . . made a lawe.* This detail of David comes from 1 Kings 30:24.

585–86   *Alixandre of Macedone cam on a tyme lyke a symple knyght unto the court of Porus.*
           According to Collet, this story is derived from Book 2, chapter 26 of Julius
           Valerius' *Res gestae Alexandri Macedonis,* a fourth-century translation of Pseudo-
           Callisthenes' *History of Alexander.*

607   *Ovyde saith that he that taketh yeftes, he is glad therwyth.* This quotation comes from
           Ovid's *Art of Love,* Book 3, lines 653–54 (pp. 164–65). In Latin versions of the
           Liber, Ovid is quoted directly — "Munera, crede mihi, capiunt hominesque
           deosque / Placatur donis Iuppiter ipse datis" — and these lines are spliced
           together with two more lines of apparently original verse.

615   *We rede that Cadrus, duc of Athenes, shold have a bataylle agayn them of Polipe.* The
           story of Codrus comes from Valerius, *Memorable Doings and Sayings,* Book 5.6,
           ext. 1 (1:520 and 521). Gower retells the story in *CA* 7.3163–3214.

628   *Therfore we rede that Scilla.* The story of Sulla's battle with the Romans comes
           from Orosius, *Historiae adversum Paganos,* Book 5, chapters 20–21 (p. 217).

637–39   *Therfore Joab ordeyned, whan Absalon was slayn . . . And in like wyse dyd he whan he
           faught ayenst Abner.* These two references are to 2 Kings 18:16 and 2 Kings 2:28.

649–54   *How shold a plowman be sewre in the felde . . . the costis and expencis of them bothe.* This
           section seems to have been added by Caxton.

655–56   *We rede that Athis sayd to Davyd, whiche was a knyght: "I make thee my kepar and
           defendar alwey."* This reference is from 1 Kings 28:2.

659   *Turgeus Pompeus rehercith of a noble knyght named Ligurgyus.* The story of Ligurius
           is found in Plutarch's *Lives of the Ten Orators* (Book 7), in Valerius Maximus'
           Memorable Doings and Sayings (Book 1.2, ext. 3), and in Herodotus' *Histories*
           (Book 1, chapter 65). In the Latin *Liber,* however, the *exemplum* is credited to
           Marcus Junianus Justinus' *History of Trogus Pompeius,* Book 3, chapters 2–3. (See
           Justin, *Epitome of the Philippic History of Pompeius Trogus,* pp. 46–47.) The story,
           followed by a list of Ligurius' laws, appears in the *Gesta Romanorum,* Tale CLXIX,
           where is it similarly credited to Trogus Pompeius (see *Gesta,* pp. 349–50). Gower
           tells the story in *CA* 7.2917–3028, followed by a history of lawgivers, rather than
           Ligurius' laws themselves.

663   *Apollo Delphynus* is another name for the Greek deity Apollo, the god of Delphi.

Chapter 5

722   *Wherof Valeryus rehercheth that there was a man that was named Themystydes.* The story
           of Themistocles comes from *Memorable Doings and Sayings,* Book 6.5, ext. 2 (2:62
           and 63).

735   *We have an ensaumple of Marcus Regulus.* The story is found in Cicero's *De officiis,*
           Book 1, chapter 13.39 (pp. 42–43), and in his *De finibus bonorum et malorum,*

Book 2, chapter 20.65 (pp. 154 and 155). It also appears in Augustine's *De civitate dei*, Book 1, chapter 14 (1:18–20).

751   *Valerius rehercith in the sixth book of one Emelie, duc of the Romayns.* The example of Camillus is found in *Memorable Doings and Sayings*, Book 6.5, 1a (2:52 and 53). In the *Liber*, this *exemplum* often follows the story of Hannibal. (See below.) It also appears in John of Salisbury's *Policraticus*, Book 5, chapter 7. See John of Salisbury, *Statesman's Book*, p. 97.

770   *We rede that Hanybal had taken a prynce of Rome.* From Cicero, *De officiis*, Book 3, chapter 32.113 (pp. 392–95).

775   *Amos Florus tellith that the phisicien of Kyng Pirrus.* This story of Pyrrhus' physician comes from Lucius Annaeus Florus' late first- or early second-century *Epitome of Roman History*, Book 1, chapter 13.21 (pp. 64–65). It can also be found in Cicero's *De officiis*, Book 3, chapter 22.86 (pp. 358–61).

794   *Valerius rehercith that there was a juge named Sangis.* The *exemplum* of the judge, the condemned woman, and her daughter comes from *Memorable Doings and Sayings*, Book 5.4.7 (1:500 and 501). Caxton adds the name "Sangis" out of a confusion of the Latin word "sanguinis" or "of noble blood," which applies to the condemned woman and not to the judge.

809   *Seneka sayth that the kyng of bees.* From Seneca's *De clementia* [*On Mercy*], Book 1, chapter 19.3. See *Moral Essays*, 1:410–11.

813   *Valerius rehercith in his fifthe book of Marchus Martellus.* The story of M. Marcellus comes from *Memorable Doings and Sayings*, Book 5.1.4 (1:446 and 447).

818   *Also, he recounteth when Pompeeé had conquerd the kyng of Germanye.* The story of Pompeius Tigranes (the king of the Armenians, not the Romans) appears in Valerius, *Memorable Doings and Sayings*, Book 5.1.9 (1:450 and 451).

824   *Also, he reherceth of a counceyllour that was named Poule.* The story of L. Paullus and the prisoner appears in Valerius, *Memorable Doings and Sayings*, Book 5.1.8 (1:448–51).

830   *Cesar, whan he hard the deth of Cathon.* The narrative of Caesar crying over Cato's death appears in Valerius, *Memorable Doings and Sayings*, Book 5.1.10 (1:452 and 453).

833–34 *Thus taught Virgyle and enseygneth the glorious prynces to rewle and governe the peple of Rome.* The *Liber* refers specifically to Book 6 of the *Aeneid*. Collet further places it at lines 851–53. See Virgil, *Virgil*, 1:592–93.

835   *And Saynt Austyn [in] De civitate dei sayth thus.* Although Jacobus and his French translators attribute Augustine's description of the Romans to *De civitate dei*, Book 9, it actually is found in Book 5, chapter 12 (1:157–61).

838   *And hyt was wryten unto Alixaunder.* This is taken from Ovid's *Epistulae ex Ponto* [*Letters from the Black Sea*], Book 1, chapter 2, lines 121–26 (pp. 278–79).

841   *rote of pyté.* I.e., his pity comes from the heart, the sense of which is the root of his compassion.

842   *We rede of the Emperour Trajan.* I have not been able to locate a source for this *exemplum.* On Emperor Trajan's pious compassion, see *CA* 7.3142–62, along with the note to 7.3144 in *CA* 3:468.

846   *Also, we rede of Alisaunder.* The story of Alexander the Great and the old soldier appears in Valerius, *Memorable Doings and Sayings,* Book 5.1, ext. 1a (pp. 452–55).

852–53   *"The gretter or in the hyer astate that thou art, so moche more oughtest thou be meker and more humble."* This quotation comes Ecclesiasticus 3:20.

854–55   *Valerius reherceth in his seventh book that ther was an emperour named Publius Cesar.* Although Jacobus attributes this to Valerius' seventh book, it actually comes from Book 4.1.1 (1:336–39).

858   *And Scipion of Affrique.* Jacobus does not give a source for this story. Nevertheless, in John of Salisbury's *Policraticus,* Book 5, chapter 7, there is a reference to Scipio's extreme poverty, which led to the Senate having to provide doweries for his daughters after his death. See John of Salisbury, *Statesman's Book,* p. 100.

863   *Valerius rehercith in his third book that Fabyan the Grete.* The narrative of Fabian's reluctance to pass his office to his son comes from *Memorable Doings and Sayings,* Book 4.1.5 (1:340 and 341). Fabian's refusal to accept the consulship appears in Book 6.4.1b (2:44 and 45). In Valerius' version, however, this act is attributed to Manlius.

874   *There was a kyng of so subtyl engyne that whan men brought hym the crowne.* This story appears in Valerius, *Memorable Doings and Sayings,* Book 7.2, ext. 5 (2:118 and 119).

881   *Vaspasian was so humble.* The story of Vespasian's humility in the face of his election appears in Tacitus' first-century *Historia,* Book 2, chapters 74–78 (pp. 519–23).

886–87   *Therfore saith the Byble that Joab, the sone of Saryne.* Joab, son of Zeruiah, was a military commander under King David. His deferral of credit for his military defeat is recorded in 2 Kings 12:26–29.

891   *Josephus rehercith that the frendes of Tyberius.* This *exemplum* comes from Flavius Josephus' *Jewish Antiquities,* Book 18, chapter 6.5. See *Jewish Antiquities,* 8:112–13. Josephus was a Jewish historian who lived from about 37 to 100 C.E., and his works were popular in the Middle Ages.

905   *As to the first, one sayd to Alisaunder that he was not worthy to reigne.* I have not been able to locate the specific source of this passage, though the Tale of Diogenes and Alexander, *CA* 3.1201–1313, rehearses a challenge to Alexander's authority, which he accepts graciously.

909   *Also, hit is rehercid that Julyus Cesar was ballyd.* This story of Caesar's baldness appears in *Lives of the Caesars,* Book 1 (Julius), chapter 45 (1:62 and 63).

918   *A knyght callyd on a tyme Scipyon of Affrique.* This story Scipio's patience appears in John of Salisbury's *Policratius*, Book 3, chapter 14. See John of Salisbury, *Frivolities of Courtiers*, p. 205.

922   *Another sayd to Vaspasion.* This story of Vespasian appears in Suetonius, *The Lives of the Caesars*, Book 8 (Vespasian), chapter 16 (2:310 and 311). In Suetonius' version, Vespasian is compared to a fox, not a wolf. John of Salisbury also records this story in his *Policraticus*, Book 3, chapter 14. See John of Salisbury, *Frivolities of Courtiers*, p. 208.

926   *Seneke rehercith that the Kyng Antygonus.* I have not been able to locate the source for this quote.

930–32 *Valerius reherceth that a tyraunt dyd do torment Anamaxymenes and thretenyd hym for to cutte of his tunge.* This story of Anaxarchus and the tyrant of Cyprus appears in *Memorable Doings and Sayings*, Book 3.3, ext. 4 (1:278 and 279).

938   *Valerius rehercith that Archyta of Tarente, that was mayster to Plato.* The *exemplum* of Archytas of Tarentum appears in *Memorable Doings and Sayings*, Book 4.1, ext. 1 (1:352 and 353).

943   *And therfore sayth Seneque.* The quotation from Seneca — "Nihil tibi liceat, dum irasceris" — is actually Seneca quoting Plato. It is found in Seneca's essay *De ira*, Book 3, chapter 12.7. See *Moral Essays*, 1:286–87. In his translation Caxton omits a story from Valerius, *Memorable Doings and Sayings* (Book 4.2, ext. 2) about Plato that Jacobus and the French translators place right before Seneca's quotation.

949–50 *And that rehercith Valerius in his eighth book that Scypyon of Affryque was accused unto the Senate.* This narrative of Scipio being accused of wealth appears in *Memorable Doings and Sayings*, Book 3.7.1e (1:300 and 301).

955   *And therfore sayth Seneque that the Kyng Altagone.* This *exemplum* of Agathocles and his earthen plates is not from Seneca but from the fourth-century *Epigrams* of Ausonius (c. 310–94 C.E.), a writer and a teacher at the University of Bordeaux. It is Epigram 2 from Book 19. See Ausonius, *Ausonius*, 2:156–57.

964   *And of this poverté speketh Saynt Augustyn in the Book of the Cyté of God.* Augustine speaks of the corruption of Romans through their love of wealth in Book 5, chapter 14 of *De civitate dei* (1:162–63).

971–72 *John the Monke, late cardynal of Rome, in the Decretal the Sixte, in the chappytre Gens sancta.* According to Axon, "John the Monk" was Giovanni d'Andrea, a canonist "who died at the plague of Bologna in 1347. His learning gained him such titles as *rabbi doctorum* and *normaque morum*" (*Caxton's Game and Playe of the Chesse, 1474*, p. lviii). Axon in turn cites Hoefer's *Nouvelle biographie universelle*. This particular reference is to Giovanni d'Andrea's *Liber sextus decretalium*.

990–91 *And we rede that Titus, the sone of Vaspasian, was so large and so lyberal.* This story of Titus' generosity appears in Suetonius' *Lives of the Caesars*, Book 8 (Titus), chapter 8 (2:330 and 331). It is also found in John of Salisbury's *Policraticus*, Book 3, chapter 14. See John of Salisbury, *Frivolities of Courtiers*, p. 209.

997   *And also, we rede of Julius Cesar.* The most likely source for this is Suetonius, Book 1 (Julius), chapter 67 (1:86–89).

1001   *And also, we rede of the same Julyus Cesar in the Book of Truphes of Philosophers.* The main source here is in John of Salisbury's *Policraticus*, Book III, chapter 14. See John of Salisbury, *Frivolities of Courtiers*, p. 207.

BOOK THREE

Chapter 1

15   *And we rede in the Bible that the first labourer that ever was was Caym.* Cain's murder of Abel appears in Genesis 4:8.

52–53   *And we rede of the Kyng Davyd, that was first symple and one of the comyn peple.* David forgets God in 2 Kings 12:9. Absalon's persecution of David is narrated in 2 Kings 15.

58   *We rede also of the children of Ysrael, that were nygh enfamyned in desert.* This story of manna in the desert comes from Exodus 16. The subsequent worship of the golden calf appears in Exodus 32.

74–75   *And Valerius rehercith in his sixt book that there was a wyse and noble maistre that was named Anthonius.* M. Antonius' adultery trial is found in *Memorable Doings and Sayings*, Book 6.8.1 (2:74 and 75).

86–87   *And also tellith Valerius that there was another labourer that was named Penapion.* From *Memorable Doings and Sayings*, Book 6.8.6 (2:78 and 79). In Valerius, the master is Ubinius Panapio, and the slave is Unnamedo.

101   *And of this speketh Claudyan.* This is a paraphrased version of the poet Claudian's late fourth- to early fifth-century *De raptu Proserpinae* Book 2, lines 294–302. Jacobus quotes Claudian directly. See Claudian, *Claudian*, 2:338–41.

109   *And therof made a noble versefyer.* The identity of the poet is unknown.

112   *meritis.* Good works. E.g., see *Everyman*, where Good Deeds alone accompanies Everyman beyond death.

113   *And herof fynde we in Vitas patrum.* The *Vitae patrum* is a collection of the lives and sayings of early Christian hermits. The copies circulating in the Middle Ages were not the Greek originals but translations into Latin, which were done primarily in the fourth through sixth centuries. The location of this particular story in the vast corpus of the *Vitae* is not known.

116   *thre causes.* A short lyric lament, popular in French and English; e.g.,

           Wanne ich þenche þinges þre
           ne mai neure bliþe be:
           þat on is ich sal awe,
           þat oþer is ich ne wot wilk day.

þat þridde is mi meste kare,
i ne woth nevre wuder i sal fare
(New College MS 88, one of four versions in Brown, *English Lyrics of the XIIIth Century*, pp. 18–19).

140–41   *And thou oughtest to knowe that Davyd preyseth moche in the Sawlter the trewe labourers.* This saying is derived from Psalm 127 ("Blessed are they that fear the Lord: that walk in His ways"), although some versions cite the Roman poet Lucan (39–65 c.e.) as the source. By contrast, Jacobus in his *Liber* includes six lines from the *Carmina* (Book 2.1, lines 5–10) of Albius Tibullus (c. 55–19 b.c.e.), a Roman elegiac poet. See "Tibullus," trans. J. P. Postgate, in *Catullus, Tibullus, and Pervigilium Veneris*, pp. 252 and 253.

148   *The first pastour that ever was was Abel.* This description of Abel can be found in Genesis 4:2–4.

152–53   *And so dyd Noe, whyche was the first that planted the vygne after the deluge and flood.* Genesis 9:20.

153–54   *For as Josephus reherceth in the Book of Naturel Thynges.* The extended story of Noah and his sons appears in the *Gesta Romanorum*, Tale CLIX, which in turn references Josephus' *Causes of Natural Things*. See *Gesta*, pp. 336–37.

173–74   *And therfore, Valerian reherceth that of auncient and in olde tyme women dranke no wyn.* This *exemplum* can be found in *Memorable Doings and Sayings*, Book 2.1.5b (1:130 and 131).

176   *And as Ovyde saith.* This derives from Book 1, lines 237–40 of Ovid's *Art of Love* (pp. 28–29). Jacobus quotes these lines in full: "Vina parant animos faciuntque caloribus aptos: / Cura fugit multo diluiturque mero. / Tunc veniunt risus, tum pauper cornua sumit, / Tum dolor et curae rugaque frontis abit."

Chapter 2

200   *And therfore sayth the phylosopher.* At least one of Jacobus' French translators attributes this quotation to Socrates. Yet as Collet notes, it most likely comes from Publilius Syrus' *Sentences*, where the saying is rendered: "Fidem qui perdit, nil pote ultra perdere" or "Whoever loses faith has nothing more to lose." See The Latin Library at: http://www.thelatinlibrary.com/syrus.html (accessed 8–17–06).

204   *Valerius rehercith that Fabius.* This story of Fabius and Hannibal appears in *Memorable Doings and Sayings*, Book 4.8.1 (1:428–31).

211–13   *But in thyse dayes it were grete folye . . . at theyr nede.* These two sentences have been added by Caxton.

225–27   Caxton's emphasis of the importance of common profit and the ways in which the avaricious ignore it to the peril of society resonates with Boethius' *Consolation of Philosophy*, the *Romance of the Rose*, and, especially, Gower's *Confessio Amantis*.

228–29   *And fortune hath of nothyng so grete plesure as for to torne and werke alwey. And nature is so noble a thyng that whereas she is, she wyl susteyne and kepe.* Although Caxton does not attribute this quote to a particular author, Jacobus in his *Liber* refers to Cicero's *Pro Q. Ligario oratio* [*Speech on Behalf of Quintus Ligarius*], chapter 12.38 and quotes his source: "Nihil habet nec fortuna tua maius quam ut possis, nec natura melius quam ut velis servare quam plurimos" ["Your situation has nothing prouder in it than the power, your character nothing in it more noble than the wish, to preserve all whom you can"]. See Cicero's "On Behalf of Libarius" in *Pro Milone*, pp. 492–93.

238–39   *And also, it is to be supposid that suche as have theyr goodes comune and not propre is most acceptable to God.* This sentence begins a paragraph that represents Caxton's most substantial addition to the *Liber*. Initially, it seems that Caxton uses this passage to reinforce the moral probity of the White Friars, or Carmelites, and thus the superiority of the regular clergy over the secular clergy. After proposing that those who "have goods in common" are "most acceptable to God," he then asks: "Would not these religious men such as monks, friars, canons, observants [Franciscans], and all others make vows and keep themselves in voluntary poverty that they are bound to?" The "would not" construction here can be taken in at least two ways. First, it might affirm the general practice of monastic poverty, "would not" serving to indicate the fact that these groups do, in fact, follow this law. Taken this way, this section might read: "if this is the most acceptable practice, then why else would these religious men keep themselves in voluntary poverty." Alternately, "would not" might call attention to the deficiencies of the monks in this regard: if shared goods are more acceptable to God, then why don't other religious orders follow this law? It is at this point that Caxton turns to the Carmelites who do, it seems, practice what they preach. Yet on closer inspection, Caxton's endorsement of the Carmelites is not so clear. In 1464, the London Carmelites began a preaching battle with the secular clergy. The battle began when Harry Parker, a young Carmelite from the Fleet Street house, preached a sermon at St. Paul's in which he declared that "Christ and his apostles had no private property, that they made their living exclusively by begging for alms, and that what they were given they possessed in common." Parker went on to add that "the state of the mendicant friars was the most perfect one to be found in the Church Militant, and that all priests ought likewise to live off alms, without benefices or private property." A good account of this battle can be found in Jotischky, *Carmelites and Antiquity*, pp. 157–58. The paraphrase of Parker's sermon can be found in Du Boulay, "Quarrel between the Carmelite Friars and the Secular Clergy."

248   *And accordyng therto, we rede in Plato.* Comments about the dangers of individualism among the guardian class run throughout Plato's *Republic*. However, this specific reference seems to come from Book 5, section 462. See Plato, *Republic*, pp. 126–27.

277–78   *For we rede that Dyonyse of Zecyle.* This story of Dionysius of Sicily (also Dionysius of Syracuse) and the misery provoked by his tyranny appears in Valerius,

Memorable Doings and Sayings, Book 9.13, ext. 4 (2:384 and 385). It can also be found in Cicero's *Tusculan Disputations,* Book 5, chapter 20 (pp. 451–52).

Chapter 3

364–73   *Alas! And in Engelond . . . to theyr synguler wele and prouffyt and not to the comyn.* This is one of the few asides that Caxton has added to the text.

376   *And Tullyus saith that frendshyp and good wylle.* These observations about friendship seem to be a paraphrase of Cicero's *Laelius,* Books 6 and 7 (pp. 38–39). The example of bees does not come from Cicero.

387–88   *And this amytie is vertuous, of the whiche Tullyus saith.* From Cicero's *De officiis,* Book 3, chapter 10.46 (pp. 312–15). This also appears in Cicero's *Laelius,* Book 11.37 (pp. 46–47).

396   *And herof sayth Seneque that amytye.* In citing Seneca, Caxton follows Jacobus, who also attributes these two quotes about friendship to Seneca. Although not an exact match, Seneca's most relevant quotes about friendship appear in *De beneficiis,* Book 2, chapter 15 (3:76–79). A more likely quote for the Latin *Liber* comes from Cicero's *Laelius,* Book 6.22: "Quid dulcius quam habere quicum omnia audeas sic loqui ut tecum?" ["What is more pleasant than to have someone with whom you can safely talk about anything whatever, just as with yourself?" (pp. 38–39)]. Likely sources for the subsequent section of the *Liber* are Books 8 and 9 of Aristotle's *Nicomachean Ethics,* in which Aristotle divides friendship into three types, those of utility, pleasure, and good. These correspond to the Latin text's division of friendship into "delectabilis, utilis, et honesta." See Jacobus, *Libellus de moribus hominum et officiis nobilium,* p. 87.

401   *And Valerian sayth that it is a foule thynge and an evyl excusasion.* The *exemplum* of Taffile, or Rutilius, appears in *Memorable Doings and Sayings,* Book 6.4.4 (2:46–49).

413   *And Varro rehercith in his sommes.* Like the above reference to Varro (see note to 1.89), this is most likely taken from the *Menippean Satires.* I have not been able to locate the exact passage.

417   *And Seneque saith that somme folowe the emperour for riches.* This same saying is cited by Chaucer's Parson in his tale. See The Parson's Tale *CT* X(I)440. Chaucer took much of the Parson's Tale from the thirteenth-century *Summa virtutem et vitiorum* [*Summa of Virtues and Vices*] of Guilelmus Peraldus, which might also have served as a source for Jacobus.

420   *And Tullyus sayth that Tarquyn the Proud had a nevewe of his suster.* This observation of Tarquin is found in Cicero's *Laelius,* Chapter XV.53 (pp. 52–53).

428   *For Cathon sayth in his book.* Jacobus credits these lines to Ovid. The first line comes from *Ex Ponto,* Book 2.3, line 8 ("Vulgus amicitias utilitate probat"); the subsequent lines are found in *Tristia,* Book 1.5, lines 33–34 ("Vix duo tresve mihi de tot superestis amici / Cetera Fortunae, non mea turba fuit" and Book 1.9,

lines 5–6 ("Donec eris sospes, multos numerabis amicos / Tempora si fuerint nubila, solus eris"). See Ovid, *Ex Ponto*, pp. 332–33, and *Tristia*, pp. 30, 31, 44, and 45.

433   *And therfore sayth the versefier thyse two versis.* The identity of the poet is unknown.

440–41   *And Piers Alphons sayth in his Book of Moralité that there was a phylosophre in Arabye.* The story of the philosopher and his son comes from Book 1 of Peter Alfonso's twelfth-century *Disciplina Clericalis*, a moral guide for the clergy. See *Scholar's Guide*, pp. 36–38. It also appears in the *Gesta Romanorum*, Tale CXXIX (p. 276).

462–63   *And yet reherceth the sayd Piers Alphons that there were two marchauntes, one of Bandach and that other of Egypt.* This story also comes from the *Disciplina Clericalis* where it follows the story of the philosopher and his son (pp. 38–41). It also appears as Tale CLXXI of the *Gesta Romanorum*, where it is similarly attributed to Peter Alfonso (pp. 351–54).

507–08   *Titus Livius reherceth that the philosopher Democreon dyd doo put out his eyen.* In the Latin *Liber* and in its French translations, this story is attributed to the late second- to early third-century author Tertullian, although they do not name the specific work. Caxton credits Livy, although Livy does not include this story of Democritus in his *History of Rome*.

511   *And Valerian tellyth that there was a yong man of Rome.* The story of the beautiful young man from Rome appears in *Memorable Doings and Sayings*, Book 4.5, ext. 1 (1:400 and 401).

518–19   *And also we rede that there was a nonne, a virgyne, dyd do put out bothe her eyen.* I have not been able to locate the source for this story.

521   *And also we rede that Plato.* I have not been able to locate the source for this story.

526   *Helemand reherceth that Demostenes.* The story about Demosthenes appears in Aulus Gellius' *Attic Nights*, Book 1, chapter 8 (1:42–45). For more information on Hélinand de Froidmont, see note to 2.265.

533–34   *And Ovyde rehercith that thys thynge is the leste that maye helpe and most greve the lovers.* This quote — "Quod iuvat, exiguum, plus est, quod laedat amantes" — comes from the *Art of Love*, Book 2, line 515 (pp. 100–01).

535–36   *And therfore Saynt Augustyn rehercith in his book, De civitate dei, that there was a right noble Romayn named Marculian.* The story of Marcellus' conquering of Syracuse appears in Book 1, chapter 5 of *City of God* (1:7). Valerius also describes Marcellus' tears in Book 5.1.4 of *Memorable Doings and Sayings* (1:446 and 447).

551–52   *For Saynt Austyn sayth . . . And also, he sayth in another place.* Presumably these passages come from *The City of God*, although Jacobus does not name his source.

559   *And herof speketh Saynt Bernard.* This quote by Bernard appears in a letter that he wrote to the monk Adam. However, Bernard in turn is citing the apocryphal Book of Wisdom 1.11, which states: "Keep yourselves therefore from murmuring, which profiteth nothing, and refrain your tongue from detraction, for an obscure speech shall not go for nought: and the mouth that belieth, killeth the soul."

561–62   *And yet sayth Saynt Austyn in another place, "For to say one thynge and do the contrarye maketh doctryne suspecious."* Like the above references to Augustine, this one does not name a specific source.

564   *For the lye that the auncient enemye maad Eve and Adam.* The fall of man is described in Genesis 3.

573   *And therfore saith Saynt Poule in a pistyl.* This passage seems to be a paraphrase of 1 Corinthians 2.

576   *And Valerian rehercith that there was a good woman of Siracusane.* This story of the woman who praises the emperor comes from *Memorable Doings and Sayings*, Book 6.2, ext. 2 (2:26–29). It also appears in the *Gesta Romanorum*, Tale LIII (p. 150).

Chapter 4

608–09   *And herof sayth Tullyus that avarice is a covetise to gete that thyng that is above necessité.* Cicero defines avarice in his *Tusculan Disputations* Book 4, chapter 11 (pp. 407–08).

613–14   *And herof sayth Seneque that all worldly thynges ben mortefyed and appetissed in olde men, reservyd avarice onely.* The covetousness of old men is proverbial. See Whiting C490.

618–21   *the wolf doth never good tyl he be dede . . . the avaricious man doth no good tyl that he be deed.* Proverbial. See Whiting W472. Compare the Latin proverb "Avarus nisi cum moritur, nil recte facit," from the *Sententiae* of Publilius Syrus, (http://www.thelatinlibrary.com/syrus.html, accessed 8–9–06).

625   *And herof rehercith Seneque, and sayth that Antigonus.* From Seneca's *De beneficiis*, Book 2.17 (3:80–81). In Seneca's essay, as well as in the *Liber*, Antigonus' interlocutor is a Cynic not "Tynque," as Caxton has renamed him. It should be noted that in Seneca's essay, he supports Antigonus and not the Cynic, adding: "the situation is intolerable that a man should ask for money when he despises it."

634–35   *And Josephus rehercith in the Book of Auncient Histories that ther was in Rome a right noble lady named Paulyne.* This *exemplum* comes from Flavius Josephus' *Jewish Antiquities*, Book 18, chapter 3.4 (pp. 50–59). In Josephus' version, Paulina does refuse Decius Mundus' advances, although he later tricks her into sleeping with him. The story recurs in Hegesippus 2.4; Godfrey of Viterbo, *Pantheon* 15; and Vincent of Beauvais, *Speculum Historiale* 7.4; but the liveliest retelling is Gower's Tale of Mundus and Paulina, *CA* 1.761–1059.

644–45   *And we rede also in the Histories of Rome that there was a noble lady of Rome whiche lyved a solytarye lyf.* I have not been able to locate a source for this quotation, although it might come from Lucius Annaeus Florus' *Epitome of Roman History*.

657   *Seneque rehercith in the Book of the Cryes of Women.* The *Liber* attributes this saying to Seneca the Elder's first-century *Declamations*, also known as the *Controversiae*. Although I have not been able to locate the precise Latin quotation, a similar sentiment is found in Book 2, chapter 6.2 of that work. See *Declamations*, 1.346–47.

657–58   *avaryce is foundement of alle vyces.* Proverbial. See Whiting C491 for dozens of citations. Compare the Latin *radix malorum est cupiditas*, recurrent from Alfred's translation of the *Pastoral Care* (73.22–23) and Wulfstan's *Homilies* (203.74–76) through Chaucer's Pardoner's Tale (*CT* VI[C]334).

659   *And Valerian rehercith that avarice is a ferdful garde or kepar of richessis.* Valerius' comments on avarice and the story of Septimuleius can be found in Book 9.4, 1 and 3 of *Memorable Doings and Sayings* (2:331–33).

670   *Ptolomé, Kyng of Egipciens, poursewed avarice in another manere.* From Valerius, *Memorable Doings and Sayings*, Book 9.4, ext. 1 (2:332–35).

680–81   *And therfore hit is said in proverbe that a man ought to seignorie over the riches, and not for to serve hit.* This proverb, "Pecuniae imperare oportet, non servire," comes from the *Sententiae* of Publilius Syrus (http://www.thelatinlibrary.com/syrus.html, accessed 8–23–06).

685–86   *And Saluste saith that avarice destroubleth fayth, poesté, honesté, and al thise other good vertues.* This comes from Book 10 of Sallust's first-century C.E. historical monograph, *Bellum Catilinae* [*War with Cataline*]. See Sallust, *Sallust*, pp. 18–19.

689–90   *For Saynt Ambrose saith upon Thoby: "Poverté hath no lawe."* This saying appears in chapter 21.81–82 of St. Ambrose's *Commentary on the Book of Tobias*, a fourth-century treatise on usury. See *De Tobia*, pp. 94–95. The *Liber*, which cobbles together various phrases from this section of Ambrose's text, reads: "Paupertas non habet crimen, sed debere vercundum est, non reddere verecundius. Dives es, pauper es, non sumas mutum."

694–95   *And it is said in the proverbis that hit is fraude to take that thou wylt not ner mayst [not] rendre and paye agayn.* This proverb, "Fraus est accipere, quod non possis reddere," comes from the *Sententiae* of Publilius Syrus (http://www.thelatinlibrary .com/syrus.htm, accessed 8–23–06).

698–99   *And Seneke saith in his auctorités that they that gladly borowe ought gladly to paye.* This saying comes from Seneca's *De beneficiis*, Book 2, chapter 25 (3:102–03).

706–07   *There was a marchaunt of Gene and also a chaungeour whos name was Albert Ganor.* This *exemplum* seems to be original to Jacobus' *Liber*.

728–29   *Wherof hit happend that ther was a marchaunt which had a good and a grete name.* This *exemplum* seems to be original to Jacobus' *Liber*.

772   *And therfore hit is sayd in proverbe, "To defraude the begiler is no fraude."* This exact proverb does not appear in the *Liber*, although Jacobus cites a similar saying from Publilius Syrus: "Quid est dare beneficium? imitari deum." See the *Sententiae* (http://www.thelatinlibrary.com/syrus.html, accessed 8–23–06), and Whiting B213, which cites this line.

774–75   *And Seneke sayth that charité enseigneth and techeth that men shold paye wel, for good payement is somtyme good confessyon.* This quote comes from Seneca's *Moral Letters*, Number 73.9–10 (2:108 and 109). Latin versions of the *Liber* quote Seneca directly: "Hoc docet philosophia praecipue, bene debere beneficia, bene solvere; interdum autem solutio est ipsa confessio."

Chapter 5

title   *medecynes.* The *OED* cites Caxton's *Aesop* for *medecyne* meaning "medical prac-titioners," which is evidently the sense here.

820   *And therfore sayth Avycenne in an Anforysme.* Avicenna (980–1037 C.E.) is the European name for Ibn Sina, a Persian philosopher and scientist, who wrote over four hundred works on medicine, theology, and philosophy. One of his most famous texts was the *Canon of Medicine*, which was translated, explicated, and rewritten repeatedly throughout the Middle Ages. An early abridgement of this work, possibly by Muhammad ibn Yusuf al-Ilaqi, was limited to the *Canon's* first book and was written in the form of aphorisms. It is this work that is most likely referenced by Jacobus and Caxton.

827–28   *and specially in the bookes of Ypocras, Galiene, and of Avycene.* Hippocrates (460–377 B.C.E.) and Galen (c. 130–200 C.E.) were both Greek physicians whose writings, like those of Avicenna, provided the foundations for Western medicine up to, and even beyond, the Renaissance.

851–63   *For Valerian rehercith that Ypocras was of mervayllous contynence of his body . . . And in semblable wyse rehercith Valeryan of Scenocrates, phylosopher.* This story of Xenocrates and his refusal of the prostitute appears in *Memorable Doings and Sayings*, Book 4.3, ext. 3a (1:380–83). There is no separate story of Hippocrates.

867   *Cornelius Scipion, that was sent by the Romayns for to governe Spayn.* This story of Scipio in Spain comes from Valerius, *Memorable Doings and Sayings*, Book 2.7.1 (1:178 and 179).

873–74   *And herof it is sayd in the fables of the poetes in the first book of the Truphes of the Philosophres.* The *Truphes of the Philosophers* is a reference to John of Salisbury's *Policraticus.* Caxton's specific citation is wrong: the saying appears in the fifth book, not the first book. Moreover, John of Salisbury's treatise refers to the fountain of Salmacis, which had the effect of turning men into women, and not to the fountains of sirens. See John of Salisbury, *Statesman's Book*, pp. 121–22.

890   *And Marcial sayth that joyes fugetyves abyde not long, but fle awey anone.* This saying comes from from Martial's *Epigrams*, Book 1, chapter 15. The Latin quote reads: "gaudia non remanent, sed fugitiva volant." See Martial, *Epigrams*, 1:52–53.

893–94   *Wherof hit happend that there was a woman named Lyna.* Although Jacobus claims to have taken this story from Valerius, *Memorable Doings and Sayings*, he modifies it beyond recognition. In Valerius' version (Book 9.12.2), it is a mother who, upon seeing her son return alive from Lake Trasimene, dies in his arms. See *Memorable Doings and Sayings*, 2.368–69.

899–900   *Also, of another woman to whom was reported by a fals messanger that her sone was deed.* See Valerius, *Memorable Doings and Sayings*, Book 9.12.2 (2:368–71).

907   *Valerie rehercith that a knyght of Rome named Instavlosus.* The story of M. Juventius
               Thalna (as he is called in the *Liber*) or Colaphe (as he is called in the French
               versions) comes from *Memorable Doings and Sayings*, Book 9.12.3 (2:370 and 371).

914–15   *And also it is sayd that Phylomenus lawghed so sore and distemperatly that he dyed al
               lawghyng.* This story of Philemon dying of laughter comes from Valerius,
               Memorable Doings and Sayings, Book 9.12, ext. 6 (2:376 and 377).

916   *And we rede that Ypocras, the phisicien, fond remedye for thys joye.* I have not been able
               to locate the source for this story of Hippocrates.

922–48   *And also, we rede that Titus, the sone of Vaspasian, whan he had conquerd Jherusalem.*
               The apocryphal story of the healing of Titus by Vespasian during the historical
               siege of Jerusalem in 70 C.E. is of uncertain origin (it does not appear in
               Josephus' own account of the siege — see note to lines 926–27), but it was
               sufficiently popular by the thirteenth century to appear in texts as different as
               chronicles and law books (see Lewy, "Josephus"). It appears variously in Middle
               English (see, for instance, *Siege of Jerusalem*, ed. Livingston, lines 1027–68),
               though its appearance here has as its ultimate source Jacobus Voragine's *Legenda
               aurea*, a text set into English by Caxton and published in 1483 (*Golden Legend*
               III, "Of S. James the Less").

926–27   *Josephus, that made the historye of the Romayns ayenst the Jewys.* Flavius Josephus was
               perhaps most widely known for the book referred to here: *Wars of the Jews*, an
               eyewitness account of events in Judaea before, during, and immediately after the
               destruction of Jerusalem by Rome in 70 C.E. He was of such fame by the later
               Middle Ages that he merits no introduction, for instance, in the Middle English
               Siege of Jerusalem (ed. Livingston, line 313).

927   *a right wyse phisicien.* Josephus was not, properly speaking, a physician of any
               kind. What few facts we have of his life portray him as a Jewish military leader
               from a priestly family, whose education and circumstances prompted him to write
               works of history and philosophy; the Middle English *Siege of Jerusalem* refers to
               him with some accuracy as a "gentyl clerke" (ed. Livingston, line 789). His repu-
               tation as a *phisicien* seems very much confined to this single apocryphal story.

935–36   *boutelers, cokes, and other officers.* These specifics regarding the servants taking
               part in Josephus' scheme are not found in Voragine's *Legenda aurea*, and Caxton
               does not include them in retelling this story for his translation of that text (see
               note to lines 922–48).

976   *And herof sayth Boecius [in] De consolacisone, in his first booke.* Boethius (c. 480–526
               C.E.) was an advisor to the Ostrogothic king Theodoric in the early sixth century
               before Theodoric had him thrown into prison. While he awaited execution,
               Boethius wrote *De Consolatio Philosophiae* [*The Consolation of Philosophy*], a work
               of alternating poetry and prose that became one of the most widely circulated
               texts of the Middle Ages. This comes from the final poem (*Metrum 7*) of the first
               book. The *Liber* gives the poem in its entirety; Caxton and the French translators
               render it in prose. See Boethius, *Consolation of Philosophy*, p. 18.

Chapter 6

1004–06   *and somtyme ben slayn or hurte unto the deth as it is wreton in Vitas Patrum, as on a tyme*
           an hermyte went for to vysite his gossibs. As with the reference to the *Vitae* in the first
           chapter of this book, the specific location of this particular story is not known.

1030   *Wherof Quyntilian saith that hit happeth ofte tymes in grete festes and dyners.* This
           saying is taken from Book 10.1.58 of Quintillian's *Institutio oratorio* (4:34–35).

1034   *And Lucan saith that "glotony is the moder of al vices."* This saying comes from
           Lucan's first century *Bellum civile* [*Civil War*], Book 4, lines 373–77. See Lucan,
           Lucan, pp. 200–03.

1039   *And Cathon saith, "In no wyse obeye to glotonye, whiche is frende to lecherye."* This
           quote comes from Book 4, Number 10 of Cato's *Distichs*. The Latin verse reads:
           "Cum te detineat Veneris damnosa libido, / Indulgere gulae noli, quae ventris
           amica est" ["When hurtful lust hath hold of thee, refrain / From giving to thy
           appetites free rein"]. See Cato, *Distichs*, pp. 36–37.

1040–41   *And the holy doctour Saynt Augustyn saith, "The wyn eschauffith the bely that falleth*
           anone to lecherye." I have not been able to locate the precise source for this quote,
           although Augustine expresses a similar sentiment in *Confessions*, Book 10.

1048   *And therfore saith Vasilly la Graunt: "Late us take hede howe we serve the bely."* This
           quote most likely comes from St. Basil the Great (329–79), author of a variety of
           homilies, sermons, and other exegetical works. I have not been able to track the
           exact source.

1052–53   *And herof sayth Boecius [in] De consolacisone in his fourth book, that a man that lyveth*
           and doth not the condicions of a man. The *Liber* paraphrases this quote, which reads:
           "qui probitate deserta homo esse desierit, cum in divinam condicionem transire
           non possit, vertatur in beluam." This comes from Book 4 (Prosa 3) of Boethuis,
           Consolation of Philosophy (p. 79).

1061   *For as Cathon sayth: "Ire enpessheth the corage."* Although there is no mention of
           Cato in most Latin or French versions of the *Liber*, these texts contain similar
           passages, which are found in Cato's *Distichs*, Book 2, Number 4: "Iratus de re
           incerta contendere noli: / Inpedit ira animum, ne possis cernere, verum" ["Strive
           not in wrath o'er something wrapped in doubt; / Wrath clouds the mind and
           puts good sense to rout"]. See Cato, *Distichs*, pp. 24 and 25.

1065–66   *And therfore saith Ovyde in his book De remedio amoris: "Yf thou take many and dyverce*
           wynes, they apparayle and enforce the corages to lecherye." The Latin *Liber* includes
           line 805 of the *Remedies of Love*: "Vina parant animum Veneri, nisi plurima sumas"
           or "Wine prepares the heart for love, unless you take too much." By contrast,
           Caxton and the *Liber*'s French translators repeat Ovid's maxim from the *Art of
           Love*, Book 1, line 237: "Vina parant animos, faciuntque caloribus aptos" or
           "Wine gives courage and makes men apt for passion." See Ovid, *Art of Love*, pp.
           28 and 29, and *Remedies of Love*, pp. 232 and 233.

1067–68   *And Thobye wytnessyth in his book that luxurie destroyeth the body and mynyssheth rychessys.* Jacobus does not include this quote, although it does appear in Caxton's most likely French copy text. I have not been able to locate its source.

1072   *Noe was one tyme so chauffyd wyth wyn.* The stories of Noah and Lot appear in Genesis 9:20–21 and 19:31–36 respectively.

1077   *And Crete rehercith that Boece.* This is most likely a reference to St. Andrew of Crete (660–740 C.E.), author of sermons, discourses, and, most famously, a collection of hymns, now commonly known as the *Great Canon.* I have not been able to locate the source for his comments about Boethius.

1084   *Herodes Antipas had not doon Saynt John Baptist to ben beheded.* The stories of Herod and John the Baptist come from Matthew 14:3–12 and Mark 6:17–29, although there is no mention of Herod having consumed alcohol.

1085–86   *Balthazar, kyng of Babylone, had not been chaced out of his kyngdom, ne be slayn.* Balthazar's killing is described in Daniel 5:30.

1099   *We rede that Loth, whan he had receyvyd the aungellys into his hows.* Lot welcomes the angels in Genesis 19:1–11.

1119–20   *Hit happend on a tyme in the parties of Lombardye in the cyté of Jene that a noble man was lodgyd in an hostelrye.* This story of a nobleman in Genoa seems to have been original to Jacobus' *Liber.*

1133   *Another caas right cruel and vilaynous fyl at Tholouse.* The story of the two pilgrims also seems to have been original to Jacobus' *Liber. Saynt James in Galice* (1139) refers to the Way of St. James, the most popular pilgrimage route in the Middle Ages. Pilgrims ended their journey at the cathedral of Compostela in Galicia, Spain.

1137   Caxton has amplified this final *exemplum.*

1156   *For semblable caas fyl in Spayn at Saynt Donne.* This story seems to be one of Caxton's own inventions.

Chapter 7

1203–04   *Hit is founden in the histories of Rome that the Emperour Frederik the Second dyd doo make a gate of marble.* Although the *Liber* makes reference to the *Histories of Rome,* there is no mention in that text of the gate that Emperor Frederick II had erected at Capua in 1240.

1216–17   *And herof we fynde in the auncient histories of Cecille that the Kyng Denys had a broder whom he lovyd sore wel.* There are several possible sources for the story of King Dionysius, which include Cicero's *Tusculan Disputations,* Book 5, chapter 21 (pp. 452–53) and Macrobius' early fifth-century *Commentary on the Dream of Scipio,* Book I, chapter 10.16 (p. 129). Boethius' *Consolatio* Book 3 (Prose 5) also contains a brief reference to this narrative (*Consolation of Philosophy,* p. 48).

1249–50   *And herof sayth Quyntilian that thys drede surmounteth alle other maleurtees and evylles.*
           Although Jacobus and his translators all cite Quintilian here, the maxim comes
           from Publilius Syrus: "Res vera est, qui a multis timetur, multos timet" or, as
           Caxton writes, "And it is verite that to hym that is doubted of moche peple, so
           muste he doubte moche." See Publilius Syrus, *Sentences* (http://www.thelatin
           library.com/syrus.html, accessed 8–25–06).

1267   *A jogheler on a tyme behelde Socrates and sayd to hym.* Although the jester in Caxton
           accuses Socrates of having eyes "of corumpour of children," other translators are
           often more explicit, referring to "les yeulx de home sodomite." I have not
           located a source for this story.

1272   *This same Socrates hymself was chidde and right foul spoken to of hys wyf.* The story of
           Xanthippe dousing Socrates with urine appears in Diogenes Laertius' *Lives of the
           Eminent Philosophers*, Book 2, chapter 5.36–37 (1:166 and 167). See also
           Chaucer's Wife of Bath's Prologue (*CT* III[D]726–29). A discussion of Socrates'
           reasons for enduring his wife's temper can be found in Aulus Gellius' *Attic Nights*,
           Book 1, chapter 17 (1:84 and 85).

1283–84   *And Cathon saith: "Whan thou lyvest rightfully, retche thee not of the wordes of evyl
           peple."* This proverb appears in Cato's *Distichs*, Book 3, Number 2: "Cum recte
           vivas, ne cures verba malorum; / Arbitrii non est nostri, quid quisque loquatur"
           ["Upright, care not if bad men thee deride; / 'T is not within our power men's
           tongues to guide"]. See Cato, *Distichs*, pp. 30 and 31.

1287–88   *And Prosper sayth that to good men lacketh no goodnes, ner to evyl men tencions, stryves,
           and blames.* The reference here is to the *Epigrams* of St. Prosper of Aquitaine
           (390–465 C.E.), an author most famous for his scriptural commentary. The Latin
           quote, "Numquam bella bonis, numquam discrimina desunt" is from Book 96,
           De bello intestino. See *Epigrammata ex sententiis Augustini* in the *PL* 51:0528A.

1289–90   *as a noble versefier saith that pacience is a right noble maner to vaynquysshe.* The
           identity of the poet is unknown.

1300–01   *And herof saith Ysaye: "Woo to thee that robbest! For thou, thyself, shalt be robbyd."* This
           seems to be a paraphrase of the prophecy of Isaias 3:11: "Woe to the wicked
           unto evil: for the reward of his hands shall be given him."

Chapter 8

1336   *Cassiodore admonesteth the fole larges to kepe their thynges.* Although Cassiodorus, a
           writer from the late sixth and early seventh centuries, is the purported source
           for this saying, Jacobus does not identify the work from which he has taken it,
           nor have I been able to locate it.

1341–42   *And Claudyan saith in like wyse in his book that hyt is a gretter thynge and better to kepe
           that is goten than to gete more.* This quote is a modification of Book 2, lines 326–27
           of Claudian's *De consulatu Stilichonis* [*On Stilicho's Consulship*]: "plus est servasse
           repertum / quam quaesisse novum" (*Claudian*, 2:26 and 27).

1345   *There was a noble man named John de Ganazath, whiche was right riche.* Collet refers
            to this story as original to Jacobus (*Le Jeu des Éschaz Moralisé*, p. 251). However,
            Axon argues that this story was a common one throughout the Middle Ages
            (*Caxton's Game and Playe of the Chesse, 1474*, pp. lx–lxii).

1417–18   *Wherof hit happend on a tyme that Saynt Bernard rode on an hors about the contrey.* Tale
            CLXX of the *Gesta Romanorum* contains a version of this story in which the dice do
            not split and Bernard simply wins the game outright. See *Gesta*, pp. 350–51.

Book Four

Chapter 1

14–16   *For as the blessyd Saynt Jherome sayth, the cité of Babylone was right grete and was maad
            al square.* In *Le Jeu des Éschaz Moralisé* Collet attributes this to Jerome's *Commentary
            on Jeremey*, Book 14.22–23. However, the version of this text that appears in *PL*
            does not seem to support this reference.

18–40   *and in Englond they be callyd myles also . . . Hit is to wete that Lombarde mylis and
            Englissh myles ben of one lengthe . . . whiche is seven myle Englissh.* These asides about
            English measurements are all added by Caxton.

28–29   *And as the blessyd Saynt Jherome sayth, upon the prophesie of Ysaye.* This comes from
            Jerome's *Commentary on Isaiah*, Book 5:13, verses 20–22. See Hieronymus
            Stridonensis [MED], *PL* 24:0163A–D.

29–31   *whiche wordes were sayd of Babylone, whiche standeth in Caldee, and nothyng of that
            Babylone that stondeth in Egypt.* The Babylon referred to here is the Biblical city,
            which is located in modern day Iraq, and not the Egyptian Babylon, an ancient
            city on the Nile.

40–41   *The walles about the toure made a woman whos name was Semyramis, as sayth Virgilius.*
            Although Jacobus refers to Virgil as the source for this story, it seems more likely
            that it is Dante's guide Virgil, who names Semiramis as a sinner in Canto V,
            verses 52–72 of the *Inferno*. The story of Semiramis and her building of the brick
            walls was common throughout the Middle Ages. In his *Metamorphoses*, Ovid
            refers to it in passing when describing Pyramus and Thisbe: "Pyramus et Thisbe,
            iuvenum pulcherrimus alter, / Altera, quas Oriens habuit, praelata puellis, /
            Contiguas tenuere domos, ubi dicitur altam / Coctilibus muris cinxisse
            Semiramis urbem" ["Pyramus and Thisbe — he, the most beautiful youth, and
            she, loveliest maid of all the East — dwelt in houses side by side, in the city which
            Semiramis is said to have surrounded with walls of brick"]. See *Metamorphoses*,
            1:182 and 183. It also appears in Justinus' *History of Trogus Pompeius*, Book 1,
            chapter 2.7 (Justin, *Epitome*, p. 15).

68–69   *And Plato sayth that the comyn thynges and the cytees ben blessyd whan they ben governed
            by wyse men, or whan the governours studye in wysedom.* From Valerius, *Memorable
            Doings and Sayings*, Book 7.2, ext. 4 (2:118 and 119).

86–95   *Alas, what habundaunce was somme tymes in the royames. . . . And noblesse of lignage wythout puyssaunce and myght is but vanyté and dyspyte.* This section is added by Caxton.

Chapter 3

231   *For Dyna, Jacob's doughter.* The story of Dinah appears in Genesis 34.

234–35   *Seneka sayth that the women that have evyl vysages ben gladly not chaste, but theyr corage desyreth gladly the companye of men.* I have not been able to locate a source for this saying.

236–37   *And Solinus sayth that no bestys femeles desire to be touched of their males whan they have conceyvyd.* This is from Pliny's *Natural History*, Book 7, chapter 11. See *Natural History*, 2:536–39.

238   *Sidrac.* Sidrak, the wise Jew, counsels and converts Bokkus with his questions and exemplary discussions. On women's sexuality, desire, pleasure in love, pregnancy, and (un)controllability, see *Sidrak and Bokkus*, pp. 260–63.

243–47   *And Ovyde sayth that there ben somme that, how wel that they eschewe the dede.* This quote comes from Ovid's *Art of Love*, Book 1, line 345: "Quae dant quaeque negant, gaudent tamen esse rogatae" ["And, grant they or deny, yet they are pleased to be asked" (pp. 36 and 37)]. In the *Liber* Jacobus adds Book 1, poem 8, line 43 of the *Amores*: "Ludunt formosae: casta est quam nemo rogavit" ["Enjoy yourselves, beautiful ones: she is chaste whom no one has pursued"].

Chapter 6

335   *And this was doon whan Cirus, kyng of Perse, and Darius, kyng of Medes.* This scriptural example comes from Daniel 5:30.

Chapter 7

374   *as we have in the historye of Davyd, that was made kyng.* The story of David is narrated in 1 Kings 16–31, 2 Kings, and 3 Kings 1–2.

377   *as of Gyges, whiche was right riche of landes and of richessis.* The story of Gyges and his riches is found in Valerius, *Memorable Doings and Sayings*, Book 7.1.2 (2:106 and 107). It appears in a modified form in Book 3, chapter 9.38 of Cicero's *De officiis* (pp. 304–07), and Pliny's *Natural History*, Book 7, chapter 46 (2:606 and 607).

388–89   *Virgyle, that was borne in Lombardye of the nacion of Mantua and was of lowe and symple lignage.* This is a modified version of what appears in Macrobius' *Saturnalia* Book 5, chapter 3.16. In this instance, Virgil is described in the third person and is compared to stealing the club from Hercules. See *Saturnalia*, pp. 292–93.

 TEXTUAL NOTES

BOOK ONE

7	*Evylmerodach.* The text reads *Enylmerodach.* See Explanatory Note.
95	*noveltees.* The text reads *novelteees.*
98	*thynges.* The text reads *thyuges.*

BOOK TWO

29	*doo.* The text reads *dooo.*
102	*the.* The text reads *tho.*
175	*Jovynyan.* The text reads *Jonynyan.* See Explanatory Note to 1.174–75.
262	*chastité.* The text reads *chasttie.*
353	*there, where.* Caxton writes *there, there,* although *there, where* captures a better sense of the meaning.
359	*Where.* Again, Caxton has used *there* when *where* seems better suited to the meaning of the sentence.
420	*Libro.* The text reads *Li.*

BOOK THREE

244	*three pence or four pence.* Abbreviated in Caxton as "iii d or iiii d."
431	*prouffyt.* The text reads "puroffyt" here.
721	*Albert.* This appears in the text as *Abbert.*
732	*tresour.* This appears in the text as *cresour.*
878	*or.* The text reads "woundes of soores" here, although the context calls for "or."

BOOK FOUR

76	*For.* Caxton has "For for" here.
162	*attributed.* The text reads *attribued.*
Title, chapter 3	*third.* Although this is the third chapter of Book Four, the word "seconde" appears in both printings.
390	*poyntes.* In the first edition Caxton uses the word "poetes" here, which makes more sense.
401–02	*thre [of] the.* The text reads *thre the.*

 **BIBLIOGRAPHY**

Sources for, and Translations of, the *Liber de ludo schachorum*

Ambrose, St. *De Tobia: A Commentary, with an Introduction and Translation.* Ed. and trans. Lois Miles Zucker. Washington, DC: The Catholic University of America, 1933.

———. *De Officiis.* Ed. and trans. Ivor J. Davidson. 2 vols. Oxford: Oxford University Press, 2001.

Augustine, St. *The City of God.* Trans. John Healey. 2 vols. London: J. M. Dent & Sons, 1931.

Ausonius. *Ausonius.* Ed. and trans. Hugh G. Evelyn White. 2 vols. London: William Heinemann, 1919.

Boethius. *The Consolation of Philosophy.* Trans. P. G. Walsh. Oxford: Oxford University Press, 1999.

Brown, Carleton, ed. *English Lyrics of the XIIIth Century.* Oxford: Clarendon Press, 1932.

Cato. *The Distichs of Cato: A Famous Medieval Textbook.* Trans. Wayland Johnson Chase. University of Wisconsin Studies in the Social Sciences and History 7. Madison, 1922.

Chaucer, Geoffrey. *The Riverside Chaucer.* Third edition. Ed. Larry D. Benson. Boston: Houghton Mifflin Company, 1987.

Cicero. *The Academic Questions, Treatise de Finibus, and Tusculan Disputations of M. T. Cicero.* Trans. C. D. Yonge. London: Henry G. Bohn, 1853.

———. *De finibus bonorum et malorum.* Ed. and trans. H. Rackham. London: William Heinemann, 1914.

———. *De re publica, De legibus.* Ed. and trans. Clinton Walker Keyes. Cambridge: Harvard University Press, 1928.

———. *Pro Milone, In Pisonem, Pro Scauro, Pro Fonteio, Pro Rabirio Postumo, Pro Marcello, Pro Ligario, Pro rege deiotaro.* Trans. N. H. Watts. Cambridge, MA: Harvard University Press, 1953. Rpt. 2000.

———. *De officiis.* Ed. and trans. Walter Miller. Cambridge, MA: Harvard University Press, 1961.

———. *Laelius, On Friendship, and The Dream of Scipio.* Ed. and trans. J. G. F. Powell. Warminster: Aris & Phillips, Ltd., 1990.

Claudian. *Claudian.* Trans. Maurice Platnauer. 2 vols. London: William Heinemann, 1922.

Collet, Alain. *Le Jeu des Éschaz Moralisé.* Paris: Honoré Champion, 1999.

Curtius, Quintus. *Quintus Curtius.* Ed. and trans. John C. Rolfe. 2 vols. Cambridge, MA: Harvard University Press, 1946.

Diogenes Laertius. *Lives of Eminent Philosophers.* Ed. and trans. R. D. Hicks. 2 vols. Cambridge, MA: Harvard University Press, 1972.

Florus, Lucius Annaeus. *The Epitome of Roman History.* Ed. and trans. Edward Seymour Forster. Cambridge, MA: Harvard University Press, 1984, rpt. 1995.

Gautier de Châtillon. *The Alexandreis of Walter of Châtillon.* Trans. David Townsend. Philadelphia: University of Pennsylvania Press, 1996.

Gellius, Aulus. *The Attic Nights of Aulus Gellius.* Ed. and trans. John C. Rolfe. 3 vols. London: William Heinemann, 1927.

Gesta Romanorum. Ed. and trans. Charles Swan. New York: E. P. Dutton & Co., 1924.

Godfrey of Viterbo. *Pantheon, sive Memoria Sæculorum. PL* 198:871–1044.

Gower, John. *Confessio Amantis.* Ed. Russell A. Peck. 3 vols. Kalamazoo, MI: Medieval Institute Publications, 2002–06.

Guillaume de Lorris and Jean de Meun. *The Romance of the Rose.* Trans. Charles Dahlberg. Princeton, NJ: Princeton University Press, 1971.

Herodotus. *Herodotus.* Ed. and trans. J. Enoch Powell. 2. vols. Oxford: Clarendon Press, 1949.

Hoefer, Jean Chrétien. *Nouvelle biographie universelle.* Paris: Firmin Didot Fréres, 1852–66.

Jacobus de Cessolis. *"Libellus de moribus hominum et officiis nobilium ac popularium super ludo scachorum."* Ed. Sister Marie Anita Burt. Ph.D. dissertation, University of Texas, Austin, 1957.

———. "A Critical Edition of *Le Jeu des Eschés, Moralisé* Translated by Jehan de Vignay." Ed. Carol S. Fuller. Ph.D. dissertation, Catholic University of America, 1974.

———. *Le Livre du jeu d'échecs, ou la society ideal au Moyen Age, XIIIeme siècle.* Ed. and trans. Jean-Michel Mehl. Paris: Editions Stock, 1995.

Jerome, St. *Adversus Jovinianum. PL* 23:211–338. A good English translation of this text can be found online at: http://www.ccel.org/fathers2/NPNF2-06/Npnf2-06-10.htm#TopOfPage (accessed 8-8-06).

———. *On Illustrious Men.* Trans. Thomas P. Halton. Washington, DC: Catholic University of America Press, 1999.

John of Salisbury. *The Statesman's Book.* Ed. and trans. John Dickinson. New York: Russell and Russell, 1963.

———. *Frivolities of Courtiers and Footprints of Philosophers.* Trans. Joseph B. Pike. Minneapolis: University of Minnesota Press, 1938.

———. *Policraticus: Of the Frivolities of Courtiers and the Footprints of Philosophers.* Ed. and trans. Cary J. Nederman. Cambridge: Cambridge University Press, 1990.

Josephus, Flavius. *Jewish Antiquities.* Ed. and trans. Louis H. Feldman. 9 vols. Cambridge, MA: Harvard University Press, 1930–65.

Justin. *Epitome of the Philippic History of Pompeius Trogus.* Trans. J. C. Yardley. Atlanta: Scholars Press, 1994.

Lewy, Hans. "Josephus the Physician: A Mediaeval Legend of the Destruction of Jerusalem." *Journal of the Warburg Institute* 1.3 (1938), 221–42.

Livy. *Ab urbe condita.* Ed. and trans. B. O. Foster. 14 vols. Cambridge, MA: Harvard University Press, 1922–67.

Lucan. *Lucan.* Trans. J. D. Duff. London: William Heinemann, 1928.

Macrobius. *Commentary on the Dream of Scipio.* Trans. William Harris Stahl. New York: Columbia University Press, 1952.

———. *The Saturnalia.* Trans. Percival Vaughan Davies. New York: Columbia University Press, 1969.

———. *The Saturnalia.* A good online Latin edition of this text can be found at: http://penelope.uchicago.edu/Thayer/E/Roman/Texts/Macrobius/Saturnalia/home.html (accessed 8-8-06).

Martial. *Epigrams.* Ed. and trans. D. R. Shackleton Bailey. 3 vols. Cambridge, MA: Harvard University Press, 1993.

Migne, J. P. *Patrologiae cursus completus . . . Series Latina.* 221 vols. Paris 1844–82. [I have identified the texts by the author's name, the abbreviation *PL*, the volume number, the column number and the location within the column.]

Orosius, Paulus. *The Seven Books of History against the Pagans.* Trans. Roy J. Deferrari. Washington, DC: Catholic University of America Press, 1964.

Ovid. *Metamorphoses.* Ed. and trans. Frank Justus Miller. 2 vols. Cambridge, MA: Harvard University Press, 1916.

———. *Tristia, Ex Ponto.* Ed. and trans. Arthur Leslie Wheeler. Cambridge, MA: Harvard University Press, 1924.

———. *The Art of Love, and Other Poems.* Ed. and trans. J. H. Mozley. Cambridge, MA: Harvard University Press, 1929.

Paul the Deacon. *History of the Langobards.* Trans. William Dudley Foulke. Philadelphia: The Department of History, University of Pennsylvania, 1907.

Plato. *Republic.* Trans. Raymond Larson. Arlington Heights, IL: AHM Publishing, 1979.

Pliny. *Natural History*. Ed. and trans. H. Rackham. 10 vols. Cambridge, MA: Harvard University Press, 1938–63.

Plutarch. *Moralia*. Ed. and trans. Frank Cole Babbitt. 14 vols. London: William Heinemann, 1927–76.

Quintilian. *The Institutio Oratoria of Quintilian*. Ed. and trans. H. E. Butler. 4 vols. Cambridge, MA: Harvard University Press, 1920–22.

Sallust. *Sallust*. Ed. and trans. J. C. Rolfe. London: William Heinemann, 1931.

Seneca the Elder. *Declamations*. Ed. and trans. Michael Winterbottom. 2 vols. Cambridge, MA: Harvard University Press, 1974.

Seneca. *Ad Lucilium Epistulae Morales*. Ed. and trans. Richard M. Gummere. 3 vols. London: William Heinemann, 1917–25.

———. *Moral Essays*. Ed. and trans. John W. Basore. 3 vols. London: William Heinemann, 1928–35.

The Scholar's Guide: A Translation of the Twelfth-Century Disciplina Clericalis of Pedro Alfonso. Trans. Joseph Ramon Jones and John Esten Keller. Toronto: Pontifical Institute of Mediaeval Studies, 1969.

Sidrak and Bokkus: A Parallel-text Edition from Bodleian Library, MS Laud Misc. 559 and British Library, MS Lansdowne 793. Ed. T. L. Burton. EETS o.s. 311–12. Oxford: Oxford University Press, 1998–99.

Siege of Jerusalem. Ed. Michael Livingston. Kalamazoo, MI: Medieval Institute Publications, 2004.

Stoneman, Richard, ed. and trans. *Legends of Alexander the Great*. London: J. M. Dent, 1994.

Suetonius. *Suetonius*. Ed. and trans. J. C. Rolfe. 2 vols. Cambridge, MA: Harvard University Press, 1913–14.

Syrus, Publilius. *Sententiae* [*Sayings*]. The Latin Library: http://www.thelatinlibrary.com/syrus.html (accessed 8-10-06).

Tacitus. *The Complete Works of Tacitus*. Trans. Alfred John Church and William Jackson Brodribb. New York: Modern Library, 1942.

Tibullus, Albius. "Tibullus." In *Catullus, Tibullus, and Pervigilium Veneris*. Ed. J. P. Postgate. London: William Heinemann, 1913. Pp. 185–339.

Valerius Maximus. *Memorable Doings and Sayings*. Ed. and trans. D. R. Shackleton Bailey. 2 vols. Cambridge, MA: Harvard University Press, 2000.

Varro, Marcus. *Saturarum Menippearum reliquiae*. Ed. Alexander Riese. Leipzig: B. G. Teubner, 1865.

Vincent of Beauvais. *Speculum quadruplex; sive, Speculum maius: naturale, doctrinale, morale, historiale*. Graz: Akademische Druck-u. Verlaganstalt, 1964–65.

Virgil. *Virgil*. Ed. and trans. H. Rushton Fairclough. 2 vols. Cambridge, MA: Harvard University Press, 1999.

Whiting, Bartlett Jere, and Helen Wescott Whiting. *Proverbs, Sentences, and Proverbial Phrases: From English Writings Mainly before 1500*. Cambridge, MA: Belknap Press, 1968.

Historical and Cultural Contexts for *The Game and Playe*

Adams, Jenny. *Power Play: The Literature and Politics of Chess in the Late Middle Ages*. Philadelphia: University of Pennsylvania Press, 2006.

Antin, David. "Caxton's The Game and Playe of the Chesse." *Journal of the History of Ideas* 29 (1968), 269–78.

Axon, William A. E. See Caxton, *Caxton's Game and Playe of the Chesse, 1474*.

Batt, Catherine. "Recreation, the Exemplary and the Body in Caxton's *Game and Playe of the Chesse*." *Ludica* 2 (1996), 27–44.

Blades, William. *The Life and Typography of William Caxton, England's First Printer, with Evidence of His Typographical Connection with Colard Mansion, the Printer at Bruges*. 2 vols. London: J. Lilly, 1861–63. Rpt. New York: Burt Franklin, 1966.

Blake, N. F. *Caxton and His World*. London: Andre Deutsch, 1969.

———. *Caxton: England's First Publisher*. London: Osprey, 1976.

———. "Continuity and Change in Caxton's Prologues and Epilogues: The Bruges Period." *Gutenberg-Jahrbuch* (1979), 72–77.

———. *William Caxton: A Bibliographical Guide.* New York: Garland, 1985.

———. *William Caxton and English Literary Culture.* London: Hambledon Press, 1991.

Carlson, David R. "A Theory of the Early English Printing Firm: Jobbing, Book Publishing, and the Problem of Productive Capacity in Caxton's Work." In *Caxton's Trace: Studies in the History of English Printing.* Ed. William Kuskin. Notre Dame, IN: University of Notre Dame Press, 2006. Pp. 35–68.

Caxton, William. *Raoul Lefèvre's The Recuyell of the Historyes of Troye.* Ed. H. Oskar Sommer. 2 vols. London: David Nutt, 1894.

———. *The Game of the Chesse by William Caxton.* Ed. Vincent Figgins. London: John Russell Smith, 1860.

———. *Caxton's Game and Play of the Chesse, 1474.* Ed. William E. A. Axon. London: Elliot Stock, 1883. (Available online at: http://www.gutenberg.org/dirs/1/0/6/7/10672/10672-h/10672-h.htm)

———. *Jacobus de Cessolis, The Game of Chess: Translated and Printed by William Caxton, c. 1483.* Ed. N. F. Blake. London: The Scholar Press, 1976.

Cooper, Lisa. Crafting Narratives: Artisans, Authors, and the Literary Artifact in Late Medieval England. Unpublished monograph.

Desmond, Marilynn. *Reading Dido: Gender, Textuality, and the Medieval Aeneid.* Minneapolis: University of Minnesota Press, 1994.

Driver, Martha W. *The Image in Print: Book Illustration in Late Medieval England and Its Sources.* London: British Library, 2004.

Du Boulay, F. R. H. "The Quarrel between the Carmelite Friars and the Secular Clergy of London, 1464–1468." *Journal of Ecclesiastical History* 6 (1955), 156–74.

Epstein, Steven A. *Genoa and the Genoese, 958–1528.* Chapel Hill: University of North Carolina Press, 1996.

Gill, Louise. "William Caxton and the Rebellion of 1483." *English Historical Review* 112 (1997), 105–18.

Green, Richard Firth. *A Crisis of Truth: Literature and Law in Ricardian England.* Philadelphia: University of Pennsylvania Press, 1999.

Harriss, Gerald L. "Political Society and the Growth of Government in Late Medieval England." *Past and Present* 138 (1993), 28–57.

Jotischky, Andrew. *The Carmelites and Antiquity: Mendicants and Their Pasts in the Middle Ages.* Oxford: Oxford University Press, 2002.

Kaeppeli, Thomas. "Pour la biographie de Jacques de Cessole." *Archivum Fratrum Praedicatorum* 30 (1960), 149–62.

Knowles, Christine. "Caxton and His Two French Sources: The 'Game and Playe of the Chesse' and the Composite Manuscripts of the Two French Translations of the 'Ludus Scaccorum.'" *Modern Language Review* 49.4 (1954), 417–23.

Kolata, Judith. "*Livre des Echecs Moralisés.*" Master's thesis, University of Chicago, 1987.

Kuskin, William. "Caxton's Worthies Series: The Production of Literary Culture." *ELH* 66 (1999), 511–51.

Mizobata, Kiyokazu. "Caxton's Revisions: The *Game of Chess,* the *Mirror of the World,* and *Reynard the Fox.*" In *Arthurian and Other Studies Presented to Shunichi Noguchi.* Ed. Takashi Suzuki and Tsuyoshi Mukai. Cambridge: D. S. Brewer, 1993. Pp. 257–62.

Murray, H. J. R. *A History of Chess.* Oxford: Clarendon, 1913.

Painter, George D. *William Caxton: A Biography.* New York: G. P. Putnam's Sons, 1977.

Poole, William. "False Play: Shakespeare and Chess." *Shakespeare Quarterly* 55 (2004), 50–70.

Rutter, Russell. "William Caxton and Literary Patronage." *Studies in Philology* 84 (1987), 440–70.

Wilson, Robert H. "Caxton's Chess Book." *Modern Language Notes* 62 (1947), 93–102.

Wiseman, D. J. *Nebuchadnezzar and Babylon.* Schweich Lectures of the British Academy. Oxford: Oxford University Press, 1985.

❧ GLOSSARY

a(d)voultrie(y) *adultery*
alphyns *chess bishops*
alwey *always*
anon(e) *immediately*
axe *ask*

behoveth *is necessary*
bren(ne) *burn*
but if *unless*

chese (chase) *choose (chose)*
consul *a member of the Roman Senate*
convenable *suitable*

debonayr (-air) *gracious*
doubt(e) *fear*

ensey(i)ne *teach*
envyrone *surround*

feet (fait) *act*
figured *depicted*
for as moche as *because*
frende *friend*

geve *give*
grauntdame *grandmother*
grauntsire *grandfather*
gu(y)rdel *belt*

heeris *hair*
her *their; her*
hows *house*

lasse *less*
lever *rather*

maad *made*
membris *body parts*
metis(es) *meats*
meve *move*
mo(o) *more*

ner *nor*

oonly (onely) *alone*
oost(e) *army*
ordonaunce *care*
otherwhyle *sometimes*

parelle(eil) *peril*
pi(y)etous *merciful*
poure *poor*

requyre *request*

sauf *except*
semblable *same*
sewre *sure*
sithen *afterwards*
slear *slayer*
sonner *sooner*
subget(tis) *subject*

tofore *before*

ver(r)ay *true*
vy(i)sage *face*

wene(th) *believe*
wyst *knew*

✒ Middle English Texts Series

The Floure and the Leafe, The Assembly of Ladies, The Isle of Ladies, edited by Derek Pearsall (1990)

Three Middle English Charlemagne Romances, edited by Alan Lupack (1990)

Six Ecclesiastical Satires, edited by James M. Dean (1991)

Heroic Women from the Old Testament in Middle English Verse, edited by Russell A. Peck (1991)

The Canterbury Tales: Fifteenth-Century Continuations and Additions, edited by John M. Bowers (1992)

Gavin Douglas, *The Palis of Honoure*, edited by David Parkinson (1992)

Wynnere and Wastoure and The Parlement of the Thre Ages, edited by Warren Ginsberg (1992)

The Shewings of Julian of Norwich, edited by Georgia Ronan Crampton (1994)

King Arthur's Death: The Middle English Stanzaic Morte Arthur and Alliterative Morte Arthure, edited by Larry D. Benson, revised by Edward E. Foster (1994)

Lancelot of the Laik and Sir Tristrem, edited by Alan Lupack (1994)

Sir Gawain: Eleven Romances and Tales, edited by Thomas Hahn (1995)

The Middle English Breton Lays, edited by Anne Laskaya and Eve Salisbury (1995)

Sir Perceval of Galles and Ywain and Gawain, edited by Mary Flowers Braswell (1995)

Four Middle English Romances: Sir Isumbras, Octavian, Sir Eglamour of Artois, Sir Tryamour, edited by Harriet Hudson (1996; second edition 2006)

The Poems of Laurence Minot, 1333–1352, edited by Richard H. Osberg (1996)

Medieval English Political Writings, edited by James M. Dean (1996)

The Book of Margery Kempe, edited by Lynn Staley (1996)

Amis and Amiloun, Robert of Cisyle, and Sir Amadace, edited by Edward E. Foster (1997; second edition 2007)

The Cloud of Unknowing, edited by Patrick J. Gallacher (1997)

Robin Hood and Other Outlaw Tales, edited by Stephen Knight and Thomas Ohlgren (1997; second edition 2000)

The Poems of Robert Henryson, edited by Robert L. Kindrick with the assistance of Kristie A. Bixby (1997)

Moral Love Songs and Laments, edited by Susanna Greer Fein (1998)

John Lydgate, *Troy Book Selections*, edited by Robert R. Edwards (1998)

Thomas Usk, *The Testament of Love*, edited by R. Allen Shoaf (1998)

Prose Merlin, edited by John Conlee (1998)

Middle English Marian Lyrics, edited by Karen Saupe (1998)

John Metham, *Amoryus and Cleopes*, edited by Stephen F. Page (1999)

Four Romances of England: King Horn, Havelok the Dane, Bevis of Hampton, Athelston, edited by Ronald B. Herzman, Graham Drake, and Eve Salisbury (1999)

The Assembly of Gods: Le Assemble de Dyeus, or Banquet of Gods and Goddesses, with the Discourse of Reason and Sensuality, edited by Jane Chance (1999)

Thomas Hoccleve, *The Regiment of Princes*, edited by Charles R. Blyth (1999)

John Capgrave, *The Life of Saint Katherine*, edited by Karen A. Winstead (1999)

John Gower, *Confessio Amantis*, Vol. 1, edited by Russell A. Peck; with Latin translations by Andrew Galloway (2000; second edition 2006); Vol. 2 (2003); Vol. 3 (2004)

Richard the Redeless and Mum and the Sothsegger, edited by James M. Dean (2000)

Ancrene Wisse, edited by Robert Hasenfratz (2000)

Walter Hilton, *The Scale of Perfection*, edited by Thomas H. Bestul (2000)

John Lydgate, *The Siege of Thebes*, edited by Robert R. Edwards (2001)

Pearl, edited by Sarah Stanbury (2001)

The Trials and Joys of Marriage, edited by Eve Salisbury (2002)

Middle English Legends of Women Saints, edited by Sherry L. Reames, with the assistance of Martha G. Blalock and Wendy R. Larson (2003)

The Wallace: Selections, edited by Anne McKim (2003)

Richard Maidstone, *Concordia (The Reconciliation of Richard II with London)*, edited by David R. Carlson, with a verse translation by A. G. Rigg (2003)

Three Purgatory Poems: The Gast of Gy, Sir Owain, The Vision of Tundale, edited by Edward E. Foster (2004)

William Dunbar, *The Complete Works*, edited by John Conlee (2004)

Chaucerian Dream Visions and Complaints, edited by Dana M. Symons (2004)

Stanzaic Guy of Warwick, edited by Alison Wiggins (2004)

Saints' Lives in Middle English Collections, edited by E. Gordon Whatley, with Anne B. Thompson and Robert K. Upchurch (2004)

Siege of Jerusalem, edited by Michael Livingston (2004)

The Kingis Quair and Other Prison Poems, edited by Linne R. Mooney and Mary-Jo Arn (2005)

The Chaucerian Apocrypha: A Selection, edited by Kathleen Forni (2005)

John Gower, *The Minor Latin Works*, edited and translated by R. F. Yeager, with *In Praise of Peace*, edited by Michael Livingston (2005)

Sentimental and Humorous Romances: Floris and Blancheflour, Sir Degrevant, The Squire of Low Degree, The Tournament of Tottenham, and The Feast of Tottenham, edited by Erik Kooper (2006)

The Dicts and Sayings of the Philosophers, edited by John William Sutton (2006)

"Everyman" and Its Dutch Original, "Elckerlijc," edited by Clifford Davidson, Martin W. Walsh, and Ton J. Broos (2007)

The N-Town Plays, edited by Douglas Sugano, with assistance by Victor I. Scherb (2007)

The Book of John Mandeville, edited by Tamarah Kohanski and C. David Benson (2007)

John Lydgate, *The Temple of Glas*, edited by J. Allan Mitchell (2007)

The Northern Homily Cycle, edited by Anne B. Thompson (2008)

Codex Ashmole 61: A Compilation of Popular Middle English Verse, edited by George Shuffelton (2008)

Chaucer and the Poems of "Ch", edited by James I. Wimsatt (revised edition 2009)

🖋 COMMENTARY SERIES

Haimo of Auxerre, *Commentary on the Book of Jonah*, translated with an introduction and notes by Deborah Everhart (1993)

Medieval Exegesis in Translation: Commentaries on the Book of Ruth, translated with an introduction and notes by Lesley Smith (1996)

Nicholas of Lyra's Apocalypse Commentary, translated with an introduction and notes by Philip D. W. Krey (1997)

Rabbi Ezra Ben Solomon of Gerona, *Commentary on the Song of Songs and Other Kabbalistic Commentaries*, selected, translated, and annotated by Seth Brody (1999)

John Wyclif, *On the Truth of Holy Scripture*, translated with an introduction and notes by Ian Christopher Levy (2001)

Second Thessalonians: Two Early Medieval Apocalyptic Commentaries, introduced and translated by Steven R. Cartwright and Kevin L. Hughes (2001)

The "Glossa Ordinaria" on the Song of Songs, translated with an introduction and notes by Mary Dove (2004)

🖋 DOCUMENTS OF PRACTICE SERIES

Love and Marriage in Late Medieval London, selected, translated, and introduced by Shannon McSheffrey (1995)

Sources for the History of Medicine in Late Medieval England, selected, introduced, and translated by Carole Rawcliffe (1995)

A Slice of Life: Selected Documents of Medieval English Peasant Experience, edited, translated, and with an introduction by Edwin Brezette DeWindt (1996)

Regular Life: Monastic, Canonical, and Mendicant "Rules," selected and introduced by Douglas J. McMillan and Kathryn Smith Fladenmuller (1997); second edition, selected and introduced by Daniel Marcel La Corte and Douglas J. McMillan (2004)

Women and Monasticism in Medieval Europe: Sisters and Patrons of the Cistercian Reform, selected, translated, and with an introduction by Constance H. Berman (2002)

Medieval Notaries and Their Acts: The 1327–1328 Register of Jean Holanie, introduced, edited, and translated by Kathryn L. Reyerson and Debra A. Salata (2004)

✒ MEDIEVAL GERMAN TEXTS IN BILINGUAL EDITIONS SERIES

Sovereignty and Salvation in the Vernacular, 1050–1150, introduction, translations, and notes by James A. Schultz (2000)

Ava's New Testament Narratives: "When the Old Law Passed Away," introduction, translation, and notes by James A. Rushing, Jr. (2003)

History as Literature: German World Chronicles of the Thirteenth Century in Verse, introduction, translation, and notes by R. Graeme Dunphy (2003)

✒ VARIA

The Study of Chivalry: Resources and Approaches, edited by Howell Chickering and Thomas H. Seiler (1988)

Studies in the Harley Manuscript: The Scribes, Contents, and Social Contexts of British Library MS Harley 2253, edited by Susanna Fein (2000)

The Liturgy of the Medieval Church, edited by Thomas J. Heffernan and E. Ann Matter (2001; second edition 2005)

✒ TO ORDER PLEASE CONTACT:

Medieval Institute Publications
Western Michigan University
Kalamazoo, MI 49008-5432
Phone (269) 387-8755
FAX (269) 387-8750
http://www.wmich.edu/medieval/mip/index.html

Typeset in 10/13 New Baskerville
and Golden Cockerel Ornaments display
Designed by Linda K. Judy
Manufactured by McNaughton & Gunn, Inc.

Medieval Institute Publications
College of Arts and Sciences
Western Michigan University
1903 W. Michigan Avenue
Kalamazoo, MI 49008-5432
http://www.wmich.edu/medieval/mip

 WESTERN MICHIGAN UNIVERSITY